Understanding
Jane Eyre

The Greenwood Press "Literature in Context" Series
Student Casebooks to Issues, Sources, and Historical Documents

UNDERSTANDING
Jane Eyre

A STUDENT CASEBOOK TO ISSUES, SOURCES, AND HISTORICAL DOCUMENTS

Debra Teachman

The Greenwood Press
"Literature in Context" Series
Claudia Durst Johnson, Series Editor

GREENWOOD PRESS
Westport, Connecticut • London

Library of Congress Cataloging-in-Publication Data

Teachman, Debra, 1955–
    Understanding Jane Eyre : a student casebook to issues, sources, and historical
documents / Debra Teachman.
        p.   cm.—(Greenwood Press "Literature in context" series, ISSN 1074–598X)
    Includes bibliographical references and index.
    ISBN 0–313–30939–6 (alk. paper)
    1. Brontë, Charlotte, 1816–1855. Jane Eyre—Sources. 2. Literature and
history—England—History—19th century—Sources. 3. Governesses in literature.
I. Title. II. Series.
PR4167.J3T43 2001
823'.8—dc21   00–049069

British Library Cataloguing in Publication Data is available.

Library of Congress Catalog Card Number: 00–049069
ISBN: 0–313–30939–6
ISSN: 1074–598X

First published in 2001

Greenwood Press, 88 Post Road West, Westport, CT 06881
An imprint of Greenwood Publishing Group, Inc.
www.greenwood.com

Printed in the United States of America

The paper used in this book complies with the
Permanent Paper Standard issued by the National
Information Standards Organization (Z39.48–1984).

10 9 8 7 6 5 4 3 2 1

Contents

Acknowledgments

I could not have undertaken and completed this book without the support of family, friends, and colleagues. I thank them all for their help.

I thank Claudia Durst Johnson, series editor, and Lynn Malloy, acquisitions editor for Greenwood Press, for their encouragement, understanding, and assistance throughout the writing process.

For assistance with research, I express my gratitude to the staff at Townsend Library at New Mexico State University at Alamogordo. Without their help, most especially the help of interlibrary loan librarian, Lois Knowles, the tasks of finding and accessing the materials for this volume would have been much more difficult. To former head librarian, Anne Moore, a special thank you for all your work in making electronic access to information so much easier and more efficient during your tenure at NMSU-A.

I thank my colleagues in the Humanities Division at New Mexico State University at Alamogordo for their encouragement and support throughout the research and writing process.

To Sally Tree Sutton and Sky Guse, I express my deepest appreciation for providing me with the wonderful writer's retreat at which much of the material in this book was drafted and organized. I also thank you for your support of this project in other important but less tangible ways.

Finally, to my family, Wayne and Andrew Jones, thank you for your understanding, your support, and your patience. Without your assistance, this book would never have been completed.

Introduction

Jane Eyre was published in 1847, in the early years of the Victorian period. The revolutionary fervor of the Romantic period was at bay. The American Revolution was almost three-quarters of a century in the past; the French Revolution had run its course; the Napoleonic Wars had ended before Charlotte Brontë was even born. Life in Brontë's England was relatively stable, with everyone knowing his or her place in the social order and most people accepting that place without public complaint. The agitation for women's rights that had resulted from the revolutionary ideas that all people were entitled to equal opportunities had gone underground. Late eighteenth-century proponents of rights for women, such as Mary Wollstonecraft, had been discredited because of lifestyles that were considered wholly inappropriate during Victorian times. Those who espoused similar ideas tended to be pilloried in the press, tarred, as it were, by the same brush as their predecessors merely for publicly supporting women's rights.

Into this world came Charlotte Brontë, the writer. Brontë had been raised by a father who taught his children to think for themselves. She, together with her sisters and brother, had been given the freedom as children to allow their imaginations to soar, creating imaginary worlds in which difference of gender meant very little. They even *wrote* their imaginary stories of their imaginary

Charlotte Brontë. From an oil painting by J. H. Thompson in *Jane Eyre*, vol. 2 (1905).

worlds, providing them with an expectation that writing imaginary tales was an acceptable behavior, even though many of their contemporaries, girls especially, were trained to believe that fiction was, at best, a distraction from one's duties, and at worst, an invitation to immoral beliefs and behaviors. Through her flights of imagination and her tendency to write the stories that came to her, Charlotte Brontë learned to trust her instincts, instincts that encouraged her to believe that women, as well as men, had a need to dream, to explore, that they "need exercise for their faculties, and a field for their efforts as much as their brothers do" (*Jane Eyre*, 130). Brontë wrote in a world in which the rebellions were not so much those of political entities against one another as of individuals who recognized a need to stretch their wings and explore their abilities and desires more fully than the society of the day allowed.

As sources of material for her fiction, Brontë used the experiences she, her sisters, and her female friends had at school and work. While neither she nor any of her sisters or friends fell in love with and married an employer like Mr. Rochester, the experiences of school, as student and teacher, and of governess work, were based strongly on experience. Brontë's experiences at Cowen Bridge School provided the foundation for much of Jane's experience as a student at Lowood, and Brontë's experiences at Roe Head School provided her with an understanding of the experiences Jane would have undergone as a teacher at Lowood. Brontë worked for two separate families as a governess. Those experiences, together with those of her sister Anne, gave her a clear understanding of the restrictions involved in the life a governess was supposed to lead in Victorian England. All these experiences combined with her own ideas of romantic love, gleaned primarily from Romantic novels and poetry, to create the novel *Jane Eyre*.

To understand the world that Charlotte Brontë was a part of, and how unlikely it was that women like Charlotte, Anne, and Emily Brontë would come to write novels as full of romantic ideas and thoughts of freedom for women as they did, one must examine the ideas that dominated the early Victorian world and dictated its lifestyle. Twenty-first–century readers of Brontë's works can hardly imagine a world in which women are not allowed to enter professions, in which married women are not permitted to control their own money, in which mothers do not even have the right to be a part of their own children's lives unless their father gives permission. Attitudes and laws concerning love and marriage were vastly different then than they are today. Divorce was almost an impossibility. Mental health disorders were treated as "insanity" and "madness" and were so little understood that most individuals who displayed behaviors that were considered a threat to other people (whether physically or morally) were simply locked away, either in their own homes or in asylums in which they usually received little or no legitimate mental treatment.

In this book, such attitudes are displayed primarily through excerpts from writings of the Romantic and Victorian periods. These writings enable the twenty-first–century reader to approach the novel with a greater understanding of the society and the social mores in force when the novel was first published. That understanding will enable contemporary readers to incorporate ideas and attitudes from Brontë's own time as well as from the twenty-first century into their personal interpretations of the novel.

The first chapter offers a literary analysis of *Jane Eyre*, focusing on the ways in which different characters within the novel provide insight into other characters and into the novel as a whole. The literary technique of the double is examined. Physical locations that double each other thematically as well as characters that double behaviors and feelings of others are explored. Attention is also given to the role of Nature in the novel, as a place in which the restrictions placed on women in society can temporarily be thrown off and the fullness of a woman's humanity can be felt. Such freedom can threaten a woman's physical safety, but it does, at least, give her a place in which to experience a kind of freedom that is unavailable to her in society.

The second chapter explores the formal education that was available for girls in Brontë's time. Women of the upper classes were usually educated at exclusive boarding schools, which focused more on the "accomplishments" the girls could attain (that might attract the notice of a wealthy mate) than on intellectual stimulation and knowledge. Those who did not attend such boarding schools generally were educated at home by a governess and a series of "masters" in various fields such as music, drawing, dancing, and the like. Among the lower classes, most girls attended no school whatsoever, but those who did generally attended one of three varieties: a charity school, in which the girl's needs for food, clothing, and occupation were taken care of as she was trained to be a good worker of the servant class or a worker in industry; the industrial school, in which a girl was trained in the principles and activities most useful to the owner of the industry in which she was expected to work; or the Sunday School, in which girls who worked the other six days of the week came for religious instruction as well as to learn basic reading, writing, and arithmetic. Middle-class girls, like the Brontë sisters, tended to attend either boarding schools or day schools (if they attended school at all), where they learned the basics of reading, writing, and arithmetic. Many were also trained in many of the "accomplishments" of the upper classes, especially those who were expected to make their own living, since teaching was the only occupation most girls of the middle classes were permitted to consider entering. Those who did not attend school generally were taught by their mothers to run households, the expectation being that most girls would marry and have husbands who would provide for their basic needs.

Chapter 3 discusses the life of the governess. Most middle-class women who did not marry and who did not have family who could provide for them went into the teaching profession. Women who did not have the financial backing to start a school of their own often went into service as governesses, serving the needs of those wealthier (though not necessarily of more genteel birth) than themselves. Such women were usually very isolated, above the other servants in education and birth but on an unequal footing with their employer because they were, in fact, hired help. This chapter addresses specific situations that some governesses found themselves in, as well as published "advice" for women who were considering or who already were involved in working as governesses.

In Chapter 4, the issue of "madness" is examined. We delve into medical and social attitudes of the time toward those who did not fit neatly into the roles that society dictated. Various medical experts are cited with respect to diagnosing and treating "lunatics," both in and out of asylums. Most of the medical men (and they were almost all male) writing about lunacy were associated with asylums of one kind or other and, therefore, believed that most people diagnosed as insane should spend time in such institutions. But the state of mental institutions and of the treatment of the insane in the nineteenth century prompted many families to care for their own insane at home, as Mr. Rochester does. The science of psychiatry did not begin until very late in the nineteenth century, and did not gain credence until well into the twentieth century; a scientific understanding of the psychological causes of behaviors diagnosed as madness was, therefore, not available to those of Brontë's time.

Chapter 5 provides insight into the legalities underlying the structure of Charlotte Brontë's world. The rights of the landowner and the ways in which land was transmitted from one owner to another, particularly within families, is at the core of the marriage between Edward Rochester and Bertha Mason. The rights of a husband over his wife's property and her person also provide much of the impetus for the novel's storyline. If women had more freedom to control their lives and their money in the early Victorian period, Bertha's situation would have been quite different, and Jane would not have found herself facing some of her most difficult dilemmas in the novel.

Chapter 6 examines the issues raised in *Jane Eyre* from a twenty-first–century perspective. Laws and customs have changed dramatically regarding issues such as women's rights, the ownership of property, and the diagnosis and treatment of mental illness. But by comparing Victorian attitudes and understandings about those issues with attitudes of the present day, we can see the roots of some of our more conservative beliefs and attitudes.

Excerpts from and references to a wide variety of documents are included in these chapters, all of them chosen to expand one's understanding of the novel *Jane Eyre* and the society from which it grew. These documents include the following:

- a literary study
- commentaries on nineteenth-century English law
- eighteenth- and nineteenth-century advice manuals
- eighteenth- and nineteenth-century educational treatises
- nineteenth-century novels and biographies
- historical reports
- journal and magazine articles

Each issue explored, as well as each of the supporting documents, is introduced by an essay explaining its significance to *Jane Eyre*.

Also included are topics for written or oral exploration and suggested readings.

Page numbers in parentheses following quoted material refer to the texts listed in the suggested readings at the end of each chapter. Original spellings and punctuation have been maintained in most cases; some have been modified, however, to provide greater clarity. Quotations from *Jane Eyre* have been taken from the Haworth Edition, published by Harper and Brothers in 1900.

1

Literary Analysis: *Jane Eyre*

"Such a strange book! Imagine a novel with a little swarthy governess for heroine, and a middle-aged ruffian for hero." Such was the evaluation of one reviewer in *Sharpe's London Magazine* soon after the publication of *Jane Eyre* (qtd. in Smith, v). Coming on the heels of the young, dark, and handsome Byronic antiheroes of Romantic literature, Mr. Edward Fairfax Rochester is, indeed, quite an ordinary looking, middle-aged man, with his "ugly" features and rough demeanor. He is also older than most literary heroes, nearly thirty-five years of age, and has already lived for a significant time in the West Indies and on the European continent. His father and elder brother have both died, leaving him as the last surviving Rochester with two moderately sized estates in the country and no need to work at a profession. His future seems laid out for him and eminently secure. Jane Eyre's character is far from the traditional Victorian heroine. She is very plain, and her low social position (despite a genteel birth) and lack of any fortune with which to attract a husband make her very unlikely to marry, unlikely even to have a clandestine relationship with a man in nineteenth-century literature. She has more in common with various minor characters like Miss Bates or Mrs. Goddard in Jane Austen's *Emma* than with the traditional literary heroine. And yet, the novel *Jane Eyre* was an instant success with many early Victorian readers.

Jane Eyre takes the form of both a fictional autobiography and a bildungsroman. As an autobiography, it presents the story of Jane's life from her own adult perspective and in her own words. As a bildungsroman, it is the story of the education of an individual, both through formal education and by growing into maturity. Most bildungsromans of the nineteenth century and before were written about men, but *Jane Eyre* is the story of a woman's education into life. The novel focuses the reader's attention primarily on those experiences, academic and otherwise, from which Jane learns the most about herself and the world she lives in. It displays the process of her growth in knowledge and wisdom as she experiences life.

LOCATIONS

Jane Eyre can be divided into five parts based on the five primary locations of activity within it: Gateshead, Lowood, Thornfield, Marsh End, and Ferndean. The first two locations are those Jane experiences as a child. The next two are the locations in which she learns the most about herself and the world as an adult. The final location, Ferndean, is the place in which she is able to integrate all that she has learned as she creates the life she wants to live. At Ferndean, she finally reaches the end of her bildungsroman and enters mature adulthood.

At Gateshead, Jane begins her journey through life. Although she was born elsewhere, her earliest memories are of Gateshead and the Reed family. Thus, the Reeds' home is the "gate" at the "head" of her journey through life. Gateshead is the place in which the passions of childhood are given free rein. Jane's young cousins are free to insult her whenever they choose. John Reed, the heir apparent of the Reed estate and fortune, even punches and pushes her without fear of punishment. Jane, unlike her cousins, is punished for her fits of passion, but she experiences passions at Gateshead, nonetheless. Jane's sensitivity to acts of injustice develops while she lives at Gateshead, where she sees herself treated as less worthy even than a servant, while her cousins, who are significantly less well-behaved than she is, receive all the privileges and honors.

Gateshead is also a place filled with disappointment for Jane. There she experiences brief moments of hope—that she will have some privacy in which to read a book, that her cousins will avoid her rather than tormenting her, that Mrs. Reed and the servants will be fair to her—but those hopes are inevitably crushed.

Jane's move to Lowood is the result of one of her hopes that is quickly crushed. Jane is sent to school on the advice of a doctor her aunt, Mrs. Reed, calls in to take care of her when she becomes ill after a particularly cruel and unfair punishment. The doctor understands that Jane's life at Gateshead is a life of torment and hopes that getting her away from the Reed family will make her life easier. Mrs. Reed's choice of Lowood as the school to which Jane is sent, however, does not fulfill Jane's need for a less tormented life. Lowood is a charity school for girls of lower genteel standing whose relatives do not have the means or the desire to care for them. At Lowood emphasis is placed on the need for the girls to accept their station in life, to learn to endure hardship and deprivation without complaint, and to restrain their passions in the process. The food provided for the girls is limited in quantity and poor in quality. Their clothing is inadequate for long walks in cold temperatures, which they take every Sunday throughout the winter as they walk miles to and from church. They remain at the unheated stone church in that inadequate clothing throughout the long day, eating a skimpy, cold-packed lunch as they wait for the second service and the long, cold walk home following it. Punishments for infractions of the rules at Lowood are cruel, both physically and psychologically. Yet, as poor girls dependent on "charity," they are expected to be grateful for everything they receive. At Lowood they are trained to support themselves through teaching and sewing, the two professions by which a single, genteel woman without other means of support could manage to sustain herself. Jane learns her academic lessons well and is qualified, by the end of her training at Lowood, to hire herself out as a governess, by which means she is convinced that she will be able to earn her keep and, thus, take care of her future.

When Jane leaves Lowood, she is eighteen years old and ready to enter the world as an adult. She advertises for a position as a governess and is hired, sight unseen, by Mrs. Fairfax of Thornfield Hall. Thornfield is, in fact, a "field" for her activities that will become very "thorny" for her before she leaves. At Thornfield, Jane enters adulthood. Passions reign at Thornfield, just as they did at Gateshead, but at Thornfield the passions are those of an adult man and woman rather than childish cousins. Despite Jane's years

The Rydings, Birstall. The manor house that inspired Brontë's creation of Thornfield Hall. From *Jane Eyre*, vol. 1 (1905).

of training in restraint at Lowood, her passions get the better of her common sense as she allows herself to fall in love with her employer, Edward Rochester. An excess of passion, on the parts of both Jane and Mr. Rochester, ultimately causes her to run from Thornfield Hall with no plans for the future, ending up starving and delirious on the doorsteps of the Rivers family at Marsh End. Had she and Mr. Rochester been more restrained initially, and had Rochester been honest with Jane about his circumstances sooner, her escape from Thornfield in the middle of the night, an event which put her life in danger, would never have happened.

Marsh End, like Lowood, is a place where restraint of passion is a way of life. St. John Rivers is a clergyman with a strong desire to be of service as a missionary in India. That desire, however, is at odds with his romantic interest in Rosamund Oliver, the daughter of a local landowner. She is a good woman, with great integrity and beauty, but she is not (in St. John's mind, at least) the sort of woman who could stand up under the strain of missionary work in India, the work to which St. John is determined to dedicate his life. Upon arriving at Marsh End, Jane finds herself in the kind of self-sacrificing environment that should enable her to restrain her own desires and passions, if ever any environment could. In fact, St. John even makes Jane an offer of marriage and a life performing missionary work with him in India, which would give her a means by which to protect herself from acting on her feelings for Mr. Rochester as well as a way to be of service, the purpose for which she has been trained throughout her life. Jane almost accepts his offer but ultimately cannot turn her back on passion. While she cares deeply for St. John, she knows that she would never be able to love him with the kind of passion she feels for Rochester. She is also aware that St. John is not capable of the warmth of passion Rochester shows; in fact, St. John's passion is "ice" compared to Jane's "fire." Jane is a woman who, having once known true passion, cannot settle for anything less in marriage.

Ferndean is the final location of the novel. When Jane, recognizing that she must see Rochester again, leaves Marsh End, she returns to Thornfield to find it burned to the ground. After inquiring in the nearby town, she discovers that Mr. Rochester is now living at the smaller estate he owns, Ferndean. In that location, passions have been moderated to some degree by both time and experience. Rochester has suffered life-changing injuries in the fire at Thornfield which have rendered him dependent on others for his daily care. Jane thus finds him changed from a vital and some-times threateningly passionate man into a man tamed by both emo-tional and physical trauma. Jane, in the meantime, has found loving cousins with whom she has experienced a loving family. She has also inherited her uncle's fortune, making her an independent woman with no need of the financial support of an employer or husband. Jane finds that her emotions continue to run as deep for Rochester as they ever did, but that her experiences with the Rivers family, together with her inheritance from her uncle, has made her less dependent than before, both emotionally and physically. As a result of this increased level of independence, she is able to reg-ulate her passions, indulging them when she feels it appropriate and choosing not to act on them at other times. This final section of the novel reveals the integration of essential parts of Jane's per-sonality and education into a strong adult woman, who also at this time becomes a mother and a true partner to her husband. Al-though the entire life is not finished at this point (Jane is approx-imately thirty), the bildungsroman has been completed. Jane has learned the lessons she needed to become a strong, adult woman.

THE DOUBLE

The literary technique of the double has been used throughout history for many purposes. In Shakespearean comedies, we see characters doubled (as twins, most especially) in order to achieve comic effects. In novels such as *Dr. Jekyll and Mr. Hyde*, the dou-ble is used for more serious purposes, to demonstrate two sides of a single self: the civilized self and the primal being that lies just below the surface of civilization's veneer. In *Jane Eyre*, Charlotte Brontë uses the technique of the double in several ways. Locations double one another (Gateshead and Thornfield as places to learn to be passionate and to indulge those passions; Lowood and Marsh End as places in which to learn and develop restraint of passion and self-sacrifice), creating a structure of the novel that has its foundation on the effects of doubling. But there are also doublings of characters throughout the novel. Sometimes those doubles op-erate on a surface level, demonstrating overt similarities. But the doubling effect also, at times, betrays the shadow side of char-acters, the actions and attitudes that characters sometimes feel tempted to display but cannot because of social mores.

THE COUSINS

Among the minor characters, the clearest set of doubles is Jane's two sets of cousins. The Reed siblings and the Rivers siblings consist of three children each, an older brother and two younger sisters. The cousins of Jane's childhood are selfish and spiteful, excluding Jane whenever possible and mistreating her whenever they are forced to be with her. The cousins Jane meets as an adult appear to be exactly the opposite. They take her into their home, not even knowing her true name and having no idea that she is related to them by blood. They nurse her to health, having saved her from an almost certain death, and provide her with a job and a place to live.

Despite their money and position in the world, the Reed cousins are not, by the end of the novel, successful. John Reed, having gotten himself deeply into debt (with hints of more sinister troubles), kills himself. Of his sisters, one is a frivolous woman concerned only about appearances who plans to move to London and live the fashionable life after the death of her mother. The other is an austere spinster who intends to spend her life cloistered in a nunnery, as isolated as possible from the world. Her intent is not to be of service to God and to those in need, but to find a place of comfortable retirement for herself where she can indulge her desire to live a life of isolated contemplation.

The world of the Rivers cousins is considerably more productive. St. John actively works at his profession. When we first meet him, he is a clergyman, serving a parish in the English countryside near his father's home. After his father's death, he goes to India as a missionary. There he spends the remainder of his life in service to God and humanity. His sisters, Diana and Mary, also work. When Jane meets them, they are visiting their late father's home from the homes of the families for whom they work as governesses. Jane decides to share the inheritance she received from her uncle with her cousins, enabling Diana and Mary to resign from their positions in other people's households so that they may create a household of their own from which they can do good in their home community.

And yet the contrast between the Reeds and the Rivers is not complete. Jane faces difficulties in both cousins' homes. Both John Reed and St. John Rivers attempt to control her. Both use coercion—the child John Reed resorting to physical coercion as well as emotional torment; the adult St. John Rivers to emotional and spiritual coercion. Jane suffers under the heat of John Reed's passionate outbursts in childhood. As an adult, she suffers from the coldness of St. John's determination to marry her (despite the fact that the only passion he feels toward her has to do with the work they could perform together) and take her to India as his partner in missionary work.

With the Reeds, Jane is made to feel alone in the world—even while living with blood relatives. With the Rivers, Jane finds the family she had wished for as a child. Even before they know of the blood bond, the Rivers siblings accept Jane into their home and into their lives as though she belongs with them. St. John Rivers, like John Reed, believes that he, as the man of the family, has the right to determine how she should spend her time and her future, but unlike the young John, St. John eventually accepts Jane's right to exist and to thrive in a world that had previously brought her little more than pain. With the Reeds, Jane's orphan status and dependency are apparent at every turn; with the Rivers, she truly becomes a member of a close-knit and loving family.

TEACHERS

Since *Jane Eyre* is a bildungsroman, focusing on the education of a young woman, teachers abound in the novel. Some are teachers by profession, others merely individuals who teach Jane valuable lessons. Within the ranks of the professional teachers, Brontë depicts two specific individuals who provide Jane with models for her own behavior, both as a teacher/governess and as an adult woman. One is a negative model; the other positive.

Miss Scatcherd is the epitome of the bad teacher in Brontë's work. Her emphasis is on punishment for infractions of the rules. The punishments she inflicts are painful both physically and emotionally. She uses corporal punishment (beating girls with birch branches) and shame (pinning signs on girls for sloppiness, making them stand on stools for all to see their shame, etc.) as ways of trying to change behaviors of which she disapproves. The reasons behind those behaviors are irrelevant to her. For instance, when Helen Burn's fingernails are dirty because the water in the basin in the dormitory that morning was frozen, Miss Scatcherd refuses to hear the explanation. The fact of unclean fingernails is all she needs or wants to know before doling out punishment.

Miss Temple, on the other hand, is the epitome of the good teacher. As superintendent of the entire school, her responsibilities are far greater than those of any of the other teachers; yet she takes the time necessary to get to know her students, to provide for their needs emotionally as well as physically and, to the extent allowable, intellectually. When the porridge is so burnt at breakfast that it is inedible, she arranges, against the orders of Mr. Brocklehurst, the clergyman in charge of the school, to have the children fed a different, better meal. When Mr. Brocklehurst announces to the entire school that Jane is a bad and deceitful girl, based on information given to him by her aunt, Mrs. Reed, Miss Temple takes the time to hear her side of the story and to promise that, if her story is corroborated by the doctor who had recommended she be sent to school, her name will be cleared before the entire school. Miss Temple then follows up on the information and, when receiving corroboration from the doctor, does indeed announce to the entire school that Jane has been exonerated of the charges Mr. Brocklehurst made. Miss Temple teaches Jane that it is her present and future behavior that matter most, that if she behaves herself well at Lowood, her reputation will be based on that behavior, not on the criticisms of someone from her past.

The intellectual rigor of Lowood, like that of most early nineteenth-century schools for girls, is not strong. More attention is paid to suitable behavior and rote learning of basic information than to advanced knowledge or critical thinking skills. In the early nineteenth century, girls were not expected (nor desired) to have rigorous intellectual lives. Miss Temple does, however, make certain that those girls who are capable of learning basic intellectual (as well as practical) skills receive some education in them. As a result, by the time Jane leaves Lowood at age eighteen, she has sufficient knowledge and skills to be hired as a governess in a well-to-do family. Her knowledge of French, a requirement in most schools for those of genteel birth, is essential to her work with Adele Varens, the young French girl who is Mr. Rochester's ward and Jane's student. Her knowledge of reading, writing, and arithmetic is sufficient for Adele's educational needs, and her understanding of and adherence to the rules of propriety for young women in society make her a satisfactory model of behavior for the young girl. These qualities and skills are ones that Miss Temple made certain Jane developed while at Lowood, not through punishment and shame (Miss Scatcherd's means of teaching young women), but through positive reinforcement of those qualities and skills whenever she saw them displayed.

When Jane becomes a teacher herself, she models her own behavior on that of Miss Temple. She recognizes the potential loneliness and isolation a child like Adele can feel—alone in a strange country with people who don't even speak her language—and she tries to provide comfort and security for the child, along with proper training of her morals and her mind. Miss Scatcherd is a good reminder to Jane of what she does not want to become as a teacher or as a woman. The small-minded, embittered spinster is not a happy person. Miss Temple, on the other hand, is that all too rare individual: a working woman with neither fortune nor strong family ties who, on the basis of her goodness and open-heartedness, is found by a good man who marries her and provides her with a happy home of her own. Few women who were reduced to teaching or governess work in the late eighteenth or early nineteenth centuries ever found their way into such domestic happiness as Miss Temple. Jane Eyre, like her creator Charlotte Brontë, was fortunate in finding such a felicitous domestic situation after having worked for years as a teacher and governess.

THE MEN IN JANE'S LIFE

Jane spends much of her life under the thumb of various men, all of whom, to differing extents, bully her. John Reed believes he has a right to bully her because of her dependent status in his family. *He* will inherit everything at Gateshead, and *she* has no right even to be there, let alone to touch the books or anything else in the house. Such is his rationale. When he chooses, he hits her or pinches her, knowing that he will suffer no repercussions because of his importance and her complete insignificance to the household. When Jane does fight back, she is punished in a fear-inspiring manner; she is locked in the "red room," the room in which her uncle died. Locked in that room for hours with the thought of her uncle's ghost still haunting it terrifies young Jane so much that she falls seriously ill from the terror. This illness, while horrendous at the time, actually precipitates a positive outcome—her removal from Gateshead. Thus, Jane learns in this situation that rebellion can eventually work to one's benefit where bullies are concerned—even if one must sometimes endure severe trauma in the process.

When Mr. Brocklehurst arrives at Gateshead to arrange for Jane's admission to Lowood, he too bullies her. When Jane does not agree that she is the deceitful and morally corrupt girl Mrs. Reed makes her out to be, Mr. Brocklehurst threatens her with the full exposure of what he has been told are her misdeeds. When he follows through with his threats, Jane feels as though she has been branded for life, that no one will ever believe that she is, in fact, a truthful girl. She also watches as Mr. Brocklehurst berates Miss Temple for coddling the girls by giving them additional food when the porridge was badly prepared. She sees Miss Temple stand up to him, insisting that she had done what was right and taking responsibility for her own actions. From watching Miss Temple's adult responses to Mr. Brocklehurst's bullying, Jane learns that standing up for oneself and for what one believes to be right can, in fact, end in something other than pain and shame.

As Jane enters adulthood, she is faced with yet another man who, despite his love for her, at times, presents himself as a bully. Mr. Rochester, like most men of property in nineteenth-century England, is used to getting his own way in almost everything. Because he dislikes the bustle involved in getting the house ready for full occupancy after it has been closed up due to his absence, Mrs. Fairfax keeps the house ready for full occupancy at all times, despite the extra work it creates for her and the servants. When Mr. Rochester decides to take a trip at a moment's notice, he does so. When he decides to return, he returns without notifying the staff. His comings and goings are completely unrestricted, despite the trouble that fact often causes others, especially the dependents of his household.

For a man like Mr. Rochester, who is not used to restriction or argument from those dependent on him, a woman like Jane Eyre is an enigma. She performs her duties as Adele's governess admirably and is a help to Mrs. Fairfax in other ways as well, but she does not show Mr. Rochester the degree of deference to which he has been accustomed. She shows him respect, but she does not try (initially, at least) to anticipate his desires and satisfy them before he is even aware they exist, as Mrs. Fairfax and many of the other women in his life do and have done in the past. As a result, he finds Jane fascinating, because she is different. He insists on having her company and often, when finding himself using the commanding tone with her that he is used to using with other

Illustration of Jane Eyre, Edward Rochester, and Adele Varens. From an early edition of *Jane Eyre* (The Haworth Edition, 1900).

women, apologizes for his rudeness to her. Most of the time his behavior toward her is respectful, but, at times, her rebellion and insistence on being treated as his equal as a human being (while recognizing her dependency on him as an employee) become serious irritants to him, causing him to behave in ways that cause her emotional pain. For instance, when Mr. Rochester wants to know whether Jane is as emotionally attached to him as he is becoming to her, he forces her to watch as he courts Blanche Ingram, a local heiress of great beauty who intends to marry him. He forces Jane into conversations about Blanche, trying to get her to feel (and admit) some jealousy over his attentions to the dark beauty. Jane is clearly pained by such conversation and struggles to get away from it and him, but Mr. Rochester refuses to allow her to leave him, sadistically enjoying, it seems, his ability to cause her discomfort at the idea of his marriage to Miss Ingram.

When Jane discovers on her wedding day that Mr. Rochester is not free to marry her, that he is legally married to another woman, she is tormented by the thought of the cruelty of the deception Mr. Rochester has practiced upon her, as well as the moral degradation into which she has almost sunk (a woman of her time who had sexual relations without being properly married was considered "ruined" regardless of whether she has knowingly and willingly done anything wrong). Mr. Rochester does not, however, allow her peace and privacy in which to deal with her situation. Instead, he tries to bully her into staying with him, into going with him to the Continent where they could live as though they were married, with no one knowing the difference. Jane knows that whether others know the difference or not is not important. She and Mr. Rochester would know, and they would be living in sin; those are the important issues in Jane's mind. Also, Jane is well aware, from the manner in which Mr. Rochester has spoken about previous mistresses, that he could not continue to respect her if she gave in to his demands. His attempts to bully her into agreement are so strong, however, that she finds it necessary to face the dangers of running from Thornfield in the middle of the night rather than staying to face Mr. Rochester's coercive manipulations.

Whereas Mr. Rochester's attempts to bully Jane into a semblance of marriage are based on the deep passions of the heart, St. John Rivers attempts to bully her into marriage with him by appealing to her sense of duty, honor, and gratitude. He uses the fact that he saved her life and provided her with a means of supporting herself as a way to try to make her feel guilty for refusing his proposal. He reminds her that there is something in her past (she has not told him the entire story, though he suspects it has to do with disreputable behavior on the part of a man) that she must avoid reverting to, something that had almost cost her her innocence and her honor. He reminds her of her duty to God and uses that reminder as a means of trying to force her into an acceptance of his advances. She assures him that she could never marry without love, but he insists that love such as she refers to is overrated, that it is, in fact, almost blasphemous in that it can get in the way of one's service to God.

Ultimately, Jane is able to resist St. John's bullying, but only with great difficulty. She is influenced by his arguments; they make sense to her intellectually even though they leave her heart cold. In a time when many more marriages were entered into for practical reasons than for passionate love, St. John had every reason to expect that Jane would accept his proposal to marry him and share his missionary work in India. When she doesn't, he takes it as an affront not only to himself, but also to God. He believes that Jane's return to Mr. Rochester, albeit an honorable return after his first wife dies in the fire that destroys Thornfield, demonstrates a rejection of duty on Jane's part to both God and propriety. St. John goes to India to perform his work as a missionary without her, but he is cold toward her and her marriage to Mr. Rochester for the remainder of his life.

Jane Eyre was written in a period when men believed they had a right to determine what was best for the women in their families and under their hire. Women were taught that their duty was to submit. *Jane Eyre* is the story of a woman who is unwilling to submit to anything she perceives as wrong or unfair. She believes that she should have the right to determine her future for herself, that she should have the right to make her own choices, and that she should be considered the equal of any man as a human being, even if she is his subordinate in terms of money, position, or employment. Such a position was difficult for any Victorian woman to adhere to. For a woman raised as an orphan, dependent for her very existence on the compassion of others, it would have been quite remarkable. Perhaps that is one of the reasons the novel touched so many of its earliest readers so deeply.

THE WOMEN IN JANE'S LIFE

Jane Eyre believes in her right to be a full and complete human being, to be treated as the equal of any other human being in terms of basic human rights. In the twenty-first century, this idea is commonplace. In Charlotte Brontë's time, however, it was quite revolutionary. Women were considered to be subordinate to men according to the laws of both God and Nature. Under the law, married women were unable to own property in their own name; they were not permitted to sue in their name or even to have legal rights to their own children. They were legally the property of their husbands, who could treat them as well or as poorly as they chose. A respectable woman was expected never to fall in love, but only to allow herself to grow to love the man she marries out of gratitude for his love of her. Respectable women were expected to service their husbands' needs sexually and to give them children (preferably at least one son), but never to enjoy themselves sexually. To enjoy the pleasures of the body was considered coarse and disreputable for a Victorian woman. Nor were women expected to have a love of intellectual activity. In fact, most nineteenth-century doctors recommended against women receiving a classical education or reading in too much depth, claiming that it would make them "unwomanly." Intellectual pursuits would, so it was believed, redirect a woman's vital energies from the production of children and the maternal instincts. As a result, it was believed that her uterus and ovaries would atrophy, and she would not only be unable to have and/or to nurture children (the role a Victorian woman was supposedly born to play), but she would begin to act and look more like a man than a woman. For a woman like Jane Eyre, who felt and thought so deeply, such restrictions on feeling passion and thinking philosophical thoughts would be wholly intolerable.

In *Jane Eyre* Charlotte Brontë presents several women who represent one or another aspect of the early Victorian woman. Some coincide with the ideal of the "angel in the house," a phrase coined by Coventry Patmore to describe the ideal Victorian lady. Others represent the shadow side of the Victorian woman, the energies and demeanors that must remain repressed if one is to be considered an ideal, or even respectable, lady. Not one of these single-faceted individuals lives a fully productive or satisfying life. Only when all the qualities are combined and integrated into a single individual, the novel seems to say, can a truly satisfactory life result.

Helen Burns represents the extreme of amiability and self-deprecation. She is the "good girl" who never has a bad word to say against anyone except herself. She is willing to accept any and all criticism of herself, believing that she is, in fact, a very slatternly and willful girl. She undergoes painful corporal punishment from Miss Scatcherd without a protest or a whimper, certain that she must endure the punishment in order to learn the lessons she is supposed to learn in life. She is continually shamed in front of the other students, often as punishment for circumstances beyond her control, and she takes her punishment in stride, as her due. Jane recognizes Helen's essential goodness, but detests the fact that Helen refuses to stand up for herself. Such denial of one's essential selfhood is beyond Jane's understanding. It is also, the novel would seem to imply, something that cannot effectively be maintained for an entire lifetime. Helen dies young, seemingly too good for this world.

Blanche Ingram is another single-faceted individual in the novel, representing the antithesis of Jane in terms of wealth and beauty. Blanche is, outwardly, the perfect marital partner for Mr. Rochester. She is a dark beauty, solid and strong, a good horsewoman, and apparently a good match for him physically. She is also an heiress. She is born into his social class and would be able to bring her own fortune to his estate. She is, thus, exactly what a man in Mr. Rochester's position is expected to desire in a mate. She is also, however, cold and haughty, especially where servants and children are concerned. She speaks in Jane's presence of her opinion that all governesses are detestable women with nothing of substance to offer and of her determination to have Adele sent away to school the moment she becomes Mrs. Rochester. She displays no evidence of even the slightest warmth, human kindness, or compassion. In Blanche Ingram, Jane sees the kind of woman that society expects men like Mr. Rochester to marry. Similarity of vision, compatibility of character, and shared passions are qualities that Rochester shares with Jane, not Blanche, but they are not qualities that society considers to be important for a husband and wife. Since childhood, Jane has been told that she is nothing but a dependent, someone who will never be truly significant in anyone else's life. In Blanche Ingram, she comes face to face with the kind of woman who is significant, according to the societal rules of the time, and finds her extremely distasteful.

Jane finds Mr. Rochester's apparent interest in marrying Blanche Ingram difficult to understand on a personal level, but she recognizes the practical and social aspects of such a marriage and assumes that he is behaving true to form for a gentleman of his time and class. In fact, he does not intend to marry Blanche, only to lead her on and, in the process, to try the heart and spirit of the woman he truly loves, Jane Eyre. But Mr. Rochester's reluctance to marry Blanche Ingram does not come as a result of his intellectualizing about the possible problems involved in a marriage with someone so incompatible with his personality; it comes from actual experience. Rochester did, when he was younger, marry someone very much like Blanche Ingram, a woman of position and money with whom he had little in common intellectually or emotionally.

Bertha Mason Rochester is the living wife of Edward Fairfax Rochester at the time Jane comes to Thornfield to live. Jane, unaware that Bertha lives in the attic, or even of Bertha's very existence, allows herself to fall in love with her employer as they discover their essential compatibility. Bertha, in her present state, represents the shadow side of the proper Victorian lady, for Bertha has become a madwoman, kept locked away from sight and public awareness.

All of the inhabitants of Thornfield know about the existence of Bertha except Jane and Adele. For Adele, the knowledge is considered too adult. Jane is not told because Mr. Rochester initially feared she might not stay to teach Adele if she knew. But no one at Thornfield is aware of Bertha's exact relationship to Mr. Rochester. Some believe she may be one of his former mistresses who has gone mad and whom he has chosen to care for. Others believe that she may be a bastard half-sister, or even a former employee. Some may suspect the relation to be marital, but no one living at Thornfield knows for sure. All they know for certain is that she remains locked in the attic under the watch of Grace Poole, the coarse woman who serves as her caregiver.

By the time we see Bertha in the novel, she has degenerated into a creature with animalistic characteristics. She continues, however, to have great human cunning, as is apparent on those occasions when she manages to sneak away from her keeper and wreak havoc in select areas of the house. She attempts to burn her husband to death in his bed one night, only to have Jane wake him in time. When her stepbrother, Richard Mason, visits her, she attacks him with both a knife and her teeth, sinking her teeth so deeply into his shoulder that he requires medical attention. She visits Jane's room on the night before her wedding to Rochester is scheduled, and destroys the veil that symbolizes their imminent nuptials.

As the shadow side of the respectable Victorian woman, Bertha displays the rage and violence that women were required to repress in Victorian life. She was discarded by her family, essentially sold to a complete stranger for her fortune, then taken, against her will, to England, a land so different in culture and climate from the Caribbean Island on which she was born and raised that, had she not already been exhibiting serious signs of mental imbalance, the move itself would have likely driven her mad.

When finally forced into revealing Bertha as his wife, Rochester describes her heritage:

> Bertha Mason is mad; and she came of a mad family:—idiots and maniacs through three generations! Her mother, the Creole, was both a mad woman and a drunkard!—as I found out after I had wed the daughter: for they were silent on family secrets before. Bertha, like a dutiful child, copied her parent in both points. (355)

Bertha's madness reveals itself to Rochester after their marriage through her drinking, her irrational (in his opinion, at least) behavior, and her lustiness. No respectable and responsible woman could, according to the standards of Victorian society, act as Bertha acted unless she were mad. In fact, madness in women was often described in the medical articles of the day as a tendency toward drunkenness and lascivious desires. Bertha indulges her desires; therefore, she must be ill. Such was the logic of Victorian social mores and medical practices.

Brontë does not show the reader a young Bertha, capable of winning Rochester with her dark beauty and her fortune. We do not know, therefore, how Bertha interacted with the world before her marriage, whether her impending madness would have been apparent to a wiser man than her husband or not. Nor do we know how quickly her illness progressed or what her husband may have done to accelerate the process. Brontë leaves those details to the imagination of the reader. One may freely accept Rochester's version of the story, or one may look beyond it, blaming, at least in part, the very essence of Victorian culture for Bertha's degeneration into the mad creature we meet in the novel.

But regardless of the course of her illness and the reasons behind it, once Bertha is defined as mad and locked away from the world, her condition worsens, resulting in the animalistic creature Rochester displays to his thwarted wedding party:

> In the deep shade, at the further end of the room, a figure ran backwards and forwards. What it was, whether beast or human being, one could not, at first sight, tell: it groveled, seemingly, on all

fours; it snatched and growled like some strange wild animal: but it was covered with clothing; and a quantity of dark, grizzled hair, wild as a mane, hid its head and face. (356)

Bertha represents that part of the Victorian woman that is not to be seen, not even to be admitted to exist. She reflects the instinctive animalistic part of the woman's nature, filled with violent rage at being repressed. The consequences for a woman of showing her deepest passions publicly in Victorian England were severe. A woman could be considered "unnatural" merely for allowing anyone, including her husband, to be made aware that she enjoys sex or that she feels intense anger or frustration. The respectable woman of this time was calm, passive, and subservient. The only aggression she was permitted to show was passive aggression—illnesses (real or feigned) that prevented her from meeting her husband's expectations, or indirect manipulations that enabled her to get her way without others being aware that they had been manipulated. Such "feminine wiles" were permissible, though dangerous in that they could easily backfire. Bertha's aggression, however, is far from passive. She is the most direct female in the entire novel. Her emotions and desires are clear in each of her actions. She is not passive toward others; she is active. And the actively aggressive woman in Victorian culture is, by definition, a madwoman.

The character of Jane Eyre strives to be a fully developed human being, instead of a mere Victorian lady. She recognizes the need of a human being to take action in her life, not merely to be reactive. She believes that, as a human being, she has a right to want more than the proper Victorian lady is expected to want. "Anybody may blame me who likes," Jane challenges her readers,

That, now and then . . . I climbed the three staircases, raised the trap-door of the attic, and having reached the leads, looked out afar over sequestered field and hill, and along dim skyline: that then I longed for a power of vision which might overpass that limit; which might reach the busy world, towns, regions full of life I had heard of but never seen: that then I desired more of practical experience than I possessed; more of intercourse with my kind, of acquaintance with variety of character, than was here within my reach. . . .

Who blames me? Many no doubt; and I shall be called discontented. I could not help it: the restlessness was in my nature; it agitated me to pain sometimes. Then my sole relief was to walk along the corridor of the third story, backwards and forwards, safe in the silence and solitude of the spot, and allow my mind's eye to dwell on whatever bright visions rose before it . . . to let my heart be heaved by the exultant movement which, while it swelled it in trouble, expanded it with life; and, best of all, to open my inward ear to a tale that was never ended—a tale my imagination created, and narrated continuously; quickened with all of incident, life, fire, feeling, that I desired and had not in my actual existence. (129)

Jane, in order to feel fully alive, in order to dream the dreams and have the visions that keep her sane, must go to the third floor and into the attic (the floor, though not the room, where the insane Bertha is kept) and out onto the roof (from which Bertha eventually leaps to her death) to look out and experience the world that has, thus far, been closed to her. She knows that "many" will condemn her for even the need to dream such dreams, but she must dream them. And, when the frustration of having her vision and actions so restricted gets the better of her, she paces, "backwards and forwards," along the corridor, just as Bertha runs "backwards and forwards" within her cell. And, in case the reader misses that particular connection, Brontë encloses Jane's entire speech about desiring so much more than is available to her within two loud laughs, laughs that we discover later in the novel originate from Bertha Rochester herself. Bertha would seem to be laughing at Jane's dreams and desires, the knowing laugh of one who has experienced those dreams and desires herself, but who has found herself, because of them, to be more greatly restricted than she ever could have imagined by the very man with whom Jane will soon fall in love.

The Victorian woman can be imminently respectable, like Helen Burns, but be victimized by those in power over her. She can appear to be perfect in appearance and social position, like Blanche Ingram, but be cold, aloof, and haughty. Or she can be completely disreputable like Bertha, indulging her desires to the point of madness (at least as it was defined by the Victorians). Jane wants to do what is right; she wants to do her duty and to remain a respectable woman. But she also wants to experience the fullness of her humanity, with all its potential action and excitement as well. To find a means of doing both, in Victorian society, was extraordinarily difficult, if not impossible, for women.

NATURE VERSUS CIVILIZATION

Civilized society in *Jane Eyre* is the place in which women are not free to express their feelings and experience their desires without risking being declared mad. And yet Nature dictates, so Brontë seems to say, that women will have the same feelings, dreams, and needs for activity that men have. To underscore this point, the novel associates images of nature with ideas and events that place Jane beyond the bounds of acceptable feminine behavior. Images of nature in general and the moon in particular occur on several occasions when Jane experiences more emotion than a respectable Victorian woman should.

The first association of moonlight with Jane's excesses of emotion occurs when she is locked in the red room at Gateshead. There, as she becomes more and more frightened of the possibility that her uncle's ghost will visit, she sees, or imagines seeing, a streak of light move across the wall. "Was it, I asked myself, a ray from the moon penetrating some aperture in the blind? No; moonlight was still, and this stirred: while I gazed, it glided up to the ceiling and quivered over my head" (13). Jane never finds out precisely what caused the light, but her association of it with the natural light of the moon introduces the idea of using images of nature to indicate feelings that are more in tune with nature than with societal expectations.

Another image of moonlight follows Jane's emotional speech about her need for more excitement and activity than her life has thus far provided. After she comes down from the roof, she goes for a walk under "the rising moon; pale yet as a cloud, but brightening momentarily" (132). While walking under this moon, she hears the beat of horse's hooves and sees, suddenly coming into view, a large dog followed by a horse and rider. In this moment of passionate otherworldliness, she meets Mr. Rochester, her future husband, for the first time.

It is not moonlight, but thunder and lightning that accompany Jane's excess of emotion when Mr. Rochester proposes marriage. Her joy is as overwhelming as the storm itself, but the storm is also destructive: lightning strikes the large horse-chestnut tree, causing it to split in two. Mr. Rochester's proposal is likewise destructive. He asks Jane to marry him because of his passion for her, but he knows that he cannot be truly married to her in the eyes of the church or the law. The divided tree represents his divided loyalties, "blasted" by the violence of his passion.

When Jane leaves Thornfield, with no friend to go to and no job to support her needs, she decides that Nature, "the universal Mother," is now her only friend (394). She sees Nature as "benign and good" and believes that she will protect her in her time of need (394). This "mother," she believes, "would lodge me without money and without price" (394). She sleeps that night in the bosom of her mother, Nature, trusting her more than she has ever been able to trust mankind to take care of her. In the light of day, however, Jane realizes that Nature cannot and will not provide for all her needs. She must find a way to survive that acknowledges the civilized world of humanity as well as Nature. Thus, Jane goes back into society to look for a means of supporting herself.

The final image of moonlight associated with extremes of emotion for Jane comes when, having almost given in to St. John's demands to marry him, she hears Rochester's voice calling to her, seemingly from across a mysterious void. Her feelings intensely affected, she notices that "the room was full of moonlight" (513). Moonlight, associated in folk traditions with the emotional depths of the soul, here suggests an almost supernatural connection with Jane's deepest feelings for Rochester.

Such depth of feeling was not something that a proper Victorian lady could admit to. In fact, having such depth of feeling was considered to be a sin against propriety for such a lady. Much of the criticism directed at the novel when it was first published was directed at Jane's feeling and expressing such depth of emotion. Charlotte Brontë, in trying to create a strong female character who feels "just as men feel," creates a novel that was considered downright dangerous by some readers, but with which multitudes of Victorian women could identify and approve (130).

CONCLUSION

Jane Eyre was a very unusual novel for its time. It presents the experiences of a young girl in a very honest and straightforward manner, in the voice of the character herself. It claims a need for women to have equal experiences with men—not the same, but equal in quality and depth of meaning. It insists that women are, in fact, the equal of men, that "they need exercise for their faculties, and a field for their efforts as much as their brothers do," that they "suffer from too rigid a restraint, too absolute a stagnation" in this culture, "precisely as men would suffer" (130). In *Jane Eyre* a very young, plain, and penniless girl claims the right to have a field for her actions as large as that of any man. Such a claim was revolutionary in the world to which Jane Eyre—and Charlotte Brontë—belonged.

TOPICS FOR WRITTEN OR ORAL EXPLORATION

1. Choose one of the minor characters in *Jane Eyre* for whom the novel does not provide extensive details about childhood experiences. Write a character study in which you analyze his or her character as it is presented in the novel and then invent a history that would account for the way he or she behaves. Be able to defend the history you create. Possible subjects for analysis include Mrs. Reed, Bessie, Mr. Brocklehurst, Miss Temple, Miss Scatcherd, Mrs. Fairfax, Bertha Rochester, Grace Poole, and St. John Rivers.

2. Discuss the role that organized religion plays in the novel.

3. Imagine that Helen Burns does not die at Lowood School. Discuss what kind of adult she would become and what kind of friendship she and Jane would be likely to have as adults.

4. Compare the characters of the clergymen in the novel: Mr. Brocklehurst and St. John Rivers. How are their religious values similar to and/or different from those of each other and those that the novel supports?

5. Imagine life for the characters after the novel ends. Write a description of the lives of the following individuals ten years later: Georgiana and Eliza Reed, Diana and Mary Rivers, Adele Varens, Mrs. Fairfax, Blanche Ingram, Richard Mason, and St. John Rivers.

6. Write an essay in which you explain why, how, and when Mr. Rochester fell in love with Jane Eyre. Be sure to use details from the novel to support your perspective.

7. Write an essay in which you explain why, how, and when Jane fell in love with Mr. Rochester. Be sure to use details from the novel to support your perspective.

8. Write an essay on the significance of class differences in *Jane Eyre*.

9. Discuss the role that education plays in *Jane Eyre*. What aspects of education seem to be most emphasized in Jane's childhood? What aspects are most emphasized for Adele?

10. Discuss the similarities and differences among Mr. Rochester's various romantic interests: Bertha Mason Rochester, Celine Varens, Blanche Ingram, and Jane Eyre. What are the common traits among the women? What are their differences? What do his choices say about his character?

11. Write an essay explaining why the values that *Jane Eyre* upholds would or would not be appropriate values for people to live by in the twenty-first century.

12. Write an essay on the theme of duty in the novel.

13. Write an essay on the theme of personal responsibility in the novel.

14. Create a list of the various symbols of love within the novel. Then write an essay in which you define love as it is displayed in *Jane Eyre*.

15. View one or more film versions of *Jane Eyre*. Discuss the choices the director made in creating the film. Write an essay in which you analyze the relative success or failure of the film version(s) you watched in terms of faithfulness to the novel.

SUGGESTED READINGS

Allott, Miriam, ed. *The Brontës: The Critical Heritage*. London: Routledge, 1974.

Auerbach, Nina. *Woman and the Demon: The Life of a Victorian Myth*. Cambridge: Harvard University Press, 1982.

Barker, Juliet. *The Brontës*. New York: St. Martin's Press, 1994.

Brontë, Charlotte. *Jane Eyre*. The Haworth Edition. London: Harper and Brothers, 1900.

Dunbar, Janet. *The Early Victorian Woman*. London: Harrap, 1953.

Eastlake, Elizabeth Rigby. "Vanity Fair and Jane Eyre." *Quarterly Review* 83 (1848): 153–185.

Ewbank, Inga Stina. *Their Proper Sphere: A Study of the Brontë Sisters as Early Victorian Female Novelists*. London: Edward Arnold: 1966.

Fraser, Rebecca. *Charlotte Brontë*. London: Metheun, 1988.

Gerin, Winifred. *The Brontës. I. The Formative Years*. Essex: Longman Group, 1973.

———. *The Brontës. II. The Creative Work*. Essex: Longman Group, 1974.

———. *Charlotte Brontë: The Evolution of Genius*. Oxford: Oxford University Press, 1967.

Gilbert, Sandra, and Susan Gubar. *The Madwoman in the Attic: The Woman Writer and the Nineteenth-Century Literary Imagination*. New Haven, CT: Yale University Press, 1979.

Gordon, Lyndall. *Charlotte Brontë: A Passionate Life*. New York: W. W. Norton, 1994.

Gregor, Ian, ed. *The Brontës: A Collection of Critical Essays*. Englewood Cliffs, NJ: Prentice-Hall, 1970.

Guerard, Albert J. *Stories of the Double*. Philadelphia: J. B. Lippincott, 1967.

Martin, Robert Bernard. *Accents of Persuasion: Charlotte Brontë's Novels*. London: Faber, 1966.

Michie, Helena. *The Flesh Made Word: Female Figures and Women's Bodies*. Oxford: Oxford University Press, 1989.

Moglen, Helene. *Charlotte Brontë: The Self Conceived*. New York: Norton, 1976.

Poovey, Mary. *Uneven Developments: The Ideological Work of Gender in Mid-Victorian England*. London: Virago, 1989.

Smith, Margaret. "Introduction." In *Jane Eyre*, by Charlotte Brontë. Oxford: Oxford University Press, 1993.

Thaden, Barbara. *Student Companion to Charlotte and Emily Brontë*. Westport, CT: Greenwood Press, 2001.

2

Education for Victorian Girls

Jane Eyre is a bildungsroman, the story of the moral education of an individual. As a bildungsroman, it focuses on both the formal and the informal education of the main character, Jane Eyre, examining what she learns from the experience of life as well as the classroom as she comes of age.

In the Victorian period, the form and content of one's education depended largely on one's economic and social standing. Girls of the lower classes, if they attended school at all (most did not), attended charity schools or schools of industry that were geared toward training their students to be good workers in factories, small businesses, and household servant staffs. Most of these schools taught a minimum of what we would consider to be educational subjects today, focusing instead on training the students in tasks such as sewing or weaving. These schools were supported through subscriptions paid by industrialists and charitable wealthy individuals, whose primary interest was that these girls would be trained to be productive workers, not that they would receive an education in the intellectual sense. Many of the girls who attended these schools went on to apprenticeships as servants or factory workers when they were old enough.

Girls from wealthier, genteel families were provided with a very different sort of education. Often the intellectual content was only slightly more rigorous than that of the industrial school curriculum, but women from this level of society were not expected to have to earn their own livings; therefore, the emphasis on learning marketable skills was negligible. Instead, they focused on becoming "accomplished": learning to dress appropriately, discuss appropriate subjects, play musical instruments, sing, dance, speak French, and read fashionable works of both fiction and nonfiction. In the better schools (better in terms of the quality of learning, not necessarily better in social reputation), girls also learned enough arithmetic to balance the household books and were taught how to supervise a staff. Girls from these families were not expected to be put into the position of having to support themselves, nor were they expected to have to do any of the real labor of household work, since they would have servants to perform those services for them.

Two methods of educating daughters were available to the wealthy families of Charlotte Brontë's time. One was to send the girls away to fashionable boarding schools, where they would learn from a variety of different teachers along with other girls of approximately the same social class. This method had the advantage of keeping the daughters out of the house, providing the parents with greater freedom and fewer obligations while at home. It also enabled the daughters to meet girls from other families in the same social class—girls who might have brothers at home who were in the market for an appropriate marital partner. Such schools, therefore, often became a kind of marketplace in which wealthy young men might find suitable marriage partners.

The second method of educating daughters of wealthy families was to hire a governess. The governess was usually a woman whose pedigree was genteel, but who had fallen on hard times, either because her father's income was not large enough to support her or because it was tied up legally in such a way as not to be available to her. The daughters of many clergymen with limited incomes spent significant parts of their lives teaching, either as governesses in private families or in boarding schools. Charlotte Brontë worked both as a private governess and as a teacher in several schools in order to support herself. Girls taught by private governesses received a quality education if their governesses were well-trained and their parents allowed the governesses a free hand in teaching. But often the governesses were not well-trained and/or the parents interfered with the progress of their daughters' education to the point of making hiring a governess more of a status symbol for the family than an educational advantage for their daughters.

The character of Jane Eyre is forged in neither the lower class's charity schools nor in the wealthier boarding schools. Her path, like that of many girls born into genteel families with little money, integrates aspects of both. Jane is born into an impoverished, but genteel, family. Her father is a clergyman and her mother the daughter of a wealthy gentleman. Therefore, despite the fact that Jane is orphaned and left with no money of her own (her parents having lived on the income from Mr. Eyre's church and having no savings to leave to their daughter), it does not occur to Jane's aunt to send her to a poor working class charity school or a school of industry. Jane is entitled, by reason of her birth into the genteel classes, to a life within that level of society, albeit one on the fringes. Jane is, therefore, sent to Lowood, an institution established for the education of daughters of clergymen. It is a school run primarily on charity, the families of the girls being able to provide only a small amount toward the total required to lodge and teach the girls, but it is not what was traditionally referred to as a charity school. At schools like Lowood, girls were trained to fit into the world of their betters in order that they might become governesses, school teachers, or lady's companions as a means of providing for themselves when reaching adulthood. Many of the "accomplishments" taught at the schools for girls of wealthy families were taught at schools like Lowood, but they were taught with the intent of providing the girls with the ability to teach those accomplishments to wealthier girls rather than to use them to attract husbands for themselves. They were, in fact, trained to believe that they would never find husbands since they had no financial assets to offer. They were taught at these schools to be self-effacing, to endure deprivation without complaint, and to expect little out of life.

Whether of the poor working classes, the wealthier classes, or somewhere in between, whether educated at home by a mother or a governess or sent to school, a major portion of the education of a girl in Victorian times focused on learning proper morals and behavior. The onus of propriety was always on the woman in Victorian times. The single woman was expected to remain an innocent, not even knowing what sex was or having any sexual desires, and yet to be able to avoid any situation in which a man might be able to take advantage of her in any way (even to taking her hand or giving her a kiss). Even the *appearance* of impropriety could affect a woman's future in Victorian England, especially if her family had limited funds and the daughter was not being sought after as a financially profitable marriage partner. And yet, because the future of most women was only considered secure if they married, they also had to make themselves as attractive as possible to men of their social class so that they would be considered acceptable as marriage partners. Learning the accepted rules of proper behavior for her station in life, therefore, was an essential part of every girl's education.

THE CHARITY SCHOOL

The charity school movement began in England at the beginning of the eighteenth century as a means of providing children of the poor with a sufficient education to be able to become productive citizens in a culture that was moving away from being a completely agrarian culture and moving toward industrialization. Charity schools provided children with a relatively standardized education, not only in the fundamentals of reading, writing, and arithmetic, but also in the kind of values that would be most beneficial to their future employers. The schools taught children to be prompt, to be thorough, to keep themselves clean, and to obey authority. The teaching of these values was probably the most important aspect of the schools from the perspective of those who supported them with their money and employed the students later in life.

Whether the schools truly benefited the majority of students is somewhat questionable. Josephine Kamm, noted scholar of the history of education, writes:

> In the charity school proper—as distinct from the industrial school—the teaching was often lifeless and mechanical and the discipline and austerities unnecessarily severe, girls as well as boys being flogged for minor offences. There were exceptions, of course, but on the whole the existence of the charity school child was dreary and dull. Much depended on the master or mistress, but good teachers were all too rare, the vast majority were undistinguished and insignificant. All the same, critics complained that the charity school girl was getting ideas above her station.
>
> What in fact was happening was that the institutional atmosphere of the charity school was turning out girls who were too listless and lethargic to show any enthusiasm for work or for any of the other active duties of life. (91)

To women of the upper classes, the severity of the charity schools was not a problem. They expected such an institution to be severe in order to prepare students to be good workers who were not prone to the vices so often associated with members of the lower classes.

MRS. SARAH TRIMMER

Mrs. Sarah Trimmer (1741–1810) was a strong proponent of education in England in the late eighteenth and early nineteenth centuries. Known best as a writer of moral tales and devotional stories for children, Mrs. Trimmer advocated a particular educational method developed by Dr. Andrew Bell. She used his "monitorial" system of education in teaching her own twelve children and encouraged many schools throughout England to adopt the system in which older students, supervised by a master teacher, taught the young ones. Her work eventually led to the founding of the National Society for Promoting the Education of the Poor in the Principles of the Established Church. Her ideas about education became well known and respected as a result of her publication of several books, including *An Essay Introduction to the Knowledge of Nature* (1782), and the *Comparative View of the New Plan of Education* (1805), as well as her editing of *The Family Magazine* (1788–1789) and the *Guardian of Education* (1802–1806).

Mrs. Trimmer was a strong advocate of the Charity School movement throughout England. She encouraged others to support the Charity School movement as well as supporting it herself with her time, her money, and her writing. She wrote *The Economy of Charity; or, an Address to Ladies; Adapted to the Present State of Charitable Institutions in England*, a defense of the Charity School system. She also wrote textbooks that she believed would better serve students than many that had been in use in English classrooms for quite some time. Trimmer died in 1810, but her influence on education remained strong years after her death. Charlotte Brontë would have been well aware of Mrs. Trimmer's educational ideas as well as her moral and devotional tales from her experience as a teacher at Roe Head School.

In *The Economy of Charity; or, an Address to Ladies; Adapted to the Present State of Charitable Institutions in England*, Mrs. Trimmer encourages other English ladies to assist in her crusade to provide an education to the children of the poor in England. Such an education will, she asserts, not only assist the children themselves, but will help those who employ them and even the nation itself, as the children will be educated in such a way as to enable them to avoid many of the improprieties their parents have fallen into. According to Mrs. Trimmer, children educated in the Charity Schools will be better prepared to perform the tasks expected of those in their station in life with efficiency and judiciousness than those who are raised entirely by their parents.

Mrs. Trimmer also discusses other kinds of schools that were available for the poor: Sunday Schools and Schools of Industry. Each type of school had its own purpose and, therefore, its own reason for existing. Sunday Schools were established to teach young workers to read and write, as well as to provide religious instruction to those who worked the other six days of the week. Schools of Industry were training grounds for youth who would be going to work in factories and mines. They taught the fundamental skills necessary to produce efficient workers for hire by the captains of industry. The Charity Schools that Mrs. Trimmer writes in support of are full-time schools that provide a somewhat more well-rounded education for those among the poor who will be working primarily in the households and on the estates of the wealthy.

FROM MRS. SARAH TRIMMER, *THE ECONOMY OF CHARITY; OR, AN ADDRESS TO LADIES; ADAPTED TO THE PRESENT STATE OF CHARITABLE INSTITUTIONS IN ENGLAND*
(London, 1801)

Whoever seriously considers the present manners of the lower order of people, must surely see the necessity of vigilant attention towards the rising generation; since no less than the safety of the nation probably depends upon the education of those children, who are now growing up to maturity, whose parents are not only incapable of giving them proper instruction, but are likely, it is to be feared, to lead them astray by their own bad example, if the hand of charity is not seasonably stretched out to guide them in the paths of religion and virtue.

It is a general complaint that domestic servants, instead of being attached to their masters and mistresses, act merely upon selfish and mercenary principles; and that no confidence is to be placed in the lower kinds of labourers and workmen.—It is certainly of great consequence to the welfare and happiness of families to have faithful and conscientious servants. But how frequent of late years have instances occurred of domestics being detected in league with house-breakers and thieves; of others who have set fire to their master's houses, eloped with considerable sums of money, or betrayed important trusts? Does not every mistress of a family complain that the expenses of housekeeping are considerably increased by the wastefulness and dishonesty of servants; and is it not generally lamented that the frauds practiced by labourers and workmen, keep their employers in a constant state of suspicion and uneasiness; and that a spirit of insubordination prevails amongst the lower orders which sets them above all control, and endangers the safety of the state? These evils according to the opinion of the first writers of the present day, who have considered the subject maturely, are imputable in a great measure to the want of early instruction; in consequence of which the generality of youth of both sexes go out into the world without a proper sense of the duties of their station. The education of the poor children therefore should not be left to their ignorant and corrupted parents; it is a public concern, and should be regarded as a public business, so far as is consistent with that freedom, which it would be an injury to the community to infringe; and it is much to be lamented, that this important concern should ever be neglected; for the peace and welfare, not only of Parishes, but of the Kingdom at large, greatly depend upon the training of the younger members of the lower classes, who are usually made the tools of sedition, when a design is formed for raising civil commotions. . . . The poor might probably resist in these times of licentious freedom, that authority, which would force them to give up their children entirely to the state, but they are in general glad to accept of eleemosynary education for them; and the bounty of the rich cannot be better employed than in providing it. Nor would it be a difficult task to furnish education for all the poor children in the nation at a moderate expence, if those who have ability would contribute their money, their leisure, or their talents, to the accomplishment of this object, as circumstances would admit. There are already many Charity Schools in the kingdom of various descriptions, liberally endowed and supported, which furnish instruction and employment for great numbers of poor children; nothing therefore appears to be wanting for the accomplishment of this desirable end, but to multiply these Schools—to see that the plan of instruction is suited to the condition of the children, and the circumstances of the times in respect to religion—and that it is executed with judgment and kindness. (10–14)

• • •

It is well known that those useful establishments called Charity Schools, have owed their chief support, from the beginning, to annual subscriptions and voluntary benefactions, collected at the preaching of Charity Sermons; we cannot therefore wonder that some of the trustees and managers of these Schools, from zeal for their welfare, should at first have viewed with a jealous eye the rapid progress of other institutions for the instruction of poor children, from an apprehension that the success of the one might interfere with the interests of the other, as they mutually depend on the same means for support. But the institutions of modern date Sunday Schools and Schools of Industry have already existed long enough, to prove that these fears were ill-grounded: and it is much to be lamented, that institutions respectively calculated, by their reflective and united benefits to complete the long-desired end, of educating all degrees of people in the lower ranks of life, should ever be regarded in the light of rivalship and competition. Charity Schools hold out such superior advantages, in some respect as to give them a decided pre-eminence over all the subsisting establishments for gratuitous instruction; as the money collected for them is usually sufficient to afford clothing to the children, as well as learning; and in many Charity Schools, the children are entirely maintained in the house, and some of them afterwards apprenticed to trades and manufactures.

But Sunday Schools and Schools of Industry, though the emoluments of the children are less, are of equal importance with the above institutions as they afford instruction to unlimited numbers of children, who could not be admitted into Charity Schools, on account of the expense attending them: neither could such multitudes be trained up as Charity Children are, without great injury to society: for, however desirable it may be to rescue the lower kinds of people from that deplorable state of ignorance, in which the greatest part of them are suffered to remain, it cannot be right to train them *all* in a way which will most probably raise their ideas above the very lowest occupations of life, and disqualify them for those servile offices, which must be filled by some of the members of the community, and in which they may be equally happy with the highest, if they will do their duty.

Many ill consequences are observed to arise among the higher orders of people, from educating the children of persons, whose opulence is the fruit of their own industry, and who have made themselves respectable without the aid of literary acquirements, with those whose parents are of high rank and independent fortune; but this injudicious practice we cannot expect to see abolished, while in the education of youth, so much regard is paid to externals, and so little to the regulation of the heart and the improvement of the understanding. It will, however, readily be allowed, that the children of the poor should not be educated in such a manner, as to set them above the occupations of humble life, or so as to make them uncomfortable among their equals, and ambitious of associating with persons moving in a higher sphere, with whom they cannot possibly vie in expense or appearance, without manifest injury to themselves.

But there are degrees of poverty as well as of opulence; and if it be improper to educate the children of the higher classes promiscuously, it surely must be equally so to place all the children of the poor upon the same footing, without any regard to the different circumstances of their parents, or their own genius and capacity. It would be thought cruel to send the child, or orphan, of a pious clergyman, or a respectable but reduced tradesman, to be brought up among the offspring of thieves and vagabonds, in the schools so happily and judiciously founded for those most wretched of all poor children, by the Philanthropic Society; and it would appear very absurd to send a boy designed for husbandry, to the Marine Society to be educated in the art of navigation. Yet nothing is more common than to mix poor children together in Charity Schools, whose separate claims to the superior advantages which these institutions hold out are by no means equal, and whose mental abilities will bear no comparison.

It would be justly deemed very illiberal to refuse to lads of bright parts, and uncommon activity of mind, the learning which Charity Schools afford; and consign them to the labours of the field; but is it not equally injurious, both to society and individuals, to condemn those who are invincibly dull and stupid to literary studies, as irksome to them as the most servile occupations are to boys of quick parts and aspiring tempers?

If there be among the poor children of a parish any who have been born to good prospects, who have enjoyed in their earliest years the comforts of affluence, and who still have respectable connections, it will be an act of particular kindness to place them in Charity Schools, where they will receive such an education as may hereafter prove a means of restoring them to their former station. And if there be others whose bright genius breaks through the thick clouds of ignorance and poverty, reason and humanity plead in their behalf, that they should be indulged with such tuition as may enable them to advance themselves, by the exertion of their abilities, to a higher station, and fill it with propriety. It certainly would be very unjustifiable to deny such children a chance of bettering their condition. . . .

In Charity Schools a comprehensive plan of tuition holds forth advantages for the first degree among the lower orders, who in these seminaries might be qualified for teachers in schools supported by charity, for apprentices to common trades, and for domestic servants in respectable families. (20–27)

• • •

With the domestic arrangements of Charity Schools in London, I am very little acquainted, but from the account of them collectively in the report of the Society for Promoting Christian Knowledge, it appears that very few of them furnish manufactory work for the children; this, as I have before observed, does not seem to me to be an object of regret, in respect to those Schools, which are liberally endowed: yet, I am far from wishing the children, whether boys or girls, to be brought up in idleness, or to spend their whole time in literary acquirements and going to Church. A small portion will suffice for the attainment of all that the poor have occasion to know or practice; and even those Charity Children who are separated from the multitude, to receive a greater portion of learning, may have time to do many useful things besides, as well as to recreate their minds by innocent amusements, which are particularly requisite for those young people who have sedentary employment.

For girls it is very easy to find intermediate employments; spinning wheels, both for wool and flax, should be constant appendages to Charity Schools, not only upon the principle of economy, but for exercise, particularly the long running-wheel, which will be found very conducive to the health of those children especially, who belong to Charity Schools in London. They should also, by turns, do all the household work belonging to the School. Plain work is so evidently useful to women in general, but to the poor in particular, that no Charity Girl can be deemed properly educated who has not attained to a tolerable proficiency at her needle; and there cannot be a want of this kind of work in a Charity School, if each girl be required not only to spin her own clothing, knit her own stockings, and make and mend her own clothes; but also be allowed to work occasionally for other branches of the family, in order to ease her mother. But if a sufficiency of work be not supplied by these means, Charity Girls might contribute greatly to the comfort and conveniency of a neighbourhood, by working for such poor women as are obliged to go constantly to day labour, or who cannot use a needle themselves. It would be a great addition to the comforts of the indigent and necessitous, if Ladies would kindly furnish materials, either old or new, to be made by Charity Girls into baby linen, or other articles of apparel for the poor. Occupations of this kind, under the direction of a clever mistress, would produce reciprocal benefits to those who work, and those who receive the fruits of their labour, for by these means girls would be trained up not only in habits of industry, but of contrivance and economy; and if the generality of Charity Girls learnt to write a tolerable hand, and to do common sums in the two first rules of arithmetic, it would be quite sufficient. (92–99)

THE GENTEEL BOARDING SCHOOL

Jane Eyre attends Lowood, a boarding school that provides education for destitute daughters and orphans of clergymen. Charlotte Brontë herself attended such a school, one that has much in common with Lowood. The school Jane attends in the novel is not unique in Victorian culture. In fact, many accounts of life in similar Victorian boarding schools can be found in autobiographies, biographies, and diaries, as well as fiction of the period.

Boarding schools for girls in Victorian times were run in a variety of ways by many kinds of people. Some were dedicated to educating girls from the most fashionable families, preparing them for the upper levels of the marriage market as thoroughly as cattle are prepared for market. Others prepared impoverished girls to teach—their own children if they were fortunate enough to marry; other people's if they remained single. Yet others were primarily organized to teach religious principles and a life of self-sacrifice. Some were well provisioned; others provided barely enough food and other essentials to enable the girls to survive. Some provided good teachers in a wide variety of subjects; others provided little more than a place for parents to send daughters they did not want to keep at home.

What follows are accounts of several boarding schools for girls of genteel backgrounds. While each of the accounts contains specific idiosyncratic details, when examined in total, one can recognize patterns common to most girls' boarding schools of the day. One can see that Lowood was not a figment of Charlotte Brontë's vivid imagination, but that it was, in fact, based on the experiences of Charlotte, her sisters, and her friends.

FRANCES POWER COBBE

Frances Power Cobbe was the only daughter of a well-to-do English Victorian family who owned considerable property in Ireland. She spent much of her early life on the family's estate near Dublin. There she was educated by her mother and a series of governesses until she turned fourteen. At that point she was sent to a very expensive and fashionable school for girls in Brighton, England. She describes her experience of the school in her autobiography.

FROM FRANCES POWER COBBE, *LIFE OF FRANCES POWER COBBE, AS TOLD BY HERSELF*
(London, 1904)

When it came to my turn to receive education, it was not in London but in Brighton that the ladies' schools most in estimation were to be found. There were even then (about 1836) not less than a hundred such establishments in the town, but that at No. 32, Brunswick Terrace, of which Miss Runciman and Miss Roberts were mistresses, and which had been founded some time before by a celebrated Miss Poggi, was supposed to be *nec pluribus impar*. It was, at all events, the most outrageously expensive, the nominal tariff of £120 or £130 per annum representing scarcely a fourth of the charges for "extras" which actually appeared in the bills of many of the pupils. My own, I know, amounted to £1,000 for two years' schooling.

I shall write of this school quite frankly, since the two poor ladies, well-meaning but very unwise, to whom it belonged have been dead for nearly thirty years, and it can hurt nobody to record my conviction that a better system than theirs could scarcely have been devised had it been designed to attain the maximum of cost and labour and the minimum of solid results. It was the typical High Education of the period, carried out to the extreme of expenditure and high pressure.

Profane persons were apt to describe our school as a Convent, and to refer to the back door of our garden, whence we issued on our dismal diurnal walks, as the "postern." If we in any degree resembled nuns, however, it was assuredly not those of either a Contemplative or Silent Order. The din of our large double schoolrooms was something frightful. Sitting in either of them, four pianos might be heard going at once in rooms above and around us, while at numerous tables scattered about the rooms there were girls reading aloud to the governesses and reciting lessons in English, French, German, and Italian. This hideous clatter continued the entire day till we went to bed at night, there being no time whatever allowed for recreation, unless the dreary hour of walking with our teachers (when we recited our verbs), could so be described by a fantastic imagination. In the midst of the uproar we were obliged to write our exercises, to compose our themes, and to commit to memory whole pages of prose. On Saturday afternoons, instead of play, there was a terrible ordeal generally known as the "Judgment Day." The two schoolmistresses sat side by side, solemn and stern, at the head of the long table.

Behind them sat all the governesses as Assessors. On the table were the books wherein our evil deeds of the week were recorded; and round the room against the wall, seated on stools of penitential discomfort, we sat, five-and-twenty "damosels," anything but "Blessed," expecting our sentences according to our ill-deserts. It must be explained that the fiendish ingenuity of some teacher had invented for our torment a system of imaginary "cards," which we were supposed to "lose" (though we never gained any) whenever we had not finished all our various lessons and practisings every night before bed-time, or whenever we had been given the mark for "stooping," or had been impertinent, or had been "turned" in our lessons, or had been marked "P" by the music master, or had been convicted of "disorder" (*e.g.*, having our long shoe-strings untied), or, lastly, had told lies! Any one crime in this heterogeneous list entailed the same penalty, namely, the sentence, "You have lost your card, Miss So-and-so, for such and such a thing;" and when Saturday came round, if three cards had been lost in the week, the law wreaked its justice on the unhappy sinner's head! Her confession having been wrung from her at the awful judgment-seat above described, and the books having been consulted, she was solemnly scolded and told to sit in the corner for the rest of the evening! Anything more ridiculous than the scene which followed can hardly be conceived. I have seen (after a week in which a sort of feminine barring-out had taken place) no less than nine young ladies obliged to sit for hours in the angles of the three rooms, like naughty babies, with their faces to the wall; half of them being quite of marriageable age, and all dressed, as was *de rigueur* with us every day, in full evening attire of silk or muslin, with gloves and kid slippers. Naturally, Saturday evenings, instead of affording some relief to the incessant overstrain of the week, were looked upon with terror as the worst time of all. Those who escaped the fell destiny of the corner were allowed, if they chose, to write to their parents, but our letters were perforce committed at night to the school-mistress to seal, and were not as may be imagined, exactly the natural outpouring of our sentiments as regarded those ladies and their school.

Our household was a large one. It consisted of the two schoolmistresses as joint proprietors, of the sister of one of them and another English governess; of a French, an Italian, and a German lady teacher; of a considerable staff of respectable servants; and finally of twenty-five or twenty-six pupils, varying in age from nine to nineteen. All the pupils were daughters of men of some standing, mostly country gentlemen, members of Parliament, and offshoots of the peerage. There were several heiresses amongst us. . . . On the whole, looking back after the long interval, it seems to me that the young creatures there assembled were full of capabilities for widely extended usefulness and influence. Many were decidedly clever and nearly all were well disposed. There was very little malice or any other vicious ideas or feelings, and no worldliness at all amongst us. . . .

But all this fine human material was deplorably wasted. Nobody dreamed that any one of us could in later life be more or less than an "Ornament of Society." That a pupil in that school should ever become an artist, or authoress, would have been looked upon by both Miss Runciman and Miss Roberts as a deplorable dereliction. Not that which was good in itself or useful to the community, or even that which would be delightful to ourselves, but that which would make us admired in society, was the *raison d'être* of each acquirement. Everything was taught us in the inverse ratio of its true importance. At the bottom of the scale were Morals and Religion, and at the top were Music and Dancing; miserably poor music, too, of the Italian school then in vogue, and generally performed in a showy and tasteless manner on harp or piano. I can recall an amusing instance in which the order of precedence above described was naively betrayed by one of our schoolmistresses when she was admonishing one of the girls who had been detected in a lie. "Don't you know, you naughty girl," said Miss R. impressively, before the whole school: "Don't you know we had *almost* rather find you have a P——" (the mark of Pretty Well) "in your music, than tell such falsehoods?"

It mattered nothing whether we had any "music in our souls" or any voices in our throats, equally we were driven through the dreary course of practicing daily for a couple of hours under a German teacher, and then receiving lessons twice or three times a week from a music master . . . and a singing master. Many of us, myself in particular, in addition to these had a harp master. . . . Lastly there were a few young ladies who took instructions in the new instruments, the concertina and the accordion!

The waste of money involved in all this, the piles of useless music, and songs never to be sung, for which our parents had to pay, and the loss of priceless time for ourselves, were truly deplorable; and the result of course in many cases (as in my own) complete failure. . . . Yet so hopeless a pupil was compelled to learn for years, not only the piano, but the harp and singing.

Next to music in importance in our curriculum came dancing. The famous old Madame Michaud and her husband both attended us constantly, and we danced to their direction in our large play-room . . . till we had learned not only all the dances in use in England in that antepolka epoch, but almost every national dance in Europe, the Minuet, the Gavotte, the Cachucha, the Bolero, the Mazurka, and the Tarantella. To see the stout old lady in her heavy green velvet dress, with furbelow a foot deep of sable, going through the latter cheerful performance for our ensample, was a sight not to be forgotten. Beside the dancing we had "calisthenic" lessons every week from a "Captaine" Somebody, who put us through manifold exercises with poles and dumbbells. How much better a few good country scrambles would have been than all these calisthenics it is needless to say, but our dismal walks were confined to parading the espalanade and neighbouring terraces. Our parties never exceeded six, a governess being one of the number, and we looked down from an immeasurable height of superiority on the processions of twenty and thirty girls belonging to other schools. The governess who accompanied us had enough to do with her small party, for it was her duty to utilize these brief hours of bodily exercise by hearing us repeat our French, Italian or German verbs, according to her own nationality.

Next to Music and Dancing and Deportment, came Drawing, but that was not a sufficiently *voyant* accomplishment, and no great attention was paid to it; the instruction also being of a second-rate kind, except that it included lessons in perspective which have been useful to me ever since. Then followed Modern Languages. No Greek or Latin were heard of at the school, but French, Italian and German were chattered all day long, our tongues being only set at liberty at six o'clock to speak English. . . .

Naturally after (a very long way after) foreign languages came the study of English. We had a writing and arithmetic master (whom we unanimously abhorred and despised, though one and all of us grievously needed his instructions) and an "English master," who taught us to write "themes," and to whom I, for one, feel that I owe, perhaps, more than to any other teacher in that school, few as were the hours which we were permitted to waste on so insignificant an art as composition in our native tongue!

Beyond all this, our English studies embraced one long, awful lesson each week to be repeated to the schoolmistress herself by a class, in history one week, in geography the week following. Our first class, I remember, had once to commit to memory—Heaven alone knows how—no less than thirteen pages of Woodhouselee's *Universal History!*

Lastly, as I have said, in point of importance, came our religious instruction. Our well-meaning schoolmistresses thought it was obligatory on them to teach us something of the kind, but, being very obviously altogether worldly women themselves, they were puzzled how to carry out their intentions. They marched us to church every Sunday when it did not rain, and they made us on Sunday mornings repeat the Collect and Catechism; but beyond these exercises of body and mind, it was hard for them to see what to do for our spiritual welfare. . . .

It almost needless to add, in concluding these reminiscences, that the heterogeneous studies pursued in this helter-skelter fashion were of the smallest possible utility in later life; each acquirement being of the shallowest and most imperfect kind, and all real education worthy of the name having to be begun on our return home, after we had been pronounced "finished." Meanwhile the strain on our mental powers of getting through daily, for six months at a time, this mass of ill-arranged and miscellaneous lessons, was extremely great and trying. . . .

If true education be the instilling into the mind, not so much Knowledge as the desire for Knowledge, mine at school certainly proved a notable failure. I was brought home (no girl could travel in those days alone) from Brighton by a coach . . . to Bristol, from whence I embarked for Ireland. My convoy-brother naturally mounted the box, and left me to enjoy the interior all day by myself; and the reflections of those solitary hours of first emancipation remain with me as lively as if they had taken place yesterday. "What a delightful thing it is," so ran my thoughts, "to have done with study! Now I may really enjoy myself! I know as much as any girl in our school, and since it is the best school in England, I *must* know all that it can ever be necessary for a lady to know. I will not trouble my head ever again with learning anything; but read novels and amuse myself for the rest of my life."

This noble resolve lasted I fancy a few months, and then, depth below depth of my ignorance revealed itself very unpleasantly! I tried to supply first one deficiency and then another, till after a year or two, I began to educate myself in earnest. (60–69)

HANNAH LYNCH

In her *Autobiography of a Child*, Hannah Lynch describes her own experience of boarding school. Her school, unlike the one Frances Power Cobbe attended, was run by a religious order of nuns in Ireland. Instead of emphasizing fashionable accomplishments, they emphasized self-sacrifice and religious teachings. She writes quite passionately about her life there, a life filled with mismanagement, mistreatment, and even torture, with only a small amount of anything remotely resembling education. The only reading she remembers is that which fed her taste for gothic mysteries, not anything that would help her to develop her understanding or increase the quantity of practical knowledge in her brain. Such an education, Lynch indicates, is worthless for a young girl except as it teaches her how unfair the world can be and how necessary it is for her to learn to fight against what injustice she can and to bear that which she cannot fight.

FROM HANNAH LYNCH, *AUTOBIOGRAPHY OF A CHILD*
(New York, 1899)

Do the ladies of Lysterby continue to train atrociously and mismanage children, to starve and thwart them, as they did in those far-off days, so remote that on looking back it seems to me now that somebody else and not I, a pacific and indifferent woman, content with most things round about me, lived those five years of perpetual passion and frantic unhappiness? Or has the old convent vanished, and carried off its long tale of incompetence, ignorance, cruel stupidity, and futile vexation?

For the seeds of many an illness were stored up in young bodies by systematic under-feeding, and hunger turned most of us into wistful little gluttons, gazing longingly into the cake-shops as we marched two by two through the tiny city, dreaming at night of Barmecide feasts, and envying the fate of the happier children at home, who devoured all the sweet things we with our empty little stomachs so bitterly remembered.

Sweet things only! Enough of bread-and-butter would have satisfied our craving. When one of us sickened and rejected the single thin slice of bread-and-butter allowed the children at breakfast, oh, the prayer and expectation of each pair of hungry eyes fixed upon the sufferer, to see to whom she would offer her neglected slice! The slice was cut in two, and usually offered, while the nun was not looking, to the children on either side. This miscarriage of appetite, we noted with regret, more frequently happened at the two tables of the big girls, where such windfalls were constantly amplifying the meager breakfasts of somebody or other in long skirts. But we were only ten, and our appetite was pretty steady and never satisfied. Now it taxes all my heroism to visit the dentist; but then I knew each visit was a prospective joy, for, if I did not cry, the lay-teacher who conducted me thither always allowed me to buy jam-tart, which I ate as slowly as possible in the confectioner's shop, noting the ravages of my teeth in the cake of delight with melancholy and dismay. I so loved the recompense that I used to watch anxiously for the first sign of a shaky tooth. . . .

But I would not have it thought that those early school-days were days of untempered bitterness and constant ache. We were a merry lot of little savages as far as the authorities permitted us to enjoy ourselves, and life continually revealed its quaint surprises and thrilling terrors. I learnt to read with amazing rapidity, and my favourite books were of a kind liberally supplied by the convent library—Tyburn, wonderful tales of the escapes and underground adventures of Jesuits, double walls, spring-doors, mysterious passages, whitened bones in long-forgotten boxes. Thanks to my ingenuity and vivid imagination, our days became for us all a wild romance. Relegated to the infirmary by prolonged illnesses, the result of semi-starvation, naturally I had leisure to read laboriously the various volumes of this edifying literature. . . .

What surprises me most when I recall those days is my own rapid development. The tiny inarticulate pensive creature of Ireland is, as if by magic, turned into a turbulent adventurer, quick with initiation, with a ready and violent word for my enemies, whom I regarded as many. . . . How did it come about? It needed long months of unhappiness at home to make me revolt against the most drastic rule, and here it sufficed that a nun should doubt my word to turn me into a glorified outlaw.

I confess that whatever the deficiencies of my home training, I had not been brought up to think that anybody lied. My mother never seemed to think it possible that any of her children could lie. In fact, lying was the last vice of childhood I was acquainted with. You told the truth as you breathed, without thinking of it, for the simple reason that it could not possibly occur to you not to tell the truth. This was, I knew, how I took it, though I did not reason so. . . .

The Grand Inquisitor was a lovely slim young nun, with a dainty gipsy face, all brown and golden, full-cheeked, pink-lipped, black-browed. I see her still, the exquisite monster, with her long slim fingers as delicate as ivory, and the perfidious witchery of her radiant dark smile.

"You mustn't tell lies. . . . You were seen to break the statue."

I stood up in vehement protest, words poured from me in a flood; they gushed from me like life-blood flowing from my heart, and in my passion I flung my books on the floor, and vowed that I would never eat again, but that I'd die first, to make them all feel miserable because they had murdered me. And then the pretty Inquisitor carried me off, dragging me after her with that veiled brutality of gesture that marks your refined tyrant. I was locked up in the old community-room, then reserved for guests, a big white chamber, with a good deal of heavy furniture in it.

"You'll stay here . . . until I come to let you out," she hissed at me.

I heard the key turn in the lock, and my heart was full of savage hate. I sat and brooded long on the vengeance I desired to wreak. . . .

Had any one else except Sister Esmeralda come to the door, I should have behaved differently, for I was a most manageable little creature when not under the influence of the terrible exasperation injustice always provoked in me. But there she stood. . . .

A blur of light, the anger of madness, the dreadful tense sensation of my helplessness, and before I knew what I had done I had caught up the stool and wildly hurled it at her triumphant visage. Oh, how I hated Sister Esmeralda! How I hated her!

The moment was one of exceptional solemnity. I was not scolded, or slapped, or roughly treated. My crime was too appalling for such habitual treatment. One would think I already wore the black shroud of death, that the gallows stood in front of me, and beside it the coffin and the yawning grave. . . .

My wickedness was past sermonizing. I was simply led upstairs to a brown cell, and here the red-cheeked lay-sister, a big brawny creature, stripped me naked. Naked, mind, though convent rules forbid the whipping of girls. I was eight, exceedingly frail and delicate. The superioress took my head tightly under her arm, and the brawny red-cheeked lay-sister scourged my back with a three-pointed whip till the blood gushed from the long stripes, and I fainted. I never uttered a groan, and I like to remember this infantine proof of my pride and resolute spirit. (129–142)

ELIZABETH GASKELL

Elizabeth Gaskell was acquainted with Charlotte Brontë in her adult years and wrote the first official biography of the author, with the approval and assistance of Patrick Brontë, Charlotte's father, after the author's death. She included in that biography a detailed account of the Cowan Bridge School, which Charlotte and her sisters attended when they were children and from which Brontë gleaned many of the details that she used in creating the fictional Lowood School for *Jane Eyre*.

Gaskell makes clear that her information about Cowan Bridge comes primarily from sources other than Charlotte Brontë, that Charlotte was, in fact, disturbed that so many people recognized Cowan Bridge as the source of her fictional Lowood. In creating Lowood, she concentrated on the most negative experiences she had at Cowan Bridge, but she wanted Gaskell, and everyone else who thought Lowood was a complete depiction of her own childhood experience at Cowen Bridge, to know that she had received much that she considered to be beneficial from her early experiences at the school.

Gaskell tries, in accordance with what she perceives to be Brontë's will, to present the evidence she has gathered about the years of Brontë's attending Cowan Bridge in the most positive light possible. She tries, in particular, to present a more balanced image of Mr. Carus Wilson, the prototype of Mr. Brocklehurst in the novel *Jane Eyre*.

FROM ELIZABETH GASKELL, *THE LIFE OF CHARLOTTE BRONTË*
(London, 1857)

I do not know whether Miss Branwell taught her nieces anything besides sewing, and the household arts in which Charlotte afterwards was such an adept. Their regular lessons were said to their father; and they were always in the habit of picking up an immense amount of miscellaneous information for themselves. But a year or so before this time, a school had been begun in the North of England for the daughters of clergymen. The place was Cowan Bridge, a small hamlet on the coach-road between Leeds and Kendal, and thus easy of access from Haworth, as the coach ran daily, and one of its stages was at Keighley. The yearly expense for each pupil (according to the entrance-rules given in the Report for 1842, and I believe they had not *been increased since the establishment* of the school in 1823) was as follows:—

Rule 1. "The terms for clothing, lodging, boarding, and educating, are £14 a year; half to be paid in advance, when the pupils are sent; and also £1 entrance-money, for the use of books, etc. The system of education comprehends history, geography, the use of the globes, grammar, writing and arithmetic, all kinds of needle-work, and the nicer kinds of household work—such as getting up fine linen, ironing, etc. If accomplishments are required, an additional charge of three pounds a year is made for music or drawing, each." . . .

Rule 3rd requests that the friends [those sending the child to school, generally her parents] will state the line of education desired in the case of every pupil, having a regard to her future prospects.

Rule 4th states the clothing and toilette articles which a girl is expected to bring with her; and thus concludes: "The pupils all appear in the same dress. They wear plain straw cottage bonnets; in summer white frocks on Sundays, and nankeen on other days; in winter, purple stuff frocks, and purple cloth cloaks. For the sake of uniformity, therefore, they are required to bring £3 in lieu of frocks, pelisse, bonnet, tippet, and frills; making the whole sum which each pupil brings with her to the school—

£7 half-year in advance.

£1 entrance for books.

£1 entrance for clothes."

The 8th rule is,—"All letters and parcels are inspected by the superintendent"; but this is a very prevalent regulation in all young ladies' schools, where I think it is generally understood that the schoolmistress may exercise this privilege, although it is certainly unwise in her to insist too frequently upon it.

There is nothing at all remarkable in any of the other regulations, a copy of which was doubtless in Mr. Brontë's hands when he formed the determination to send his daughters to Cowan Bridge School; and he accordingly took Maria and Elizabeth thither in July 1824. . . .

Miss [Charlotte] Brontë more than once said to me, that she should not have written what she did of Lowood in *Jane Eyre*, if she had thought the place would have been so immediately identified with Cowan Bridge, although there was not a word in her account of the institution but what was true at the time when she knew it; she also said that she had not considered it necessary in a work of fiction, to state every particular with the impartiality that might be required in a court of justice, nor to seek out motives, and make allowances for human failings, as she might have done if dispassionately analyzing the conduct of those who had the superintendence of the institution. I believe she herself would have been glad of an opportunity to correct the over-strong impression which was made upon the public mind by her vivid picture, though even she, suffering her whole life long both in heart and body from the consequences of what happened there, might have been apt, to the last, to take her deep belief in facts for the facts themselves—her conception of truth for the absolute truth.

In some of the notices of the previous editions of this work, it is assumed that I derived the greater part of my information with regard to her sojourn at Cowan Bridge from Charlotte Brontë herself. I never heard her speak of the place but once, and that was on the second day of my acquaintance with her. A little child on that occasion expressed some reluctance to finish eating his piece of bread at dinner; and she, stooping down and addressing him in a low voice, told him how thankful she would have been at his age for a piece of bread; and when we—though I am not sure if I myself spoke—asked her some question as to the occasion she alluded to, she replied with reserve and hesitation, evidently shying away from what she imagined might lead to too much conversation on one of her books. She spoke of the oatcake at Cowan Bridge (the clap-bread of Westmoreland) as being different to the leaven-raised oatcake of Yorkshire, and of her childish distaste for it. Someone present made an allusion to a similar childish dislike in the true tale of 'The terrible knitters o'Dent' given in Southey's *Common-place Book*; and she smiled faintly that the food itself was spoilt by the dirty carelessness of the cook, so that she and her sisters disliked their meals exceedingly; and she named her relief and gladness when the doctor condemned the meat, and spoke of having seen him spit it out. These are all the details I ever heard from her. She so avoided particularizing, that I think Mr. Carus Wilson's name never passed between us.

I do not doubt the general accuracy of my informants—of those who have given, and solemnly repeated the details that follow—but it is only just to Miss Brontë to say that I have stated above pretty nearly all that I ever heard on the subject from her.

A clergyman living near Kirby Lonsdale, the Reverend William Carus Wilson, was the prime mover in the establishment of this school. He was an energetic man, sparing no labour for the accomplishment of his ends. He saw that it was an extremely difficult task for clergymen with limited incomes to provide for the education of their children; and he devised a scheme, by which a certain sum was raised annually by subscription, to complete the amount required to furnish a solid and sufficient English education, for which the parent's payment of £14 a year would not have been sufficient. Indeed, that made by the parents was considered to be exclusively appropriated to the expenses of lodging and boarding, and the education provided for by the subscriptions. Twelve trustees were appointed; Mr. Wilson being not only a trustee, but the treasurer and secretary; in fact, taking most of the business arrangements upon himself; a responsibility which appropriately fell to him, as he lived nearer the school than anyone else who was interested in it. So his character for prudence and judgment was to a certain degree implicated in the success or failure of Cowan Bridge School; and the working of it was for many years the great object and interest of his life. But he was apparently un-acquainted with the prime element in good administration—seeking out thoroughly competent persons to fill each department, and then making them responsible for, and judging them by, the result, without perpetual interference with the detail.

So great was the amount of good which Mr. Wilson did, by his constant, unwearied superintendence, that I cannot help feeling sorry that, in his old age and declining health, the errors which he was believed to have committed, should have been brought up against him in a form which received such wonderful force from the touch of Miss Brontë's great ge-nius. No doubt whatever can be entertained of the deep interest which he felt in the success of the school. As I write, I have before me his last words on giving up the secretaryship in 1850: he speaks of the "with-drawal, from declining health, of an eye, which, at all events, has loved to watch over the schools with an honest and anxious interest";—and again he adds, "that he resigns, therefore, with a desire to be thankful for all that God has been pleased to accomplish through his instrumen-tality (the infirmities and unworthinesses of which he deeply feels and deplores)."

Cowan Bridge is a cluster of some six or seven cottages, gathered to-gether at both ends of a bridge, over which the high road from Leeds to

Kendal crosses a little stream, called the Leek. This high road is nearly disused now; but formerly, when the buyers from the West Riding manufacturing districts had frequent occasion to go up into the North to purchase the wool of the Westmoreland and Cumberland farmers, it was doubtless much traveled; and perhaps the hamlet of Cowan Bridge had a more prosperous look than it bears at present. It is prettily situated; just where the Leek-fells swoop into the plain; and by the course of the beck alder-trees and willows and hazel bushes grow. The current of the stream is interrupted by broken pieces of grey rock; and the waters flow over a bed of large round white pebbles, which a flood heaves up and moves on either side out of its impetuous way till in some parts they almost form a wall. By the side of the little, shallow, sparkling, vigorous Leek, run long pasture fields, of the fine short grass common in high land; for though Cowan Bridge is situated on a plain, it is a plain from which there is many a fall and long descent before you and the Leek reach the valley of the Lune. I can hardly understand how the schools there came to be so unhealthy; the air all round about was so sweet and thyme-scented, when I visited it last summer. But at this day, every one knows that the site of a building intended for numbers should be chosen with far greater care than that of a private dwelling, from the tendency to illness, both infectious and otherwise, produced by the congregation of people in close proximity.

The house is still remaining that formed part of that occupied by the school. It is a long, bow-windowed cottage, now divided into two dwellings. It stands facing the Leek, between which and it intervenes a space, about seventy yards deep, that was once the school garden. This original house was an old dwelling of the Picard family, which they had inhabited for two generations. They sold it for school purposes, and an additional building was erected, running at right angles from the older part. This new part was devoted expressly to school-rooms, dormitories, etc. . . . The present cottage was, at the time of which I write, occupied by the teacher's rooms, the dining-room and kitchens, and some smaller bedrooms. . . . The other end forms a cottage, with the low ceilings and stone floors of a hundred years ago; the windows do not open freely and widely; and the passage upstairs, leading to the bedrooms, is narrow and tortuous: altogether, smells would linger about the house, and damp cling to it. But sanitary matters were little understood thirty years ago; and it was a great thing to get a roomy building close to the high road, and not too far from the habitation of Mr. Wilson, the originator of the educational scheme. There was much need of such an institution; numbers of ill-paid clergymen hailed the prospect with joy, and eagerly put down the names of their children as pupils when the establishment should be ready to receive them. Mr. Wilson was, no doubt, pleased by the impatience with which the realization of his idea was anticipated, and opened the school with less than a hundred pounds in hand, and with pupils, the number of whom varies according to different accounts: Mr. W. W. Carus Wilson, the son of the founder, giving it as seventy; while Mr. Shepheard, the son-in-law, states it to have been only sixteen.

Mr. Wilson felt, most probably, that the responsibility of the whole plan rested upon him. The payment made by the parents was barely enough for food and lodging; the subscriptions did not flow very freely into an untried scheme; and great economy was necessary in all the domestic arrangements. He determined to enforce this by frequent personal inspection, carried perhaps to an unnecessary extent, and leading occasionally to a meddling with little matters, which had sometimes had the effect of producing irritation of feeling. Yet, although there was economy in providing for the household, there does not appear to have been any parsimony. The meat, flour, milk, etc., were contracted for, but were of very fair quality; and the dietary, which has been shown to me in manuscript, was neither bad nor unwholesome; nor, on the whole, was it wanting in variety. Oatmeal porridge for breakfast; a piece of oatcake for those who required luncheon; baked and boiled beef, and mutton, potato-pie, and plain homely puddings of different kinds for dinner. At five o'clock, bread and milk for the younger ones; and one piece of bread (this was the only time at which the food was limited) for the elder pupils, who sat up till a later meal of the same description.

Mr. Wilson himself ordered in the food, and was anxious that it should be of good quality. But the cook, who had much of his confidence, and against whom for a long time no one durst utter a complaint, was careless, dirty, and wasteful. To some children oatmeal porridge is distasteful, and consequently unwholesome, even when properly made; at Cowen Bridge School it was too often sent up, not merely burnt, but with offensive fragments of other substances discoverable in it. The beef, that should have been carefully salted before it was dressed, had often become tainted from neglect; and girls, who were schoolfellows with the Brontës, during the reign of the cook of whom I am speaking, tell me that the house seemed to be pervaded, morning, noon, and night, by the odour of rancid fat that steamed out of the oven in which much of their food was prepared. There was the same carelessness in making the puddings; one of those ordered was rice boiled in water, and eaten with a sauce of treacle and sugar; but it was often uneatable, because the water had been taken out of the rain tub, and was strongly impregnated with the dust lodging on the roof, whence it had trickled down into the old wooden cask, which also added its own flavour to that of the original rain water. The milk, too, was often 'bingy,' to use a country expression for a kind of taint that is far worse than sourness, and suggests the idea that it is caused by want of cleanliness about the milk pans, rather than by the heat of the weather. On Saturdays a kind of pie, or mixture of potatoes and meat, was served up, which was made of all the fragments accumulated during the week. Scraps of meat from a dirty and disorderly larder could never be very appetizing; and I believe that this dinner was more loathed than any in the early days of Cowan Bridge School. One may fancy how repulsive such fare would be to children whose appetites were small, and who had been accustomed to food, far simpler perhaps, but prepared with a delicate cleanliness that made it both tempting and wholesome. At many a meal the little Brontës went without food, although craving with hunger. They were not strong when they came, having only just recovered from a complication of measles and whooping-cough—indeed, I suspect they had scarcely recovered, for there was some consultation on the part of the school authorities whether Maria and Elizabeth should be received or not, in July 1824. Mr. Brontë came again, in the September of that year, bringing with him Charlotte and Emily to be admitted as pupils.

It appears strange that Mr. Wilson should not have been informed by the teachers of the way in which the food was served up; but we must remember that the cook had been known for some time to the Wilson family, while the teachers were brought together for an entirely different work—that of education. They were expressly given to understand that such was their department; the buying in and management of the provisions rested with Mr. Wilson and the cook. The teachers would, of course, be unwilling to lay any complaints on the subject before him.

There was another trial of health common to all the girls. The path from Cowan Bridge to Tunstall Church, where Mr. Wilson preached, and where they all attended on the Sunday, is more than two miles in length, and goes sweeping along the rise and fall of the unsheltered country in a way to make it a fresh and exhilarating walk in summer, but a bitter cold one in winter, especially to children like the delicate little Brontës, whose thin blood flowed languidly in consequence of their feeble appetites rejecting the food prepared for them, and thus inducing a half-starved condition. The church was not warmed, there being no means for this purpose. It stands in the midst of fields, and the damp mist must have gathered round the walls, and crept in at the windows. The girls took their cold dinner with them, and ate it between the services, in a chamber over the entrance, opening out of the former galleries. The arrangements for this day were peculiarly trying to delicate children, particularly to those who were spiritless and longing for home, as poor Maria Brontë must have been; for her ill health was increasing, and the old cough, the remains of the whooping-cough, lingered about her.

She was far superior in mind to any of her playfellows and companions, and was lonely amongst them from that very cause; and yet she had faults so annoying that she was in constant disgrace with her teachers, and an object of merciless dislike to one of them, who is depicted as "Miss Scatcherd" in *Jane Eyre*, and whose real name I will be merciful enough not to disclose. I need hardly say that Helen Burns is as exact a transcript of Maria Brontë as Charlotte's wonderful power of reproducing character could give. Her heart, to the latest day on which we met, still beat with unavailing indignation at the worrying and the cruelty to which her gentle, patient, dying sister had been subjected by this woman. Not a word of that part of *Jane Eyre* but is a literal repetition of scenes between the pupil and the teacher. Those who had been pupils at the same time knew who must have written the book from the force with which Helen Burns's sufferings are described. They had, before that, recognized the description of the sweet dignity and benevolence of Miss Temple as only a just tribute to the merits of one whom all that knew her appear to hold in honour; but when Miss Scatcherd was held up to opprobrium they also recognized in the writer of *Jane Eyre* an unconsciously avenging sister of the sufferer.

One of their fellow-pupils, among other statements even worse, gives me the following:—the dormitory in which Maria slept was a long room, holding a row of narrow little beds on each side, occupied by the pupils; and at the end of this dormitory there was a small bedchamber opening out of it, appropriated to the use of Miss Scatcherd. Maria's bed stood nearest to the door of this room. One morning, after she had become so seriously unwell as to have had a blister applied to her side (the sore from which was not perfectly healed), when the getting-up bell was heard poor Maria moaned out that she was so ill, so very ill, she wished she might stop in bed; and some of the girls urged her to do so, and said they would explain it all to Miss Temple, the superintendent. But Miss Scatcherd was close at hand and would have to be faced before Miss Temple's kind thoughtfulness could interfere; so the sick child began to dress, shivering with cold, as, without leaving her bed, she slowly put on her black worsted stockings over her thin white legs (my informant spoke as if she saw it yet, and her whole face flushed out undying indignation). Just then Miss Scatcherd issued from her room, and, without asking for a word of explanation from the sick and frightened girl, she took her by the arm, on the side to which the blister had been applied, and by one vigorous movement whirled her out into the middle of the floor, abusing her all the time for dirty and untidy habits. There she left her. My informant says Maria hardly spoke, except to beg some of the more indignant girls to be calm; but, in slow, trembling movements, with many a pause, she went downstairs at last—and was punished for being late.

Anyone may fancy how such an event as this would rankle in Charlotte's mind. I only wonder that she did not remonstrate against her father's decision to send her and Emily back to Cowan Bridge, after Maria's and Elizabeth's deaths. But frequently children are unconscious of the effect which some of their simple revelations would have in altering the opinions entertained by their friends of the persons placed around them. Besides, Charlotte's earnest vigorous mind saw, at an unusually early age, the immense importance of education, as furnishing her with tools which she had the strength and the will to wield, and she would be aware that the Cowan Bridge education was, in many points, the best that her father could provide for her.

Before Maria Brontë's death, that low fever broke out in the spring of 1825, which is spoken of in *Jane Eyre*. Mr. Wilson was extremely alarmed at the first symptoms of this. He went to a kind, motherly woman, who had had some connection with the school—as laundress, I believe—and asked her to come and tell him what was the matter with them. She made herself ready, and drove with him in his gig. When she entered the school-room, she saw from twelve to fifteen girls lying about; some resting their aching heads on the table, others on the ground; all heavy-eyed, flushed, indifferent, and weary, with pains in every limb. Some peculiar odour, she says, made her recognize that they were sickening from "the fever"; and she told Mr. Wilson so, and that she could not stay there for fear of conveying the infection to her own children; but he half commanded and half entreated her to remain and nurse them, and finally mounted his gig and drove away, while she was still urging that she must return to her own house, and to her domestic duties, for which she had provided no substitute. However, when she was left in this unceremonious manner, she determined to make the best of it; and a most efficient nurse she proved, although, as she says, it was a dreary time.

Mr. Wilson supplied everything ordered by the doctors, of the best quality in the most liberal manner; the invalids were attended by Dr. Batty, a very clever surgeon in Kirby, who had had the medical superintendence of the establishment from the beginning, and who afterwards became Mr. Wilson's brother-in-law. I have heard from two witnesses besides Charlotte Brontë, that Dr. Batty condemned the preparation of the food by the expressive action of spitting out a portion of it. He himself, it is but fair to say, does not remember this circumstance, nor does he speak of the fever itself as either alarming or dangerous. About forty of the girls suffered from this, but none of them died at Cowan Bridge, though one died at her own home, sinking under the state of health which followed it. None of the Brontës had the fever. But the same causes, which affected the health of the other pupils through typhus, told more slowly, but not less surely, upon their constitutions. The principal of these causes was the food.

The bad management of the cook was chiefly to be blamed for this; she was dismissed, and the woman who had been forced against her will to serve as head nurse, took the place of housekeeper; and henceforward the food was so well prepared that no one could ever reasonably complain of it. . . .

All this occurred during the first two years of the establishment, and in estimating its effect upon the character of Charlotte Brontë, we must remember that she was a sensitive, thoughtful child, capable of reflecting deeply, if not of analyzing truly; and peculiarly susceptible, as are all delicate and sickly children, to painful impressions. What the healthy suffer from but momentarily and then forget, those who are ailing brood over involuntarily and remember long,—perhaps with no resentment, but simply as a piece of suffering that has been stamped into their very life. The pictures, ideas, and conceptions of character received into the mind of the child of eight years old were destined to be reproduced in fiery words a quarter of a century afterwards. She saw but one side of Mr Wilson's character; and many of those who knew him at that time assure me of the fidelity with which this is represented, while at the same time they regret that the delineation should have obliterated, as it were, nearly all that was noble or conscientious. . . .

In the spring of [1825] Maria became so rapidly worse that Mr. Brontë was sent for. He had not previously been aware of her illness, and the condition in which he found her was a terrible shock to him. He took her home by the Leeds coach, the girls crowding out into the road to follow her with their eyes over the bridge, past the cottages, and then out of sight for ever. She died a very few days after her arrival at home. Perhaps the news of her death falling suddenly into the life of which her patient existence had formed a part, only a week or so before, made those who remained at Cowan Bridge look with more anxiety on Elizabeth's symptoms, which also turned out to be consumptive. She was sent home in charge of a confidential servant of the establishment; and she, too, died in the early summer of that year. Charlotte was thus suddenly called into the responsibilities of eldest sister in a motherless family. She remembered how anxiously her dear sister Maria had striven, in her grave, earnest way, to be a tender helper and a counselor to them all; and the duties that now fell upon her seemed almost like a legacy from the gentle little sufferer so lately dead.

Both Charlotte and Emily returned to school after the Midsummer holidays in this fatal year. But before the next winter it was thought desirable to advise their removal, as it was evident that the damp situation of the house at Cowen Bridge did not suit their health." (47–61)

A REPORT ON THE STATE OF GIRLS' BOARDING SCHOOLS

In 1845, *Fraser's Magazine* published a report condemning the practices of most girls' boarding schools in England. The report found most to be inadequate as educational institutions, the focus being more on accomplishments and economics than on the development of reason, discernment, and intellect. It also found many to be dangerous. Moral danger arose from the tendency of girls to take on frivolous and immoral attitudes from other girls and even some of the staff, as well as from a tendency toward deceit encouraged by the complete lack of privacy enforced by the school rules. The schools were deemed to be dangerous physically as well because of the poor nutrition, the lack of sufficient exercise, the crowding of girls into rooms too small for their numbers, and the absence of adequate facilities and personnel for the care of those girls who became ill. These physical dangers are precisely those delineated so clearly in Charlotte Brontë's depiction of Lowood, the fictional school based on the reality she and her sisters experienced at the Cowan Bridge School.

Little was written in the report about the actual curriculum of the schools, educational content seemingly being considered of little consequence in evaluating educational institutions for girls.

"AN ENQUIRY INTO THE STATE OF GIRLS' FASHIONABLE
SCHOOLS"
(*Fraser's Magazine*, June 1845)

Before we throw out any hints on the subject of the present inquiry, we must request our readers to bear in mind, that we assume as facts the extension of womanly duties, and the necessity of more active exertion than has hitherto been required from the sex. It would take too much time and space for us to state the causes from which we have drawn such inferences; but we need only point to our machinery and our distant colonies, to the eager rush made in every profession and calling of life, to be assured that the leisure of "merry Englonde" is fast growing into "all work, and no play." Women will share in the social revolution: indeed, by every token we may know that, for the future, the bulk of English women, married and single, must bear their part in the *work* of life.

With those, therefore, whose views of womanhood do not range beyond the vista of society, we have nothing in common; but of those who believe that woman is capable of being more than a toy or a slave we would ask: "Have the means of improvement kept pace with the growing demands on the powers of women?" "Is their education suited to their extended responsibilities?" Surely, the means as yet provided are ill suited to attain the end; for, if women are henceforth to be members of a common-wealth, girls should be trained to a sense of high moral responsibility and self-dependence. Now what is the broad mark on the ordinary means of providing instruction—to wit, *schools*? Fine ladyism. Mistress, teacher, pupil, household, all bear the same impress. One might be tempted to believe, that the end most schoolmistresses propose to themselves in teaching is to get themselves handsome houses, furnish sumptuous drawing-rooms, keep livery servants, and, perhaps, equipages, and to make purses for themselves out of the credulous vanity and craving for stylishness in their employers. But when one thinks of the *homes* of her pupils, and the daily economy practiced by parent and elder sisters to obtain for them the advantages of an instruction which is to fit them for life, the strain to keep up appearances which pervades the whole estab-lishment makes one sick at heart.

The ancients regarded the teaching of the young as a trust too sacred to be undertaken for hire; and not till Greece became degenerate did the public instructors accept payment for their services. Our modern system is in the opposite extreme. We do not wish that honourable exertion should be denied its reward; but a system that is carried on by the heads in a mercenary spirit must implant in the pupils' minds a false valuation of the world's goods. Within the walls of their house of discipline girls learn to grasp after show and pomp; and, as women can rarely *acquire* these for themselves, they are taught to look at marriage as the means of making their fortune. Thus their education is but a training for somewhat in prospect; they are taught to live upon expectancy; they are to fit them-selves to catch at the straw, and wait upon the wheel of fortune. This may account in some degree for much of the instability, and for the great increase of *display* as a motive in modern women. They are brought up in a sort of panopticon; every thing they can do must be pinned to their shoulders, that the world may be advertised of their merits.

Modern teachers are so impatient, and have such a small space allotted to them in which to do their work, that they set about it like the child who constantly dug up his seeds to see if they were growing out; therefore, modern women are, in character, mere shriveled flowers, opening to the sun before a leaf has shot up to fold round them. The women of earlier days were left more to nature; true, they also were generally brought up to be married; but they had nothing to do with making the match, and we doubt whether their marriages of obedience were not entered into under happier auspices than the rash, self-willed contracts of today,—in point of *affection* between the parties; there is nothing to choose between the patriarchal marriage and the modern *"mariage de convenance."* That mighty reformer, *steam*, forbids a return to the secluded habits of the seventeenth century; and, amongst its social revolutions, it will bring women more into the world, thus making it more than ever necessary in those who have the charge of the young to give them *principles in themselves*, rather than *motives in circumstances.* . . . Amidst the distracting influences from without, which must operate more and more on the future generations of woman, it behoves the guides of their youth to train them in proportion to habits of concentration, and the principle of self-dependence, that they may have some steadfast purposes in themselves wherewith to resist the flux of mere contingencies; the incitements which, dragging every secret operation of the heart and mind to the surface, destroy all womanly delicacy, and the dignity which appeals to conscience rather than to public opinion.

Every one practically acquainted with the workings of girls' schools must admit that they are calculated to foster a spirit of distraction and self-consciousness. It may be said, that those who disapprove of the system need not commit their daughters to it. This is assuredly true; and it is to be doubted whether parents who really reflect seriously on their own responsibility, and on the duties of their daughters as beings who have work to do for this world and the next, would send them to the mere fashionable school. But the majority do not reflect; even sensible people use the Irishman's plea, and spare themselves much perplexity, "What every body does will do for them;" therefore much that might be known is not known, and the amount of knowledge is scanty, even at the greatest.

Concealment and deception prevail at the girls' schools to a degree which the uninitiated would be slow to credit. Much that goes on is never told, for very shame,—girls either fearing to confess that they have been confederates, or shrinking from being supposed to have shared in the common parlance. Many schoolmistresses make a rule of reading every letter written and received: by such a plan the girls are left at their mercy. There may be much just cause for pursuing it, but those who follow it should be worthy of the confidence they extort, and above all suspicion. It leads to collusion between the pupils and the servants,—a result fraught with mischief; it induces cunning and strategem, in order to evade the rule; in many cases, it weakens the tie between the girls and their home. True, the holydays break the restraint; children then confide to their mothers the griefs and hardships of the "half-year." But, doubtless, sensible parents would be slow in acting upon this testimony, for the wisest of us are bad judges in our own cases. Will not, then, the witness of children against teachers and companions be received with caution, as liable to the bias of passion, and selfishness, and the colourings of imagination? Yet, if not from them, whence can the truth be drawn? Say that the evil complained of be so well adduced and flagrant as not to admit of its being lightly passed over, let the parent remonstrate, what will be the consequence to the girl? She will be *marked*; the butt of every unkind speech; all eyes attracted to her by the invidious exemption from a common grievance; the mistress will regard her with distrust for ever after; her very companions will jeer and avoid her, as one who, having told the tales of the mistress, may "peach" of them at any provocation. Nowhere does privilege bring down such certain odium on its subject as at schools.

These concealments bear peculiarly on *health*,—a subject which, as connected with school, might of itself be swelled to a volume. . . . We ourselves know of a case in which the parent, before placing his daughter at school, was deliberately assured by the mistress, that no doctor had been inside her house for many half-years, "it was in such a healthy situation." The father drew the conclusion she desired, and placed his delicate child under her care. It was afterwards discovered, that at the very time one girl lay seriously ill, and another was just recovered from a severe attack of sickness. Yet the lady had spoken half the truth, for no doctor had been sent for in either case; and, in order to preserve the character of her establishment for good health, she never allowed her pupils to have medical advice, unless under fear of the parents' interference. From the difficulty of convincing women at the heads of schools that their pupils are ever ill, one would think that a hard heart and a deaf ear were among the qualifications of the superiors. Thus far we may excuse their skepticism and callousness. Illness is often shammed, in order to shirk lessons; but it is better to be deceived ten times than to let one suffer from neglect.

There are innumerable instances of girls having returned home with broken health, or the seeds of disease sown which must bring them to an untimely grave, through the blindness and want of care in those who promised to watch over them with mothers' eyes. When the malady is even acknowledged, the patient sent to bed, and the doctor called in, the *nursing* is often . . . insufficient. . . .

Illness is bad enough at the best; but, unpitied, untended, alone, who can tell the forlornness of an invalided schoolgirl? It must of necessity be difficult to provide adequately for sickness in a house full of young people, where every hand and head has its assigned duty for each hour of the day. But is not the care of the young a work of difficulty, turn it which way one will? If those who engaged in it rightly weighed the burthen of their responsibility in the outset, they would see to providing the best means in their power to meet the emergency of sickness, which, where the pupils are young, delicate girls, should be expected as a certainty, and not as a mere casualty. There should be a sick-ward in every school, so detached as to be out of the noise and bustle. No establishment for the young is complete without an experienced nurse on its staff. It is impossible that the mistress or teachers can have the time to attend to the sick: even had they it, we doubt whether those who have spent their lives over desks and pianos would possess the due qualifications of a nurse. The regulation of a sick-room is an art not picked up by chance, nor learnt in a day; and it is a cruel thing to leave any one in illness, much more a child, to the care of a hired stranger, and, worse still, to the chance offices of busy household servants, or even to the charities (seldom lacking) of companions.

Half the houses set apart for schools are not fit for the purpose; very few would be suitably airy and roomy: a garden or playground is necessary, if girls are to be kept in health; for exercise is but slightly beneficial unless taken with pleasure; and what recreation can there be in the formal walks along highroads, in a long line of two-and-two?

In many of the gaudiest establishments, the food provided is very insufficient in quantity, and bad in quality. Very often the superiors have separate tables, or only appear at the general meals to carve. This is not wise; it provokes curious questions. What is served for the pupils, who pay so highly, should be good enough for the mistress. At some places, the heads join their pupils at meals, but have their own private dishes. This practice is so unladylike, to say the least of it, that it is only to be pointed out to be condemned at once. Now it is acknowledged, that the hardest readers at the universities are the greatest eaters; and this rule holds good with girls, they require good nourishment. There is generally too great a disproportion between the meat and the vegetable and farinaceous food provided. It is a well-known fact, that most girls, in their first initiation into school, get ill, from a diet so different to what they have been accustomed to; but this evil may be remedied, and at but small expense or trouble. And here we must again enter a protest against the practice of too strict economy in an establishment of young people. Where a liberal salary is paid, it is dishonest; where the terms are low, it were more humane to cut short any expenses merely incurred on the score of appearance, than to shorten the weekly bills. Even where there is liberality in the housekeeping, the end is often defeated, by that squeamishness about eating which has led many a girl to ruin her health, rather than have the imputation of a large appetite. . . . This is a folly; but it is with the *foibles* as well as the faults that the teachers of the young have to do, and systems relative to meals prevail in most schools which promote this false shame. . . .

Much more might be said on the chapter of health and the danger incurred by a sudden rush into the regimen of schools after the watchful nurture of home. It is impossible to lay too much stress on the subject, and we would counsel parents to prosecute the investigation for themselves, for nothing is a trifle which may leave its trace on after years. Health is too often cruelly sacrificed, either through culpable neglect or ignorance, or for the sake of gaining a few more wares for the marriage-market.

We come now to that part of the matter which relates to the *over-working* of growing girls in the acquisition of tawdry accomplishments; and the fact must be known through the length and breadth of the land, since in every house drooping girls are to be seen, spiritless victims of *ennui* (the effect of a reaction after the killing excitement of school), with languid faces, and often misshapen forms. And all for what? Not for knowledge, not for an intellectual growth, which is to make up for the stunting of bodily power, for, with few exceptions, the modes of teaching which prevail in reference to women are fitted to act upon the surface alone, to accomplish the one end of attracting attention. If health were sacrificed in order to attain self-knowledge, and sources of interest which would lift the possessor above the chances of events, and make to her a world within the world, her own, beyond the touch of accident, the price would be paid for an equivalent: but health is not our own, we may not consciously barter it for the rarest gifts of mind and heart. What shall be said, then, to those who suffer their daughters to fritter it away in the pursuit of bubbles that shall break as they are breathed on? What to those who, undertaking to guide the young, destroy in them the very sap of life for the sake of a few petty acquirements, that will never solace one hour of weariness, or fit them for one practical duty of life? Woman was ordained to be the *help-meet* of man; but this high calling is utterly overlooked in the present system of female instruction.

Our limits are too small to admit of our giving more than a glance at this fruitful theme. Women learn nothing thoroughly; in their education the *reason of things* is altogether left out, they are taught by rote instead of rule. Their memories are quickened, their imaginations excited, their passions stimulated; but their understandings are left to slumber. . . . the woman who can clearly convey her reasons, or patiently follow those of another, is looked upon as an exception to her sex. But this is an error. Women are capable of being taught the three parts of a sentence in common with men; and men who have been only partially taught take one-sided views and state their notions after the fashion of all unlearned folks. But we will admit, for argument's sake (still insisting that until the experiment of sound female instruction be tried the assumed inferiority cannot be proved), that a woman's natural defect lies in her logical faculty—her thinking power; for what is education but to supply deficiency and counteract bad tendencies? And how does the ordinary system answer these purposes? . . .

Every one who reflects on the present smattering which is given to women as knowledge, and on the whole system of her education, of *home* often as well as at school, but eminently so in the latter, must see that it is calculated to produce the very converse. (704–708)

MORALITY AND PROPRIETY IN GIRLS' EDUCATION

As the reports of individuals like Frances Power Cobbe and Hannah Lynch indicate, and the report published by *Fraser's Magazine* in 1845 confirms, the intellectual content of the girls' boarding school curriculum was minimal at best. The one element that all writers of educational philosophy agreed was essential in that curriculum, however, was an emphasis on propriety and moral behavior. Women in Victorian England were expected to behave according to a very rigid set of social and moral rules. Those who failed to live up to those expectations, especially in the genteel classes, were in danger of never marrying, if they were single, and of being punished, abandoned, or locked away as lunatics by their husbands if they were married. Therefore, learning the rules of proper behavior and how to live by those rules, avoiding even the appearance of impropriety, was a vital part of the education of a Victorian lady.

HANNAH MORE

Hannah More (1745–1833) was a renowned educational moralist and Christian philosopher of the late eighteenth century. Raised by her father, Jacob More, the schoolmaster at the Free School of Fishponds, More was encouraged to develop her talents and acquire an education superior to that of most women of her age. She, together with her older sister, ran a school for young women that was nationally recognized for its religious and moral education.

In much of her writing, More concerned herself with what she perceived to be a movement in England toward teaching girls the forms of propriety without teaching the religion and morality that she believed should underlie that propriety. Such attention to form over content was, she believed, contributing to the degeneration of British culture. In *Strictures on the Modern System of Female Education*, she presents what she believes should be the foundation of education for every young woman in England, along with her arguments for it.

FROM HANNAH MORE, *STRICTURES ON THE MODERN SYSTEM OF FEMALE EDUCATION*
(London, 1799)

Propriety is to a woman what the great Roman critic says action is to an orator; it is the first, the second, the third requisite. A woman may be knowing, active, witty, and amusing; but without propriety she cannot be amiable. Propriety is the center in which all the lines of duty and of agreeableness meet. It is to character what proportion is to figure, and grace to attitude. It does not depend on any one perfection; but it is the result of general excellence. It shows itself by a regular, orderly, undeviating course; and never starts from its sober orbit into any splendid eccentricities; for it would be ashamed of such praise as it might extort by any aberrations from its proper path. It renounces all commendation but what is characteristic; and I would make it the criterion of true taste, right principle, and genuine feeling, in a woman, whether she would be less touched with all the flattery or romantic and exaggerated panegyric, than with that beautiful picture of correct and elegant propriety, which Milton draws of our first mother. (Vol 1: 6–7)

• • •

In animadverting farther on the reigning evils which the times more particularly demand that women of rank and influence should repress, Christianity calls upon them to bear their decided testimony against every thing which is notoriously contributing to the public corruption. It calls upon them to banish from their dressing rooms, (and oh, that their influence could banish from the libraries of their sons and husbands!) that sober and unsuspected mass of mischief, which, by assuming the plausible names of Science, of Philosophy, of Arts, of Belles Lettres, is gradually administering death to the principles of those who would be on their guard, had the poison been labeled with its own pernicious title. Avowed attacks upon revelation are more easily resisted, because the malignity is advertised. But who suspects the destruction which lurks under the harmless or instructive names of *General History, Natural History, Travels, Voyages, Lives, Encyclopedias, Criticism*, and *Romance?* Who will deny that many of these works contain much admirable matter; brilliant passages, important facts, just descriptions, faithful pictures of nature, and valuable illustrations of science? But while 'the dead lay lies at the bottom,' the whole will exhale a corrupt and pestilential stench.

Novels, which used chiefly to be dangerous in one respect, are now become mischievous in a thousand. They are continually shifting their ground, and enlarging their sphere, and are daily becoming vehicles of wider mischief. Sometimes they concentrate their force, and are at once employed to diffuse destructive politics, deplorable profligacy, and impudent infidelity. Rousseau was the first popular dispenser of their complicated drug, in which the deleterious infusion was strong, and the effect proportionably fatal. . . . With a metaphysical sophistry the most plausible, he debauches the heart of woman, by cherishing her vanity in the erection of a system of male virtues, to which, with a lofty dereliction of those that are her more peculiar and characteristic praise, he tempts her to aspire; powerfully insinuating, that to this splendid system chastity does not necessarily belong: thus corrupting the judgment and bewildering the understanding, as the most effectual way to inflame the imagination and deprave the heart.

The rare mischief of this author consists in his power of seducing by falsehood those who love truth, but whose principles are not yet formed. He allures the warm-hearted to embrace vice, not because they prefer vice, but because he gives to vice so natural an air of virtue: and ardent and enthusiastic youth, too confidently trusting in their integrity and in their teacher, will be undone, while they fancy they are indulging in the noblest feelings of their nature. Many authors will more infallibly complete the ruin of the loose and ill-disposed; but perhaps (if I may change the figure) there never was a net of such exquisite art and inextricable workmanship, spread to entangle innocence and ensnare inexperience, as the writings of Rousseau; and, unhappily, the victim does not even struggle in the toils, because part of the delusion consists in imagining that he is set at liberty. (Vol 1: 30–34)

• • •

[T]hough a well bred young lady may lawfully learn most of the fashionable arts, yet it does not seem to be the true end of education to make women of fashion *dancers, singers, players, painters, actresses, sculptors, gilders, varnishers, engravers*, and *embroiderers*. Most *men* are commonly destined to some profession, and their minds are consequently turned each to its respective object. Would it not be strange if they were called out to exercise their profession, or to set up their trade, with only a little general knowledge of the trades of all other men, and without any previous definite application to their own peculiar calling? The profession of ladies, to which the bent of *their* instruction should be turned, is that of daughters, wives, mothers, and mistresses of families. They should be therefore trained with a view to these several conditions, and be furnished with a stock of ideas and principles, and qualifications ready to be applied and appropriated, as occasion may demand, to each of these respective situations; for though the arts which merely embellish life must claim admiration; yet when a man of sense comes to marry, it is a companion whom he wants, and not an artist. It is not merely a creature who can paint, and play, and dress, and dance; it is a being who can comfort and counsel him; one who can reason and reflect, and feel, and judge, and discourse, and discriminate; one who can assist him in his affairs, lighten his cares, sooth his sorrows, strengthen his principles, and educate his children. (Vol 1: 97–98)

• • •

The chief end to be proposed in cultivating the understandings of women, is to qualify them for the practical purposes of life. Their knowledge is not often like the learning of men, to be reproduced in some literary composition, nor ever in any learned profession; but it is to come out in conduct. A lady studies, not that she may qualify herself to become an orator or a pleader; not that she may learn to debate, but to act. She is to read the best books, not so much to enable her to talk of them, as to bring the improvement she derives from them to the rectification of her principles, and the formation of her habits. The great uses of study are to enable her to regulate her own mind, and to be useful to others.

To woman therefore, whatever be her rank, I would recommend a predominance of those more sober studies, which, not having display for their object, may make her wise without vanity, happy without witnesses, and content without panegyrists; the exercise of which will not bring celebrity, but improve usefulness. She should pursue every kind of study which will teach her to elicit truth; which will lead her to be intent upon realities; will give precision to her ideas; will make an exact mind; every study which, imagination under dominion, will lead her to think, to compare, to combine, to methodise; which will confer such a power of discrimination that her judgment shall learn to reflect what is dazzling if it be not solid; and to prefer, not what is striking, or bright, or new, but what is just. Every kind of knowledge which is rather fitted for home consumption than foreign exportation, is peculiarly adapted to women.

It is because the superficial mode of their education furnishes them with a false and low standard of intellectual excellence, that women have sometimes become ridiculous by the unfounded pretensions of literary vanity: for it is not the really learned but the smatterers, who have generally brought their sex into discredit, by an absurd affectation, which has set them on despising the duties of ordinary life. There have not indeed been wanting (but the character is not common) *precieses ridicules*, who, assuming a superiority to the sober cares which ought to occupy their sex, claim a lofty and supercilious exception from the dull and plodding drudgeries "Of this dim speck called earth!" who have affected to establish an unnatural separation between talents and usefulness; who act as if knowledge were to confer on woman a kind of fantastic sovereignty, which should exonerate her from female duties; whereas it is only meant the more eminently to qualify her for the performance of them. For a woman of real sense will never forget, that while the greater part of her appropriate duties are such as the most moderately gifted may fulfil with credit, (for Providence never makes that to be very difficult, which is generally necessary,) yet the most highly endowed are equally bound to perform them; and the humblest of these offices, performed on Christian principles, are wholesome for the minds even of the most enlightened, and tend to the casting down of those high imaginations which women of genius are too much tempted to indulge. (Vol. 2: 1–5)

THOMAS GISBORNE

A friend of Hannah More, Thomas Gisborne (1758–1846) was Prebendary of Durham. As the clergyman in charge of the school at Durham, he acquired considerable influence as an educator. His writings on the subject of "practical morality" were widely read (nine editions were published) and received much critical acclaim in their time. In *An Enquiry into the Duties of the Female Sex*, Gisborne, like most of the practical moralists of his time, addressed the issue of appropriate education for females. He takes a less religious tone than Hannah More, but his emphasis is much the same—that girls must be taught to be virtuous by training them to live by principle, not merely to adhere to the outward form of propriety.

Much of Gisborne's work focuses on the differences between men and women, their different spheres of activity and of influence. In moral education, as in most other areas of life, Gisborne believed that the treatment of girls should differ significantly from that of boys, and that the responsibilities of the men and women who teach them should also differ.

FROM THOMAS GISBORNE, *AN ENQUIRY INTO THE DUTIES OF THE FEMALE SEX*
(London, 1797)

The primary end of education is to train up the pupil in the knowledge and application of those principles of conduct, which will lead probably to a considerable share of happiness in the present life, but assuredly to a full measure of it in that which is to come. The secondary end is to superadd to the possession of right principles, those improving and ornamental acquisitions, which, either from their own nature, or from the prevailing customs of a particular age and country, are in some degree material to the comfort and to the usefulness of the individual. The difference in point of importance which subsists between these two objects is such, that the dictates of sober judgment are palpably abandoned whenever the latter is suffered, in the slightest manner, to encroach on the priority of the former. The modes of attaining both objects, and of pursuing the second in due subordination to the first, require to be adjusted according to the circumstances which characterize the persons who are to receive instruction. Hence in female education, that instructor is ignorant or regardless of a duty of the highest concern, who, in transfusing into the youthful hearer those fundamental truths which equally concern every human being, does not anxiously point out their bearings on the particular weaknesses and errors, whether in judgment or in action, into which the female sex is in especial danger of being betrayed. An attempt to efface the discriminating features which the hand of God has impressed on the mind, is in every case impossible to accomplish; and would be in every case, presumption. To efface those of the female mind, would be to deprive women of their distinguishing excellences. But to anticipate the mistakes, to restrain the excesses, to guard against the unwarrantable passions, which originate in the very source whence those excellencies flow, is to confer on the workmanship of God the culture and the care which he intended that it should receive from the hand of man. It is humbly to contribute towards the progress of its improvement that mite of assistance, which, in the counsels of supreme wisdom, he thought fit to leave dependent on human co-operation. (37–40)

WILLIAM DUFF

Scottish clergyman William Duff (1732–1815) was probably known best for his *Essay on Original Genius* (1767), a study of the mind that anticipated many of the ideas of the major Romantic poets. But Duff was also concerned with the issue of women's intellectual and moral character. In his writings on those subjects, Duff provides his readers not only with a set of rules by which women should live but also presents a specific example of a respectable young woman who finds herself at the mercy of a disreputable man. The story of Miss Emilia Somerville is intended to be a cautionary tale for girls, letting them know the dangers that lurk around them, even when all seems proper. It is also a cautionary tale for parents and others who care for young girls, encouraging them to be as vigilant as possible over the innocence of their daughters and wards.

What to twenty-first–century readers seems particularly unfair is that Emilia is held responsible by her father as well as society for being raped. In fact, she is held more fully responsible than the actual rapist. In nineteenth-century Britain, however, the woman was *always* considered responsible for any impropriety, no matter how innocent her intentions. Just as Jane Eyre would have been considered a fallen woman had she married Mr. Rochester while he was still married to Bertha (despite the fact that Jane would have believed her marriage to be valid), so is Emilia "ruined" after Sir John Waldgrave rapes her.

FROM WILLIAM DUFF, *LETTERS ON THE INTELLECTUAL AND MORAL CHARACTER OF WOMEN*
(Aberdeen, 1807)

Miss Emilia Somerville was the daughter of Mr. Somerville, a gentleman of considerable fortune, and of an ancient family in the West of England. His wife, an agreeable and accomplished woman, having died in a few years after their marriage in child-birth, he was left with two children, a boy and a girl; the former about six years of age, the latter only a few days old at the time of her mother's death. As Mr. Somerville was much attached to his children, and at the same time solicitous for their improvement and comfortable settlement in the world, he resolved to spare no expense in giving them an education suitable to their condition and prospects in life. Having perceived in his son, early indications of a promising genius, and being flattered by his rapid progress in Greek and Latin, which he was able to read easily before he was sixteen, he determined to educate him for one of the learned professions, of which he left the choice to himself. As the young gentleman, therefore, discovered a taste for the science of Medicine, he was educated for his profession at Oxford. Having, after his education in that seminary of learning, been sent to London, where he continued three years, under the tuition of the most celebrated professors, in the different branches of medicine, he set out upon his travels to France, Germany, and Holland, in order to improve himself in his favourite science, under foreign professors of the most established reputation. After spending two years at the most distinguished foreign universities, he returned to his own country, with every advantage which genius, education, and assiduous study could bestow; and having taken his degrees in his profession, he set up as a Physician, in London, where he soon acquired a very distinguished character.

Mr. Somerville having had the pleasure to see his son, whom we shall now call Dr. Somerville, settled in so advantageous and respectable a situation in a world, had no object that could occasion his solicitude but the education of his daughter, which now began to engage his serious attention. After having laid a good foundation therefore at home, he sent her when she was about fifteen years old, to a boarding school in Bristol, where she was instructed in the usual branches of female education, in which she made singular progress; returning to her father's house highly accomplished for her age, which was then eighteen.

As Miss Somerville possessed an amiable disposition, as well as an accomplished mind, and was eminently distinguished by her filial affection to her father; the old man doated on her with all the fondness of parental love, and as he had long since given up all thoughts of a second marriage, he devoted the greatest part of his time to the innocent pleasures and useful occupations of a country life, and spent his days in uninterrupted harmony and happiness in the company of his beloved Emilia.

Mr. Somerville and his daughter passed two years in this agreeable domestic society, exhibiting in every part of their conduct the strongest proofs of an affectionate and reciprocal attachment to each other. The Doctor, however, having come on a visit to his father, at Somerville Hall, near Gloucester, was desirous of carrying his sister with him to London, in order to give the last polish to her education, by getting her introduced to genteel company, by his more distinguished female friends, and affording her an opportunity of visiting the places of the most fashionable resort in the metropolis; but as he knew that his father would feel the loss of his daughter's society, should he be left alone, he intreated him to accompany them; a favour he easily obtained.

Miss Somerville, who along with a fine face, and an elegant person, possessed a large share of good sense and good nature, united with a heart full of sensibility and tenderness, attracted, upon her first appearance in the polite world, the notice of several young gentlemen of fortune, who seemed ambitious of acquiring her favour. Among these, Sir John Waldgrave, who had lately come to the possession of a handsome estate, and was at the same time distinguished by the graces of his person and address, discovered a more particular attachment of Miss Somerville than any of the others. This young Baronet, therefore, in the hope of inspiring her with some degree of that passion, which already glowed in his heart, got himself introduced to her brother, who gave him an invitation to his house, which he very readily accepted.

As Sir John possessed not only a cultivated understanding, but a genteel person, and easy and engaging manners, he soon made an impression with these advantages upon the susceptible heart of Miss Somerville. His views, however, though artfully concealed, were base and dishonourable; but perceiving that he had to do with a woman of virtue, whose friends were watchful, and somewhat suspicious of his designs, he resolved, in order to prevent either of them from taking the alarm, to make at least honourable pretensions. With this view, he declared himself a candidate for Miss Somerville's affection, and solicited her hand in marriage, with a dissembled ardour and tenderness, which too easily imposed upon her unsuspecting mind, and made too deep an impression upon her yielding heart. In a word, Miss Somerville confessed herself neither indifferent to his merit nor to his love, and upon his earnest solicitation permitted him to mention the affair to her father.

It may be easily conceived, that so advantageous a match could not but be agreeable to Mr. Somerville, in case Sir John's character should appear upon inquiry to be favourable having applied, therefore, to some of his friends, who were considered as men of honour, though in reality their principles were not much different than his, they palliated his vices and concealed his crimes, when they were made acquainted with his professed matrimonial intentions, representing his former connections with the fair sex as ordinary affairs of gallantry, which they doubted not would now be at an end.

Though neither Mr. Somerville nor his son were satisfied with Sir John Waldgrave's former conduct, they were willing to hope that marriage might reform him, and in that hope gave their consent to the match; the accomplishment of which, it was mutually agreed to defer till after the death of a rich uncle, from whom Sir John had great expectations, and who was then supposed to be dangerously ill; lest this uncle, disapproving of the scheme, should, in resentment of his conduct, disappoint his views of succession to his fortune.

As Sir John Waldgrave had now permission to visit Miss Somerville, upon the footing of an honourable lover, who, it was expected, would soon become her husband; he paid his respects to her frequently, but had hitherto been always very decent in his addresses. Having now, however, as he imagined, thoroughly established his influence over her heart, he resolved at once boldly to accomplish the plot, which his intriguing head and corrupted heart had been gradually ripening for execution; and the daemon of malignity and mischief soon furnished him with the opportunity he desired.

Being informed, that Mr. Somerville and his son were engaged to sup one evening at the house of a friend of the Doctor's, who was a bachelor, and that Miss Somerville chose to continue at home, he determined to wait upon her that evening; and in order to facilitate the scheme he was meditating, he contrived to send the servants out of the way. Upon entering Miss Somerville's apartment, he found her reclining on a sofa in an undress [dressing gown], reading a book, in which she was so much interested, that she scarce perceived his approach, till he sat down by her side.

Struck with the contemplation of that innocence and beauty, which in the mind of a man of principle and honour might have excited love and tenderness, but would, at the same time, have checked the irregularity, and restrained the violence of passion; he felt no other effect from them than to stimulate him to the gratification of his impetuous desires. Callous as he was to remorse, and dead to every sentiment of honour, sensibility and shame, he resolved to indulge them; and through importunity and violence, he in one unguarded moment unhappily effected his detestable purpose; leaving the unhappy fair one he had ruined, to lament the misery and disgrace of her deplorable situation, with fruitless tears and heart-rending anguish.

When Sir John retired, and she had leisure to reflect on the guilt and ignominy of the condition into which she saw herself now plunged, she sunk down upon the floor in an agony of grief, bordering upon despair. At one time she accused her own weakness, at another the villainous artifices of her base seducer. Having passed a sleepless night, tortured with the keenest remorse, and agony unutterable, she resolved at last, amidst the confusion of thought that agitated and distracted her mind, to write a long letter to Sir John Waldgrave, which she immediately did, upbraiding him with his artifices and villainy, and requiring him to fulfill his often-repeated and solemn engagements to marry her.

Though this letter was no way calculated to produce the intended impression upon the mind of a man like Sir John Waldgrave, he was so conscious of the baseness of this conduct, and at the same time so desirous of her acquiescence in the plan of life which he meant to propose to her; that he wrote her with a studied smoothness and an affected contrition, imputing his trespass to the violence of his love, requesting in his letter her forgiveness; but at the same time professing his dislike of matrimony, and intreating her to leave her country and her friends, and go along with him to Paris, where he doubted not they should live in perfect harmony and happiness; promising in any event, before they set out, to settle on her a handsome annuity, as a security against any event she might dread.

This answer raised her sensibility, pride and indignation to the highest pitch. She wrote him for the last time, in the severest terms which a rankled and distracted mind could dictate; reproaching him with his insolence and perfidy, rejecting his proposal with the most contemptuous disdain, as an audacious insult upon the wretchedness of her situation, and forbidding him ever to see or write her more. Sir John finding it impossible to reconcile Miss Somerville to the plan of living he had projected, set out for France in a few days after he received this letter, in the true spirit of a man of pleasure; with a view to obliterate the remembrance of one amour, by the prosecution of others, that chance and a genius for intrigue might throw in his way.

The great difficulty now on the part of Miss Somerville, was to account to her father and brother for the breaking up of the correspondence betwixt her and Sir John, and for his abrupt departure to the continent, without taking leave of her. In the mean time, the melancholy which preyed upon her mind, was easily perceived by them both. In order therefore, to account for this change, she told them, indeed very truly, that, having lately had an interview with Sir John Waldgrave, in which he had too evidently discovered his base and dishonourable intentions, and that having since received from him a letter clearly expressive of those intentions, which in the transport of her rage, she had burnt; she had forbid him ever to see her face, or dare to repeat his detestable proposal. Both her father and brother joined in expressing the strongest indignation at such perfidious and unprincipled conduct; congratulated her upon the escape she had made; bestowed that applause on her spirit and virtue which she could not appropriate to herself, and administered to her every consolation in their power to bestow. After spending a few days longer in London, till Miss Somerville recovered a little strength, she and her father set out together on their journey to Cheshire. Soon after their arrival, Miss Somerville found herself with child, an event, in the situation in which she was placed, the most deplorable that could have happened. The experience of the present, and the anticipation of the future miseries of that situation, preyed incessantly upon her mind, and . . . [her brother] exerted his utmost assiduity and tenderness, in persuading her to adopt the means he prescribed for her recovery. His solicitude and affection stung her to the heart; and when alone drew floods of tears from her eyes, upon every recollection of his kindness, compared with her own unworthiness. At last, after much hesitation and many a conflict, she determined to discover the fatal secret, which indeed could be no longer concealed, to her brother, who, at her father's earnest desire, had come to see her. The discovery affected him exceedingly. While he glowed with the greatest indignation at the author of her wrongs, he felt more pity than resentment for the unhappy sufferer, but trembled at the apprehension of communicating the melancholy information to her father. In order to avoid this discovery, the Doctor proposed sending her immediately to Bath; but, as her father, from his anxiety and tenderness for his daughter, insisted on accompanying her; it became necessary to drop this scheme, and to communicate to him the direful tidings of her disgrace. The information threw him into an agony which it is impossible to describe. He wrung his hands, and looking up to heaven, implored his Maker to grant him a speedy death, as the only period of his misery. Having sent orders to his daughter, immediately to leave his house, her brother sent her with a confidential servant to a village at the distance of some miles, to the care of a woman who had been her nurse. The fatigue of the journey, however, and the circumstances of her disgrace, brought on her labour somewhat prematurely, and she was in two hours after her arrival at the place of her destination delivered of a girl.

The various emotions of grief, remorse and shame, which agitated the bosom of Miss Somerville, upon the present occasion, produced a fever which endangered her life. As her constitution, however, was naturally good, it enabled her to sustain the shock, though the violence of the disease reduced her to a state of weakness and languor, which, added to the melancholy that preyed upon her mind, threatened to terminate in a decay. The grief and anguish, which the circumstances of her disgrace had occasioned to so affectionate a father, in particular lay heavy on her heart. This grief would probably soon have proved fatal to her, had not her brother, whose sympathy and affection were not yet extinguished by the late instance of her frailty, for which he considered the punishment she had already suffered as a sufficient atonement, prevailed on the now relenting old man to see and forgive a daughter, who was once the delight of his eyes, and the joy of his heart. (141–156)

TOPICS FOR WRITTEN OR ORAL EXPLORATION

1. Consider the possibility of being educated in a boarding school and of being educated by a governess. If you lived in the time *Jane Eyre* is set, do you believe you would have been better educated by a boarding school or by a governess? Be prepared to discuss your reasons for choosing the educational method you have chosen.

2. In the nineteenth century, the kind of education a child received depended on a combination of gender and social class. Do you think that education in the twenty-first century should differ according to gender, social class, or any other particular factor? If so, what factors should determine the differences, and why? If no such factors should be considered, why not?

3. Based on your reading of *Jane Eyre* and the writings in this chapter, write an essay in which you evaluate the education girls received in nineteenth-century England. Be sure to use specifics from the texts to support your points.

4. Most education in Brontë's time was conducted in a single-sex atmosphere. Today, most formal education takes place in mixed-gender settings. Which environment do you believe contributes more to the intellectual development of students: single-sex or mixed-gender classrooms? Is being in a single-sex school of greater advantage to boys than to girls, to girls than to boys, or neither? After a discussion of the issues involved, divide the class into two groups: one in favor of single-sex classrooms, the other in favor of mixed-gender classrooms. Provide time for the groups to prepare; then stage a debate on the advantages and disadvantages of single-sex and mixed-gender education in the twenty-first century.

5. In groups of three or four students each, create a document that represents what you, as a group, believe the education of a young person should consist of today. Be sure to consider such factors as the need for general knowledge, skills needed to become a valuable worker in the future work force, and the kind of citizen you believe the country needs. Remember that the educational curriculum (the material to be learned) and form (tutorial study, single-sex schools, mixed-gender schools, private or public school, home study, etc.) you choose will reflect your own educational philosophy and that of the group you belong to.

6. After sharing the documents created in the above assignment, discuss the feasibility of implementing the philosophy or system presented in each document with the rest of the class. Discuss the strengths

and weaknesses of each system and examine your own education in terms of the ideal education you have detailed in your documents.

7. Based on the values that are supported in *Jane Eyre*, as well as the novel's commentary on education through the depictions of Lowood and Jane's work as a governess with Adele, draft a document that expresses what you believe to be Charlotte Brontë's educational philosophy for women. Be prepared to defend each point in that philosophy with at least one specific incident, idea, or narrator's comment from the novel.

8. If you were a schoolmistress or governess in Charlotte Brontë's time, what do you believe you would consider the most important aspects of a girl's education? Write an essay in which you describe how you would approach the education of girls in nineteenth-century England.

9. In nineteenth-century England, issues of morality and propriety were considered to be essential elements of a girl's education. Today there is much debate over whether schools should "teach" values and morality. In the United States, the separation of church and state prevents explicit religious teaching in public schools (though private schools are free to teach religion). What place do you believe morality, values, and religion should have in a student's educational life? Discuss the consequences, both positive and negative, of incorporating religion and morality into the curriculum of the public schools in the twenty-first century.

10. Interview a relative or friend who is at least thirty years older than you. Ask the individual to discuss his or her experiences with formal education. Once you have gathered the information in the form of an interview, write an analytical essay comparing that person's educational experiences with your own. In your analysis, be sure to take into account changes that have taken place in the world over the last thirty years.

SUGGESTED READINGS

Adamson, J. H. *English Education: 1789–1902*. Cambridge: Cambridge University Press, 1964.

Alexander, William. *The History of Women from the Earliest Antiquity, to the Present Time*. London: W. Strahan and T. Cadell, 1779.

Atkinson, Paul. "Fitness, Feminism and Schooling." In *The Nineteenth-Century Woman: Her Cultural and Physical World*. Ed. Sara Delamont and Lorna Duffin. New York: Barnes and Noble, 1978.

Beale, Dorothea, Lucy H. M. Soulsby, and Jane Frances Dove. *Work and Play in Girls' Schools*. London: Longmans, Green, 1898.

Bennett, John. *Letters to a Young Lady on a Variety of Useful and Interesting Subjects*. London, 1795.

Browne, Alice. *The Eighteenth Century Feminist Mind*. Detroit: Wayne State University Press, 1987.

Burstall, Sara A. *Retrospect and Prospect: Sixty Years of Women's Education*. London: Longmans, Green & Co., 1933.

Burstyn, Joan N. *Victorian Education and the Ideal of Womanhood*. London: Croom Helm, 1980.

Chapone Hester, Dr. John Gregory, and Lady Sarah Pennington. *Chapone's Improvement of the Mind; Gregory's Legacy; Lady Pennington's Advice*. London: Scott and Webster, n.d.

Chirol, J. L. *An Enquiry into the Best System of Female Education*. London, 1809.

Cobbe, Frances Power. *Life of Frances Power Cobbe, as Told by Herself*. London: Swan Sonnenschein, 1904.

Darwin, Erasmus. *A Plan for the Conduct of Female Education in Boarding Schools*. Yorkshire: S. R. Publishers Limited, 1968.

Delamont, Sara. "The Contradictions in Ladies' Education." In *The Nineteenth-Century Woman: Her Cultural and Physical World*. Ed. Sara Delamont and Lorna Duffin. New York: Barnes and Noble, 1978.

———. "The Domestic Ideology and Women's Education." In *The Nineteenth-Century Woman: Her Cultural and Physical World*. Ed. Sara Delamont and Lorna Duffin. New York: Barnes and Noble, 1978.

Duff, William. *Letters on the Intellectual and Moral Character of Women. On the Station for which They Are Destined: On the Characters They Are Qualified to Sustain: and On the Duties They Are Required to Discharge, Both in Private and Social Life*. Aberdeen, 1807.

Edgeworth, Maria, and Richard Lovell Edgeworth. *Practical Education*. London: J. Johnson, 1798.

Ellis, Mrs. [Sarah]. *The Women of England: Their Social Duties, and Domestic Habits*. New York: Edward Walker, 1848.

"An Enquiry into the State of Girls' Fashionable Schools." *Fraser's Magazine* (June 1845): 703–711.

Gardiner, Dorothy. *English Girlhood at School: A Study of Women's Education through Twelve Centuries*. Oxford: Oxford University Press, 1929.

Gaskell, Elizabeth. *The Life of Charlotte Brontë*. 1857. London: Oxford University Press, 1919.

Gisborne, Thomas. *An Enquiry into the Duties of the Female Sex.* 3rd ed. London: T. Cadell, 1797.

Gregory, John. *A Father's Legacy to His Daughters.* London: W. Strahan, T. Cadell, W. Creech, 1774.

Havergal, Maria Vernon Graham. *Memorials of Frances Ridley Havergal.* London: James Nisbet & Co., 1880.

Kamm, Josephine. *Hope Deferred: Girls' Education in English History.* London: Methuen, 1965.

Lawson, John, and Harold Silver. *A Social History of Education in England.* London: Methuen, 1973.

Locke, John. *Some Thoughts Concerning Education.* 5th ed. London, 1705.

Lynch, Hannah. *Autobiography of a Child.* New York: Dodd, Mead, 1899.

Macaulay Graham, Catherine. *Letters on Education with Observations on Religious and Metaphysical Subjects.* London: C. Dilly, 1790.

More, Hannah. *Strictures on the Modern System of Female Education.* London: T. Cadell, Jun. and W. Davies, 1799.

Myers, Sylvia H. "Learning, Virtue, and the Term 'Bluestocking.' " *Studies in Eighteenth Century Culture* 15 (1986): 279–288.

Progress of a Female Mind. By a Lady. London, 1764.

Roe, Mrs. *A Woman's Thoughts on the Education of Girls.* London, 1866.

Smith, Bonnie G. *Changing Lives: Women in European History Since 1700.* Lexington, MA: D.C. Heath, 1989.

Stoddart, Anna. *Life and Letters of Hannah E. Pipe.* Edinburgh: William Blackwood & Sons, 1908.

Sturt, Mary. *The Education of the People: A History of Primary Education in England and Wales in the Nineteenth Century.* London: Routledge and Kegan Paul, 1967.

Teachman, Debra. *Understanding Pride and Prejudice. A Student Casebook to Issues, Sources, and Historical Documents.* Westport, CT: Greenwood, 1997.

Trimmer, Mrs. [Sarah]. *The Economy of Charity; or, an Address to Ladies; Adapted to the Present State of Charitable Institutions in England.* London: J. Johnson and F. and C. Rivington, 1801.

Wakefield, Priscilla. *Reflections on the Present Condition of the Female Sex with Suggestions for Improvement.* London: J. Johnson, Darton and Harvey, 1798.

West, Mrs. [Jane]. *Letters to a Young Lady, in which the Duties and Character of Women Are Considered.* 2nd ed. London, 1806.

Wollstonecraft, Mary. *Thoughts on the Education of Daughters: With Reflections on Female Conduct, in the More Important Duties of Life.* London, 1787.

3

The Governess in Nineteenth-Century England

In nineteenth-century England, the purpose of a woman's life was generally considered to be marriage and motherhood. Yet, many women of the period did not marry at all. With the large numbers of men emigrating to India, Australia, and the Americas, many more women of marriageable age were left in England than men who wanted wives. This created what was known as a "redundancy" problem. In Victorian England, single women who were not particularly eligible for marriage (especially due to lack of fortune and suitable family ties) were considered redundant, unnecessary, superfluous. The redundant woman had few choices. If her father and/or brothers were able to provide for her, she usually lived at home and assisted with the care of the household and any children or elderly people who might live there. In the Brontë family, for instance, Patrick Brontë provided a home for his late wife's unmarried sister, while she ran his household and provided his children with a surrogate mother figure. For most middle- and upper-class women who could not be (or chose not to be) provided for by family members, the only clear reputable option was to teach, either in a school or as a governess.

Charlotte Brontë and her sister Anne both worked as governesses for wealthy families. Thus, they were very familiar with the kinds of lives governesses lived. Jane Eyre's life as a governess is actually much more romantic and much less time-consuming than the lives of most governesses of the day. Few governesses ever rose in stature through either marriage or inheritance. In fact, most sank into genteel poverty or even utter destitution by the end of their lives.

The role the governess filled was usually a very lonely one. As a woman of genteel birth and education, she did not fit in with the servant class and therefore rarely received friendship and comfort from the family's other hired help. On the other hand, her poverty and need to work for her living prevented her from being on terms of equality with her employers. And, regardless of her skill as a teacher, she was rarely allowed the freedom to teach without some measure of parental interference. The content of her students' education as well as the methods by which they were educated and disciplined were usually dictated by their mothers, who often encouraged the children to think of the governess as merely another servant deserving little respect or deference.

M. MOSTYN BIRD

At the beginning of the twentieth century, M. Mostyn Bird wrote his study of women's occupations, *Woman at Work: A Study of the Different Ways of Earning a Living Open to Women*. In it, he presents a strong positive portrait of the role that teachers play in the lives of their students. He asserts that women make the best teachers for young children because their minds are not as strong and reasonable as men's; therefore, they can relate better to the mind of a young child than a man can. Such differences between the sexes are, he claims, quite natural.

His idealized image of the teacher is one who is naturally understanding and patient. She is particularly suited for the job she fills. By contrast, the reality of the average teacher's life (whether in a school or as a governess in a family) in Victorian England was much different.

FROM M. MOSTYN BIRD, *WOMAN AT WORK: A STUDY OF THE DIFFERENT WAYS OF EARNING A LIVING OPEN TO WOMEN*
(London, 1911)

The work of instructing young children is, like the care of the home, essentially the woman's affair. Long before the word "career" was introduced into the woman's vocabulary, before history was written and even before it was made, women were occupied in training their young sons for manly tasks and their daughters to be fit mothers of men. From prehistoric times, the days of childhood, when every moment contributes its quota of information to the opening mind, and everything unconsciously learned makes its indelible impression, have been spent at the woman's knee. Savage and civilized woman alike form and develop according to their own pattern the little lives growing up about them. It is not only by custom and convenience that this is so, but because there is a natural and intimate link between the minds of the woman and the child. The stronger and more reasonable mind of the man cannot reach and touch with the same precision the unformed and changeful springs of the child's expanding existence. Women are certainly the most successful teachers of young children. They often . . . obtain a hold over the children and develop their individual minds in a way that a man seldom succeeds in doing. The gift is the teacher's, the difference is not due to the greater natural intelligence of the [student]. . . .

This prospect of success should prove an incentive to the woman with a patient and understanding love of children to enter this profession. Though it probably will not return her the money value of the life-long effort and self-discipline she will be called upon to devote to it, she will find a perennial satisfaction and stimulus in the work itself. The career can never be one of hopeless monotony; it calls for the devotion of all her time, talents, and fine qualities, but itself inspires much of the quality and devotion it demands. The successful teacher . . . must always have this fund of inner enthusiasm to draw upon. She is in love with her subject and consequently has a sympathetic understanding of it and a desire to present it in the most attractive guise to others. And she is also in close touch with her scholars, knowing what points will most appeal to them, and how they individually will be likely to view the matter she puts before them. The teacher who hews off indiscriminate chunks of a big subject and throws them down before her class will merely give them mental indigestion. In this respect the teacher is an artist, just as the painter and writer are artists. Wherever one person is concerned with the translation of an idea for the purpose of appealing to others, the immense amount of personal selection involved opens out limitless possibilities of success and failure, and all the subtle gradations between these two. The finest idea may be spoiled by the manner of its presentation; the feeblest may be dignified and idealized out of recognition. But pearls may be cast before swine and leave them as hungry as the husks that they gladly eat will leave starving human beings. The method of presentation must be decided as much by the character of the hearer as by the subject; the teacher is an alchemist and the class room the crucible in which her miracles are wrought. The unawakened mind is here brought into contact with the subject that will feed and expand it; the teacher watching over all the process of assimilation.

It is a fascinating task. By its very nature it is lifted above those careers in which a woman engages with her hands, to however useful an end, in order to gain herself an independent livelihood. As a teacher she has a wider sphere. She is helping to form the men and women of the growing generation. She is radiating influences that will spread and leave their mark upon the history of her country. It saves her life from the utter extinction that death brings to the childless woman, for something of herself will be left to live and work in the younger generation. Though she has bequeathed to it no living flesh, she has formed budding minds and moulded young wills and planted fine ideals in childish hearts. Her work will remain a living force in the world when her busy hands and thoughts are at rest. To throw open the gates of Knowledge and smooth the path for eager but tottering feet is her delightful work. To gather the resuscitated treasures of the past and show them to wondering eyes; to make hard things simple, and cruel things kind, and ugly things shine with a heavenly luster, is her high task. She cannot be too well equipped, self-disciplined, humble and yet bold, to take so much upon herself. (150–154)

MARY WOLLSTONECRAFT

Unlike M. Mostyn Bird, Mary Wollstonecraft understood life as a single woman of small means. She herself worked as a teacher and governess at the end of the eighteenth century. She recognized that there were very few possibilities open to women of her time outside of marriage, and that all options, including marriage, restricted women to a much larger degree than men were restricted. In her *Vindication of the Rights of Woman*, Wollstonecraft argued that women deserved equality with men, that they had a natural right to control their own lives, their own finances, and their own occupations. As one of the most vocal members of the women's rights movement of the later eighteenth century, she was berated by most conservative writers and thinkers, who contributed to the destruction of her reputation as a morally upright woman. But even her detractors among the single women of Victorian England tended to agree with her views on the humiliating and depressing position of the single women in a world that considered woman's purpose to be marriage and motherhood.

FROM MARY WOLLSTONECRAFT, *THOUGHTS ON THE EDUCATION OF DAUGHTERS, WITH REFLECTIONS ON FEMALE CONDUCT IN THE MORE IMPORTANT DUTIES OF LIFE*
(London, 1787)

Unfortunate Situation of Females, Fashionably Educated, and Left Without a Fortune.

I have hitherto only spoken of those females, who will have a provision made for them by their parents. But many who have been well, or at least fashionably educated, are left without a fortune, and if they are not entirely devoid of delicacy, they must frequently remain single.

Few are the modes of earning a subsistence, and those very humiliating. Perhaps to be an humble companion to some rich old cousin, or what is still worse, to live with strangers, who are so intolerably tyrannical, that none of their own relations can bear to live with them, though they should even expect a fortune in reversion. It is impossible to enumerate the many hours of anguish such a person must spend. Above the servants, yet considered by them as a spy, and ever reminded of her inferiority when in conversation with her superiors. If she cannot condescend to mean flattery, she has not a chance of being a favorite; and should any of the visitors take notice of her, and she for a moment forget her subordinate state, she is sure to be reminded of it.

Painfully sensible of unkindness, she is alive to every thing, and many sarcasms reach her, which were perhaps directed another way. She is alone, shut out from equality and confidence, and the concealed anxiety impairs her constitution; for she must wear a cheerful face, or be dismissed. The being dependent on the caprice of a fellow-creature, though certainly very necessary in this state of discipline, is yet a very bitter corrective, which we would fain shrink from.

A teacher at a school is only a kind of upper servant, who has more work than the menial ones.

A governess to young ladies is equally disagreeable. It is ten to one if they meet with a reasonable mother; and if she is not so, she will be continually finding fault to prove she is not ignorant, and be displeased if her pupils do not improve, but angry if they do so. The children treat [governesses] with disrespect, and often with insolence. In the mean time, life glides away, and the spirits with it; "and when youth and genial years are flown," they have nothing to subsist on; or, perhaps, on some extraordinary occasion, some small allowance may be made for them, which is thought a great charity.

The few trades which are left, are now gradually falling into the hands of the man, and certainly they are not very respectable. (69–73)

ADVICE TO GOVERNESSES

In 1827, the anonymous *Advice to Governesses* was published in London by John Hatchard and Son. This work, unlike the later writings of M. Mostyn Bird, recognizes that teaching is a difficult profession, that the rewards are often paltry, and that many who enter its ranks are not suited to fulfill its functions either by temperament or desire. Nonetheless, as one of a very few vocations open to an unmarried woman who has no fortune to support herself, many women seek out governess work.

The author of *Advice to Governesses* presents a realistic picture of the life a governess must expect, along with many suggestions about how she might manage to live a life of such restriction and deprivation, a life that is usually very different from the one in which she herself was brought up. A prospective governess is advised to accept that she will be required to work for those who were her equals or even her inferiors prior to her being forced into the situation of having to work to maintain herself. If this is intolerable, she had better choose some activity other than governessing, since the nature of the job is to be treated as a social inferior, despite the level of society to which the governess was born or the quality of her education.

One particular issue is dealt with in much more depth in this work than in almost any other: that of a governess attracting the romantic attentions of a gentleman who lives in the house in which she works. The author warns anyone considering becoming a governess of such danger and goes into considerable detail about her obligations to avoid any situations that might enable a gentleman to make advances. Such obligations are hers to fulfill, the essay implies, since moral conduct is an obligation of women much more than it is of men. The danger of falling in love with one's pupil's father is especially to be avoided, even if he is single and attentive to the governess. Such advice was directed particularly toward young women like Jane Eyre, whose respectability could so easily be destroyed by the advances of a gentleman whose intentions might not be honorable.

FROM *ADVICE TO GOVERNESSES*
(London, 1827)

As no one in this country is born in a state of servitude, and few would prefer it who have independence in their power; necessity, or propriety, are the usual motives which induce persons to place themselves in subordinate situations, the choice of which is left to the individual, and though a young woman may be obliged to maintain herself, and may be persuaded to undertake the office of a governess, she will do well to look to her disposition and capacity before she enters upon it. Gentlewomen, whose circumstances in life are changed, or young persons educated for this employment, or teachers and half-boarders in schools, are the description of females who usually seek such situations. . . . The gentlewoman will have much to contend with before she can resolve to serve those who are probably her inferiors in birth and education, and, unless she be a woman of high principle, she will not serve them well: sensibility to little slights, impatience at unjust requisitions, and a disposition to exact what she was once entitled to receive from all around her, will make her exceedingly burdensome to her employers, whatever real superiority she may possess. Let her not deceive herself and fancy that she shall be considered on the footing of a friend, in consequence of what she has once been. I said to Miss ——, "I do not like that you should live under the direction of persons beneath you": the thought that she was to be under their direction was so new to her, that a flood of tears was the consequence of my remark: she embarked in the office, unable to submit, and soon left it, glad to escape, and the lady who had received her into her family, still more rejoiced, to part with her. We gain nothing by shrinking from the truth; a governess is a dependent, and subject to the master and mistress of the house: she is engaged for higher employments, and requires a higher salary, than persons devoted to manual labour, because endowments of the mind must be purchased at a higher rate; she expects certain courtesies which her inferiors neither require nor understand, but she cannot demand them, yet there is this resemblance in their situations, if their abode be disagreeable to them, they are at liberty to quit it, or if they give not satisfaction they are liable to be dismissed. How often do we hear it said by mothers, "Spare me from a fallen gentlewoman [a woman of society who has fallen onto hard times financially], I shall be for ever wounding her feelings," and yet if she receive such a one into her family, she gives her children an advantage they would otherwise be deprived of; that of associating with a person whose habits and feelings resemble their own in the present, and what should be their own in the future. . . .

If a fallen gentlewoman possess sufficient magnanimity to devote herself solely to the benefit of others, in the utter forgetfulness of self, I do
not hesitate in saying that she would prove a treasure to her employers:
if her principle lead her to exact from those around her only what they
ought to bestow, to bear the slights she receives, not only without mur-
muring, but as wholesome discipline to herself, however ungraciously
administered; if she have sense enough never to remind any one what
her former station has been, but by shewing herself superior to the petty
trials which overset vulgar minds; if she give "honour to whom honour
is due" from circumstances, regardless of the narrow and inferior capacities she may have to deal with, and . . . cheerfully submit to the duties
of the state in which she is now equally placed by God, as if she had
been born in it, no prejudice could possibly exist against her from having
known, what are called, better days; indeed she will make the present
the best days of her life, by filling them with employments which will
bring her peace at the great day of account.

If a young person, on duly weighing the wishes of her friends and her
own qualifications, determine that there is no situation she is better calculated to fill, than that of a governess, she may humbly trust that the
divine blessing will rest upon her decision, but no motive of worldly
interest can justify her undertaking to instruct others, if she think under
existing circumstances this is not the line of her duty. (1–8)

• • •

A governess, on her entrance into a family, if she be inexperienced,
has often so much to contend with, that she calls powerfully for the
sympathy of those about her; though her task be hard, and her responsibility great; let her be encouraged to persevere. Although arrangements
will have been made with the intention of promoting the happiness of
all parties; no sky is always clear, nor turf always green, so there will be
dark clouds and scorching suns, in the moral as in the natural world,
and we must defend ourselves against their influences.

The first vexation a governess meets with, frequently arises from a
mother's want of confidence, and from her interference in the school-
room; from her great tenderness to her children, not suffering their instructress to use her own discretion; from indulgence breaking in upon
hours devoted to study, and from her not permitting necessary discipline,
but counteracting useful regulations. This evil is a real one and requires
great patience; but the governess must remember that a mother cannot
feel full confidence till she know how far it be merited, and must also
remember that unless she were herself a mother she cannot make sufficient allowance for the strong maternal feeling, which can scarcely bear

to place the objects of her tenderest affection in any hands but her own. Forbearance should be carried to a reasonable extent on the part of the governess, but not to a length which would be injurious to the children; she ought to remonstrate with respect and gentleness when alone with the mother; and, if she have imprudently found fault with the governess's management in the presence of her pupils, should request that this may not be repeated, as it must diminish their respect for her, expressing at the same time her willingness to be advised with, in private.

The intimacy of a mother with the teacher of her children is often a great impediment to her being of use to them, and is so tempting a snare that she knows not how to escape it. The mother has bad health and wants the attendance of a friend in whom she can confide; she wishes to be read to, or sung to, or she is afflicted and must pour out her heart to some one; she trusts the governess is prudent, at any rate she should be so, and is at hand. . . . Time, which ought to be devoted to the pupils, is thus encroached upon; the governess has a more powerful interest than that which she takes in their improvement: lessons are hurried over that the hours may be given to their mother. . . . The line of conduct which a governess so situated should pursue is so nice that without Divine help . . . it is impossible not to fail; she must look narrowly into what passes in her own heart, detect the vanity and self-love that she may find lurking there, and pursue strictly what she considers the path of duty. There are circumstances in which it may be indispensable for a governess to become the devoted nurse of the mother. There are cases in which her advice may be of infinite importance; but as a general question I should say that friendships rarely subsist where conditions are unequal. (35–40)

· · ·

There is a deference which every gentleman naturally shows to a woman. . . . If the governess be young and pretty she must scrupulously resist the slightest approach to improper familiarity; what would be unexceptionable in the conduct of any visitor might be very dangerous for her; let her manner speak, "the condition on which I live with you is, that you do not treat me as an obsequious friend." Let her not repulse attention with the air of an offended mistress, but with the decision of one who feels her rights encroached upon; and if she cannot maintain these rights, let her quit her situation without giving the reason to any human being, unless her parents demand it from her; foolishly to insinuate the cause might occasion dangerous discussion and infinite mischief.

The same conduct must be pursued where there are grown up sons, or brothers in the family in which she resides; let her not for a moment indulge the thought that a marriage with any of them may be contracted with impunity because such marriages have been made: let her be persuaded that they are usually imprudent and unhappy, and no woman has a right to suppose that there will be an exception in her own favour. If she endeavour to become the object of attachment, under these circumstances, she is guilty of a breach of trust; for who would have engaged her, expecting such a result? If her employers are careless, she ought not to take advantage of their folly or too great confidence in her. . . .

When a man has the misfortune to lose the mother of his children, the person whom he chooses for their governess is usually of an age that he would not prefer in a wife; but should he fail to consider this, she may be called upon to resist the greatest temptation to which she may ever be exposed; that of sacrificing the first earthly wish of her heart to a sense of duty. For, in addition to the inconveniences, which a man who has already been married, is subject to, in making a connexion beneath him, a new one is added of great importance; that of subjecting his children to her as a mother-in-law [stepmother], when they may have imagined themselves aggrieved by her in her former capacity, and giving them a right to judge themselves as hardly treated by their father, when they compare the birth and fortune of their own mother with those of a dependent. If it endanger the harmony of the family, when the children of two mothers abide under the same roof, this danger will be so much the more from inequality of condition, than if their mothers had always been of the equal rank in society.

I have known governesses marry the fathers of their pupils, and I have also known of one who had the magnanimity to refuse this dangerous distinction; but I respect far more highly those females who never indulged a thought of altering (by this means), their condition in life, who have tried to please, only by fulfilling the duties of their station—never sought for admiration, contented with meriting esteem. . . .

Great difficulties often arise from changes in a family, not only from the death of the mother, but from the conduct of a sister who may take her place, or the second marriage of the father. These alterations may produce a train of feelings, both in the governess and her pupils, not easily counteracted. A well principled governess, however hard the task, will suppress what is painful to herself for the sake of those under her care; she will not commit the error so frequently fallen into by superintendants under these circumstances, and, by teaching the children to resist authority, do them incredible mischief; but she will give them the most cheerful impression she can with truth, of that which is inevitable, nor suffer their discontents to create an evil of what may never prove one in itself. It is of the highest importance to them, to look up with confidence and affection, to the aunt or mother-in-law [stepmother] who takes the place of their mother. . . . The governess must herself consider, that she is as much bound to this new superintendant, as to the first who engaged her, and set an uniform example of respect, and desire to please. (41–48)

SARAH LEWIS

In April 1848, less than a year after the publication of *Jane Eyre*, *Fraser's Magazine* published an article written by Sarah Lewis that examined the position of governesses in Victorian families and society. Lewis was herself a governess, as well as a writer, and knew the difficulties and humiliations of the governess's life firsthand. She encourages the English to provide for those governesses who have had to retire from their work but do not have pensions to support them in their old age. She recognizes that some governesses are not qualified and do not earn the pittance that their employers pay them, but she points out that most governesses are worth much more than they are paid and that they have no means of saving for their elderly years or for periods of illness and/or unemployment. She makes recommendations for the better training of governesses overall, for government certification of them, and for paying them a living wage, sufficient to enable them to save for their futures as well as to pay for their present requirements.

FROM SARAH LEWIS, "ON THE SOCIAL POSITION OF
GOVERNESSES"
(*Fraser's Magazine*, April 1848).

In treating, therefore, of the wrongs, or what [the writer] conceives to be the wrongs, of governesses, she is actuated by none of the asperity of adversity, and none of the bitterness of wounded self-love. But a personal exemption from great "class evils," ought not to blind the understanding to their existence, or shut the heart to the misery which they produce. Even the perception of these evils, however, would not have sufficed to urge her to a public declaration of her sentiments, but that she feels some of the highest interests of society to be thereby compromised, and that society is even more unjust to itself than to her profession in suffering their existence.

The frequent appeals to public compassion made in behalf of governesses—the "fancy fairs," "shilling subscription cards," got up with a view to their benefit, are calculated to fill a thinking mind with painful reflections, and a cynical mind with bitter ones. There must be some great wrong—something very "rotten in the state of Denmark," before society would venture to offer, or respectable individuals could be induced to accept, such compensation for social prejudice and social injustice!

It is difficult to speak of benevolent intention, even when one thinks them ill-directed, with any thing approaching to harshness; but it remains a matter of grave consideration whether the tendency of the above-mentioned charities be not, like many of the efforts of merely impulsive benevolence, to relieve individual distress at the expense of general good.

It is too true that governesses can rarely provide for old age or contingencies. But why? Because the emolument received by governesses (however superior) is not sufficient to enable a person, required to keep up the appearance of a gentlewoman, to do so—because the general notions on this subject are notoriously such, as to have been made the subject of more than one popular burlesque! The salary of a first-rate governess is scarcely more than the interest of money which her education *ought* to have cost; and those of all under "first-rate" are not more than is given to the upper servants of good families. The profession of a private governess is the only profession which offers no premium to distinguished abilities, and we see the results, unhappily, every day. Would it not be better to pay governesses a little more, and to pity them a little less? The prejudices which would degrade, and the injustice which inadequately remunerates, the members of an honourable and useful profession, are ill compensated by a tardy and patronizing compassion. The writer knows not how the members of her profession feel *generally*, but, for her own part, she would prefer having recourse to that legal provision which the laws of her country allow all to claim,—to receiving in the form of *alms* that which had been denied in the form of *wages*. Nor can it be wondered at if the high-minded amongst the body should reject rather than be grateful for, that form of compensation which arises from public charity, and is to be sued for *in forma pauperis*.

But this is not the only, nor, in the writer's opinion, the gravest, aspect of the subject. That individuals should suffer humiliation is a light thing in comparison of a great cause suffering injury.

Education is a great cause. The public think it so; they talk of it, at least, as such! The progress of society permits no one now to *say*, whatever he may *think*, that ours is a degrading occupation. We have essays on education, essays on educators; how the tone of the one and the character of the other may be raised. Can the tone of education, or the character of educators, be raised, while society continues to offer to the members of this profession for their services . . . the wages and social position of a domestic, and for their distresses and old age . . . the provision of a pauper?

Their knowledge of human nature must be very small who do not perceive that a class, the distresses and necessities of which are thus constantly made the theme of public commiseration and the object of public charity, can never attain (as a class) to that position of social respectability which the members of so influential a profession ought to occupy; and education can never be what it ought to be, till educators do fill such a place in public estimation. How is society to learn to look up with respect to those on whom it has been first taught to look down with pity? It is impossible!

But there are two sides to every question; and where there is blame it is never altogether on one; nor is it here. Candour compels the acknowledgment, that while the respectable and meritorious are often grievously underpaid, there are but too many in our profession who would be overpaid *at any price*. And the same candour compels also the humiliating confession, that the inadequate remuneration and low social position of governesses may be greatly attributed to the assumption of the office by those whose necessities are their only title to employment. Is it not monstrous, that while a lady will not give her dress to be made to any one but a first-rate dress-maker, she will give her children to be educated by a second or third-rate governess? That she will commit their training for this world and the next to a woman whose only qualification for the task is, that she has had a twelve month's apprenticeship in an inferior boarding-school, or—that her father failed last week? One has really very little right to complain of the want of respect shewn by society to a profession which respects itself so little as to have allowed this state of things to continue without a grand simultaneous effort to remedy it. But such an effort being, it is to be feared, hopeless, some other remedy must be found. This remedy appears to lie, not in public *charity* but in public *institutions*. That governesses may be more respected, they must be better qualified; that they may be better qualified, they must be better paid; that they may be both, they must be better chosen; that they may be better chosen, there must be somebody to choose them. *That* somebody should be the Government; for the Church, which *ought* to be the curator of public education, does not sufficiently represent the people to take up its office. The Government, then, in our own, as in other countries, ought to take upon itself the office of securing the public interests by excluding the half-educated or simply necessitous from the rank of public instructors, thus giving respectability to the office and security to the public.

The public feeling on this subject has already found representatives in two bodies,—the "Queen's College," and the "College of Preceptors." To both—and especially to the latter, as organized by the Educational body itself—much gratitude is due for . . . their endeavours after a great moral and national good. But the writer (with diffidence) suggests that they are both deficient in a most important respect,—viz. They are not armed with a competent and efficient weight of authority. The power needed is a power of *exclusion*,—a power which can say, "You shall not take up this vocation unless you shew testimonials of ability." No privately organized body would, or could, assume to itself the power of such exclusion; and the assumption, that the diploma granted to the capable would amount to a virtual exclusion of the incapable, seems to be based on an insufficient consideration of the peculiar difficulties of the case.

Some of these difficulties the writer (also with diffidence) ventures to suggest. It appears to her, that while the ignorant and incapable might (by accepting low salaries) evade the requisite examination, the *very superior*—those of acknowledged merit and talent—might neglect it, not from contempt, but because nothing but a Government diploma, absolutely indispensable, and giving to the educator the dignity of a recognized public functionary, could be to such persons a sufficient desideratum to induce them to submit to the ordeal of a public examination. Now these are the very persons whom it would be desirable to tempt into that profession to which society entrusts its dearest interests. It appears also to her, that no amount of fairness or impartiality could secure the members of those bodies from the suspicion of partisanship in the exercise of their self-constituted functions; and that the clamour of injustice—first raised, perhaps, by disappointed incapacity—would soon find an echo in the public mind, and nullify the benefits expected. A Government sanction, then, appears to be the principal means by which the object so laudably attempted by these bodies can be attained; and the *only* means by which full security can be given, either to the profession or to the public, that the highest of all tasks may not often be assigned to the lowest of all minds!

But, waiting these better times, there is much misery waiting also for relief. And that Charity should stay her hand till Justice has done *her* work is not to be expected,—not even to be wished. It is, however, to be desired, that this relief could be afforded in a manner which would maintain the dignity of the profession, while it solaces the distress of the individual; that some regard (as to ways and means) be had to the feelings of those, who are many of them *in reality*, and all of them *by courtesy*, gentlewomen; that still more regard be had to the public interests, which are deeply compromised by any further degradation of a body so important to the moral interests of the community.

If these remarks prove suggestive of any useful thoughts to the public in general, the writer will be well content; but her chief object is to rouse the attention of those of her own sex and profession, who may not yet have considered the subject in its full bearings, on their own position and interests, as well as on the public good. *To* them she looks for sympathy; *from* them must come the efforts (whether pecuniary or other-wise) that are to overcome the evils which all must deplore. Why should not the heads of prosperous and respectable ladies' schools come to the rescue of their less fortunate sisters? An annual subscription of a com-paratively moderate amount from all such would effect much good in this cause. To be the pensioners of a fund having (at least for its basis) a professional combination is one thing; to be the pauperized claimants of eleemosynary public charity is another. To rescue the less fortunate members of our noble common profession from so degrading a necessity would seem to be an object needing no other recommendation than its own merits. And if this appeal rouse a few thinking heads and noble hearts (there are some such amongst us) to consideration and conse-quent action, it will not have been made in vain. (412–414)

ANNE BRONTË

Charlotte Brontë's younger sister, Anne, was, like Charlotte herself, both a governess and a writer, producing two novels, *Agnes Grey* and *Tenant of Wildfell Hall*. Although less well-known than her older sister, she likewise created fiction out of her life experience. In *Agnes Grey* she developed a main character who, like Anne Brontë herself, wanted to help her family in their financial struggles by working as a governess. The character's initial impression of what it would be like to work as a governess is very idealistic, and her parents and sister consider the very suggestion of her going out to work for another family ludicrous. But eventually she gets her chance.

Agnes's experience as a governess is a dramatized version of the anonymous advisor to governesses' warnings about a gentlewoman finding herself working for those who are her inferiors in birth. It is also an example of Sarah Lewis's argument for better preparation of women for governess work. Agnes's actual experience of working as a governess is quite different from what she had anticipated. Nonetheless, she is intent upon fulfilling her obligations to her own family and to the family who employs her, no matter how difficult she finds the situation.

FROM ANNE BRONTË, *AGNES GREY*
(London, 1847)

Through all our troubles, I never but once heard my mother complain of our want of money. As summer was coming on, she observed to Mary and me, "What a desirable thing it would be for your papa to spend a few weeks at a watering-place. I am convinced the sea-air and the change of scene would be of incalculable service to him. But then, you see, there's no money." . . .

"I wish *I* could do something," said I. . . . "I should like to be a governess."

My mother uttered an exclamation of surprise, and laughed. My sister dropped her work in astonishment, exclaiming, "*You* a governess, Agnes! What *can* you be dreaming of?"

"Well! I don't see anything so *very* extraordinary in it. I do not pretend to be able to instruct great girls; but surely, I could teach little ones: and I should like it *so* much: I am so fond of children." . . .

I was silenced for that day, and for many succeeding ones; but still I did not wholly relinquish my darling scheme. . . .

How delightful it would be to be a governess! To go out into the world; to enter upon a new life; to act for myself; to exercise my unused faculties; to try my unknown powers; to earn my own maintenance, and something to comfort and help my father, mother, and sister, besides exonerating them from the provision of my food and clothing; to show papa what his little Agnes could do; to convince mamma and Mary that I was not quite the helpless, thoughtless being they supposed. And then, how charming to be entrusted with the care and education of children! Whatever others said, I felt I was fully competent to the task: the clear remembrance of my own thoughts in early childhood would be a surer guide than the instructions of the most mature adviser. I had but to turn from my little pupils to myself at their age, and I should know, at once, how to win their confidence and affections; how to waken the contrition of the erring; how to embolden the timid, and console the afflicted; how to make Virtue practicable, Instruction desirable, and Religion lovely and comprehensible. . . .

At last, to my great joy, it was decreed that I should take charge of the young family of a certain Mrs. Bloomfield; whom my kind, prim aunt Grey had known in her youth, and asserted to be a very nice woman. Her husband was a retired tradesman, who had realized a very comfortable fortune; but could not be prevailed upon to give a greater salary than twenty-five pounds to the instructress of his children. I, however, was glad to accept this, rather than refuse the situation—which my parents were inclined to think the better plan. (8–11)

• • •

My task of instruction and surveillance, instead of becoming easier as my charges and I got better accustomed to each other, became more arduous as their characters unfolded. The name of governess, I soon found, was a mere mockery as applied to me: my pupils had no more notion of obedience than a wild, unbroken colt. The habitual fear of their father's peevish temper, and the dread of the punishments he was wont to inflict when irritated, kept them generally within bounds in his immediate presence. The girls, too, had some fear of their mother's anger; and the boy might occasionally be bribed to do as she bid him by the hope of reward; but I had no rewards to offer; and as for punishments, I was given to understand, the parents reserved that privilege to themselves; and yet they expected me to keep my pupils in order. Other children might be guided by the fear of anger and the desire of approbation; but neither the one nor the other had any effect upon these.

Master Tom, not content with refusing to be ruled, must needs set up as a ruler, and manifested a determination to keep, not only his sisters, but his governess in order, by violent manual and pedal applications; and, as he was a tall, strong boy of his years, this occasioned no trifling inconvenience. A few sound boxes in the ear, on such occasions, might have settled the matter easily enough; but as, in that case, he might make up some story to his mother, which she would be sure to believe, as she had such unshaken faith in his veracity—though I had already discovered it to be by no means unimpeachable—I determined to refrain from striking him, even in self-defence; and, in his most violent moods, my only resource was to throw him on his back, and hold his hands and feet till the frenzy was somewhat abated. To the difficulty of preventing him from doing what he ought not, was added that of forcing him to do what he ought. Often he would positively refuse to learn, or to repeat his lessons, or even to look at his book. Here, again, a good birch rod might have been serviceable; but, as my powers were so limited, I must make the best use of what I had.

As there were no settled hours for study and play, I resolved to give my pupils a certain task, which, with moderate attention, they could perform in a short time; and till this was done, however weary I was, or however perverse they might be, nothing short of parental interference should induce me to suffer them to leave the schoolroom; even if I should sit with my chair against the door to keep them in. Patience, Firmness, and Perseverance, were my only weapons; and these I resolved to use to the utmost. I determined always strictly to fulfil the threats and promises I made; and, to that end, I must be cautious to threaten and promise nothing that I could not perform. Then, I would be as kind and obliging as it was in my power to be, in order to make the widest possible distinction between good and bad conduct; I would reason with them too, in the simplest and most effective manner. When I reproved them, or refused to gratify their wishes, after a glaring fault, it should be more in sorrow than in anger: their little hymns and prayers I would make plain and clear to their understanding; when they said their prayers at night, and asked pardon for their offenses, I would remind them of the sins of the past day, solemnly, but in perfect kindness, to avoid raising a spirit of opposition; penitential hymns should be said by the naughty; cheerful ones by the comparatively good; and every kind of instruction I would convey to them, as much as possible, by entertaining discourse—apparently with no other object than their present amusement in view.

By these means I hoped, in time, both to benefit the children and to gain the approbation of the parents; and also to convince my friends at home that I was not so wanting in skill and prudence as they supposed. I knew the difficulties I had to contend with were great; but I knew (at least I believed) unremitting patience and perseverance could overcome them; and night and morning I implored Divine assistance to this end. But either the children were so incorrigible, the parents so unreasonable, or myself so mistaken in my views, or so unable to carry them out, that my best intentions and most strenuous efforts seemed productive of no better result than sport to the children, dissatisfaction to their parents, and torment to myself. . . .

About Christmas I was allowed to visit home; but my holiday was only of a fortnight's duration: "For," said Mrs. Bloomfield, "I thought, as you had seen your friends so lately, you would not care for a longer stay." I left her to think so still: but she little knew how long, how wearisome those fourteen weeks of absence had been to me; how intensely I had longed for my holidays, how greatly I was disappointed at their curtailment. Yet she was not to blame in this; I had never told her my feelings, and she could not be expected to divine them; I had not been with her a full term, and she was justified in not allowing me a full vacation. (25–33)

ELIZABETH GASKELL ON
CHARLOTTE BRONTË

Charlotte Brontë was a famous novelist, publishing novels that found an appreciative audience of readers as well as substantial acclaim from critics. Her novels have remained popular for over 150 years—especially *Jane Eyre*, a novel that continues to be taught in high schools and colleges and performed on stage (even on Broadway), as well as to be recommended from mother to daughter and grandmother to granddaughter throughout the generations.

Charlotte Brontë, her two younger sisters, and her brother had written since they were children. Writing was, for her, as natural a way to express her thoughts and feelings as talking with her siblings and friends. Nonetheless, she was not able to support herself by her writing. She worked, first as a teacher in the school from which she graduated, then as a governess in various households, while continuing to write in the brief periods of time she could carve out of such a busy life. Elizabeth Gaskell was a contemporary of Brontë and, in her biography of the author, provided considerable details about her life as a governess and her feelings about that time in her life.

FROM ELIZABETH GASKELL, *THE LIFE OF CHARLOTTE BRONTË*
(London, 1857)

Charlotte also became engaged as a governess. . . . [It] is necessary that the difficulties she had to encounter in her various phases of life should be fairly and frankly made known, before the force "of what was resisted" can be at all understood. I was once speaking to her about *Agnes Grey*— the novel in which her sister Anne pretty literally describes her own experience as a governess—and alluding more particularly to the account of the stoning [by the young boy in her charge] of the little nestlings in the presence of the parent birds. She said that none but those who had been in the position of a governess could ever realize the dark side of "respectable" human nature; under no great temptation to crime, but daily giving way to selfishness and ill-temper, till its conduct towards those dependent on it sometimes amounts to a tyranny of which one would rather be the victim than the inflicter. We can only trust in such cases that the employers err rather from a density of perception and an absence of sympathy than from any natural cruelty of disposition. Among several things of the same kind, which I well remember, she told me what had once occurred to herself. She had been entrusted with the care of a little boy three or four years old, during the absence of his parents on a day's excursion, and particularly enjoined to keep him out of the stable-yard. His elder brother, a lad of eight or nine, and not a pupil of Miss Brontë's tempted the little fellow into the forbidden place. She followed, and tried to induce him to come away; but, instigated by his brother, he began throwing stones at her, and one of them hit her so severe a blow on the temple that the lads were alarmed into obedience. The next day, in full family conclave, the mother asked Miss Brontë what occasioned the mark on her forehead. She simply replied, "An accident, ma'am," and no further inquiry was made; but the children (both brothers and sisters) had been present and honoured her for not "telling tales." From that time she began to obtain influence over all, more or less, according to their different characters; and as she insensibly gained their affection, her own interest in them was increasing. But one day, at the children's dinner, the small truant of the stableyard, in a little demonstrative gush said, putting his hand in hers, "I love 'ou, Miss Brontë." Whereupon the mother exclaimed before all the children, "Love the *governess*, my dear!"

The family into which she first entered was, I believe, that of a wealthy Yorkshire manufacturer. The following abstracts from her correspondence at this time will show how painfully the restraint of her new mode of life pressed upon her. . . .

June 8th, 1839. "I have striven hard to be pleased with my new situation. The country, the house, and the grounds are, as I have said, divine; but alack-a-day! there is such a thing as seeing all beautiful around you— pleasant woods, white paths, green lawns, and blue sunshiny sky—and not having a free moment or a free thought left to enjoy them. The children are constantly with me. As for correcting them, I quickly found that was out of the question; they are to do as they like. A complaint to the mother only brings black looks on myself, and unjust, partial excuses to screen the children. I have tried that plan once, and succeeded so notably, I shall try no more. I said in my last letter that Mrs. —— did not know me; that she cares nothing about me, except maybe to contrive how the greatest possible quantity of labour may be got out of me; and to that end she overwhelms me with oceans of needlework, yards of cambric to hem, muslin nightcaps to make, and, above all things, dolls to dress. I do not think she likes me at all, because I can't help being shy in such an entirely novel scene, surrounded as I have hitherto been by

strange and constantly changing faces. . . . I used to think I should like
to be in the stir of grand folks' society; but I have had enough of it—it
is dreary work to look on and listen. I see more clearly than I have ever
done before that a private governess has no existence, is not considered
as a living rational being, except as connected with the wearisome duties
she has to fulfil. . . ."

July 1839. [written in pencil] "I cannot procure ink without going into
the drawing-room, where I do not wish to go. . . . I should have written
to you long since, and told you every detail of the utterly new scene into
which I have lately been cast, had I not been daily expecting a letter from
yourself, and wondering and lamenting that you did not write; for you
will remember that it was your turn. I must not bother you too much
with my sorrows, of which, I fear, you have heard an exaggerated account.
If you were near me, perhaps I might be tempted to tell you all, to grow
egotistical, and pour out the long history of a private governess's trials
and crosses in her first situation. As it is, I will only ask you to imagine
the miseries of a reserved wretch like me, thrown at once into the midst
of a large family, at a time when they were particularly gay—when the
house was filled with company—all strangers—people whose faces I had
never seen before. In this state I had charge given me of a set of pam-
pered, spoilt, turbulent children, whom I was expected constantly to
amuse, as well as to instruct. I soon found that the constant demand on
my stock of animal spirits reduced them to the lowest state of exhaustion;
at times I felt—and I suppose, seemed—depressed. To my astonishment,
I was taken to task on the subject by Mrs. —— with a sternness of manner
and a harshness of language scarcely credible; like a fool, I cried most
bitterly. I could not help it; my spirits quite failed me at first. I thought
I had done my best—strained every nerve to please her; and to be treated
in that way, merely because I was shy and sometimes melancholy, was
too bad. At first I was for giving all up and going home. But after a little
reflection I determined to summon what energy I had, and to weather
the storm. I said to myself, "I have never yet quitted a school; the poor
are born to labour, and the dependent to endure." I resolved to be patient, to command my feelings and to take what came; the ordeal, I re-
flected, would not last many weeks, and I trusted it would do me good.
I recollected the fable of the willow and the oak; I bent quietly, and now,
I trust, the storm is blowing over me. Mrs. —— is generally considered
an agreeable woman; so she is, I doubt not, in general society. She behaves somewhat more civilly to me now than she did at first, and the
children are a little more manageable; but she does not know my character; and she does not wish to know it. I have never had five minutes'
conversation with her since I came, except while she was scolding me."
(138–141)

• • •

Early in March 1841, Miss Brontë obtained her second and last situation as a governess. This time she esteemed herself fortunate in becoming a member of a kind-hearted and friendly household. . . . But as her acquirements were few, she had to eke them out by employing her leisure time in needlework; and altogether her position was that of "bonne" or nursery governess, liable to repeated and never-ending calls upon her time. This description of uncertain, yet perpetual employment, subject to the exercise of another person's will at all hours of the day, was peculiarly trying to one whose life at home had been full of abundant leisure. *Idle* she never was in any place, but of the multitude of small talks, plans, duties, pleasures, etc., that make up most people's days, her home life was nearly destitute. . . . This made it inevitable that—later on, in her too short career—the intensity of her feeling should wear out her physical health. The habit of "making out," which had grown with her growth, and strengthened with her strength, had become a part of her nature. Yet all exercise of her strongest and most characteristic faculties was now out of the question. She could not (as while she was at Miss W——'s [one of the schools at which she had taught]) feel, amidst the occupations of the day, that when evening came she might employ herself in more congenial ways. No doubt all who enter upon the career of a governess have to relinquish much; no doubt it must ever be a life of sacrifice; but to Charlotte Brontë it was a perpetual attempt to force all her faculties into a direction for which the whole of her previous life had unfitted them. Moreover, the little Brontës had been brought up motherless; and from knowing nothing of the gaiety and the sportiveness of childhood— from never having experienced caresses or fond attentions themselves— they were ignorant of the very nature of infancy, or how to call out its engaging qualities. Children were to them the troublesome necessities of humanity; they had never been drawn into contact with them in any other way. Years afterwards, when Miss Brontë came to stay with us, she watched our little girls perpetually; and I could not persuade her that they were only average specimens of well-brought-up children. She was surprised and touched by any sign of thoughtfulness for others, of kindness to animals, or of unselfishness on their part: and constantly maintained that she was in the right, of their unusual excellence. All this must be borne in mind while reading the following letters. And it must likewise be borne in mind—by those who, surviving her, look back upon her life from their mount of observation—how no distaste, no suffering ever made her shrink from any course which she believed it to be her duty to engage in.

March 3rd, 1841. "I told you some time since that I meant to get a situation, and when I said so my resolution was quite fixed. I felt that, however often I was disappointed, I had no intention of relinquishing my efforts. After being severely baffled two or three times—after a world of trouble, in the way of correspondence and interviews—I have at length succeeded, and am fairly established in my new place. . . .

The house is not very large, but exceedingly comfortable and well regulated; the grounds are fine and extensive. In taking the place, I have made a large sacrifice in the way of salary, in the hope of securing comfort,—by which word I do not mean to express good eating and drinking, or warm fire, or a soft bed, but the society of cheerful faces, and minds and hearts not dug out of a lead mine, or cut from a marble quarry. My salary is not really more than 16*l*. per annum, though it is nominally 20*l*., but the expense of washing will be deduced therefrom. My pupils are two in number, a girl of eight and a boy of six. As to my employers, you will not expect me to say much about their characters when I tell you that I only arrived here yesterday. I have not the faculty of telling an individual's disposition at first sight. Before I can venture to pronounce on a character, I must see it first under various lights and from various points of view. All I can say, therefore, is, both Mr. and Mrs. —— seem to me good sort of people. I have as yet had no cause to complain of want of considerateness or civility. My pupils are wild and unbroken, but apparently well-disposed. I wish I may be able to say as much next time I write to you. My earnest wish and endeavour will be to please them. If I can but feel that I am giving satisfaction, and if at the same time I can keep my health, I shall, I hope, be moderately happy. But no one but myself can tell how hard a governess's work is to me—for no one but myself is aware how utterly averse my whole mind and nature are for the employment. Do not think that I fail to blame myself for this, or that I leave any means unemployed to conquer this feeling. Some of my greatest difficulties lie in things that would appear to you comparatively trivial. I find it so hard to repel the rude familiarity of children. I find it so difficult to ask either servants or mistress for anything I want, however much I want it. It is less pain for me to endure the greatest inconvenience than to go into the kitchen to request its removal. I am a fool. Heaven knows I cannot help it!

Now can you tell me whether it is considered improper for governesses to ask their friends to come and see them I do not mean, of course, to stay, but just for a call of an hour or two? If it is not absolute treason, I do fervently request that you will contrive, in some way or other, to let me have a sight of your face. Yet I feel, at the same time, that I am making a very foolish and almost impracticable demand. . . ."

March 21st, 1841. "You must excuse a very short answer to your most welcome letter; for my time is entirely occupied. Mrs. —— expects a good deal of sewing from me. I cannot sew much during the day on account of the children, who require the utmost attention. I am obliged, therefore, to devote the evenings to this business. Write to me often; very long letters. It will do both of us good. This place is far better than ——, but God knows I have enough to do to keep a good heart in the matter. What you said has cheered me a little. I wish I could always act according to your advice. Home-sickness affects me sorely. I like Mr. —— extremely. The children are over-indulged, and consequently hard at times to manage. Do, do, do come and see me; if it be a breach of etiquette, never mind. If you can only stop an hour, come. . . . I find it is not in my nature to get on in this weary world without sympathy and attachment in some quarter; and seldom, indeed, do we find it. It is too great a treasure to be ever wantonly thrown away when once secured."

Miss Brontë had not been many weeks in her new situation before she had a proof of the kind-hearted hospitality of her employers. Mr. —— wrote to her father, and urgently invited him to come and make acquaintance with his daughter's new home, by spending a week with her in it; and Mrs. —— expressed great regret when one of Miss Brontë's friends drove up to the house to leave a letter or parcel without entering. So she found that all her friends might freely visit her and that her father would be received with especial gladness. She thankfully acknowledged this kindness in writing to urge her friend afresh to come and see her, which she accordingly did. (160–164)

TOPICS FOR WRITTEN OR ORAL EXPLORATION

1. Research the current rules for home schooling in your state. Then determine what qualifications a governess would need to teach students in their own home in your state in the twenty-first century.

2. Research the curriculum at various schools for training nannies throughout the United States. Then discuss whether you believe that a nanny trained in one of those schools would be qualified to act as a governess for children today.

3. Imagine yourself as a young woman with no family or financial backing in nineteenth-century England. Do you believe you would have the nerve to advertise yourself as a governess and go to a distant city to live with strangers as Jane Eyre did, or do you believe you would choose to stay as a teacher at Lowood, where you knew the other teachers and had a clear sense of what was expected of you? Write a letter in that character in which you seek employment as a governess. Be sure to state your qualifications for the job and your expectations of the position to your prospective employer.

4. Some of the advice books directed at governesses in the nineteenth century warned young women not to allow themselves to become involved with men they met through their work because of the dangers of mixing social classes and the potential of losing their moral standing. If you were in Jane Eyre's position, do you believe that you would have resisted Mr. Rochester's advances? If so, to what effect? If not, why not?

5. Governesses in the nineteenth century tended to lead very lonely lives in the midst of much activity. They could not be on an equal footing with their employers because of their dependent status. They could not be on an equal footing with the rest of the staff because they had been educated to genteel standards in order to be able to provide their pupils with a proper education. If you were placed in this position, how would you cope with the isolation inherent in the position? Write a series of diary entries in which you write about your experiences as a governess.

6. Read historical accounts of various governesses in the eighteenth and nineteenth centuries (biographies, published journals, and/or diaries). Then, based on your reading, write an essay in which you generalize about what a young woman going into the governess field should expect.

7. In the novel *Emma*, Jane Austen compares going into governess work to "the slave trade." Based on your reading of *Jane Eyre* and the ex-

cerpts in this chapter, to what extent might governess work be reasonably compared to slavery? To what extent does *Emma* seem to be exaggerating the situation? Be able to support your position.

SUGGESTED READINGS

Advice to Governesses. London: John Hatchard and Son, 1827.

Alexander, Sally. *Women's Work in Nineteenth-Century London: A Study of the Years 1820–50*. London: Journeyman, 1983.

Barker, Juliet. *The Brontës*. New York: St. Martin's, 1994.

Bird, M. Mostyn. *Woman at Work: A Study of the Different Ways of Earning a Living Open to Women*. London: Chapman & Hall, 1911.

Bodichon, Barbara Leigh Smith. *Women and Work*. London: Bosworth and Harrison, 1857.

Boucherette, Jessie. "The Profession of the Teacher: The Annual Reports of the Governesses' Benevolent Institution, from 1843 to 1856." *English Woman's Journal* 1 (March 1858): 1–13.

Brontë, Anne. *Agnes Grey*. 1847. London: Oxford University Press, 1907.

Burman, Sandra, ed. *Fit Work for Women*. New York: St. Martin's, 1979.

Burstall, Sara A. *Retrospect and Prospect: Sixty Years of Women's Education*. London: Longmans, Green & Co., 1827.

Burstyn, Joan N. *Victorian Education and the Ideal of Womanhood*. London: Croom Helm, 1980.

Chirol, J. L. *An Enquiry into the Best System of Female Education*. London, 1809.

Cobbe, Frances Power. "What Shall We Do with Our Old Maids?" *Fraser's Magazine* 66 (November 1862): 594–610.

Cohen, Monica E. *Professional Domesticity in the Victorian Novel: Women, Work and Home*. Cambridge: Cambridge University Press, 1998.

The Complete Governess: A Course of Mental Instruction for Ladies: with a Notice of the Principal Female Accomplishments. By an Experienced Teacher. London: Knight and Lacey, 1826.

"An Enquiry into the State of Girls' Fashionable Schools." *Fraser's Magazine* (June 1845): 703–712.

Gaskell, Elizabeth. *The Life of Charlotte Brontë*. 1857. London: Oxford University Press, 1919.

"Going a Governessing." *English Woman's Journal* 1 (August 1858): 396–404.

Gordon, Lyndall. *Charlotte Brontë: A Passionate Life*. New York: W. W. Norton, 1994.

Gorham, Deborah. *The Victorian Girl and the Feminine Ideal*. Bloomington: Indiana University Press, 1982.

The Governess: A Repertory of Female Education. London: Darton, 1855.

The Governess, Or, Politics in Private Life. London: Smith, Elder, 1836.

"The Governess Question." *English Woman's Journal* 4 (1860): 163–170.

Hall, Edward, ed. *Miss Weeton: Journal of a Governess*. 2 vols. London, 1936, 1939.

Helsinger, Elizabeth K., Robin Lauterbach Sheets, and William Veeder. *The Woman Question: Society and Literature in Britain and America 1837–1883*. Vol 2. Chicago: University of Chicago Press, 1983.

"Hints on the Modern Governess System." *Fraser's Magazine* 30 (November 1884): 571–583.

Hoeveler, Diane Long, and Beth Lau. *Approaches to Teaching Brontë's Jane Eyre*. New York: Modern Language Association, 1993.

Horn, Pamela. "The Victorian Governess." *History of Education* 18 (1989): 333–344.

Hughes, Kathryn. *The Victorian Governess*. London: Hambledon Press, 1993.

Kamm, Josephine. *Hope Deferred: Girls' Education in English History*. London: Methuen, 1965.

Lawson, John, and Harold Silver. *A Social History of Education in England*. London: Methuen, 1973.

Lewis, Sarah. "On the Social Position of Governesses." *Fraser's Magazine* 37 (April 1848): 411–414.

Neff, Wanda F. *Victorian Working Women: An Historical and Literary Study of Women in British Industries and Professions, 1832–1850*. Reprint ed. London: Frank Cass & Co., 1966.

Parkes, Bessie Rayner. *Essays on Women's Work*. London: Strahan, 1866.

Peterson, M. Jeanne. "The Victorian Governess: Status Incongruence in Family and Society." In *Suffer and Be Still: Women in the Victorian Age*. Ed. Martha Vicinus. Bloomington: Indiana University Press, 1972: 3–19.

Poovey, Mary. "The Anathematized Race: The Governess and *Jane Eyre*." *Uneven Developments: The Ideological Work of Gender in Mid-Victorian England*. Chicago: University of Chicago Press, 1988: 126–163.

Stevens, Joan, ed. *Mary Taylor, Friend of Charlotte Bronte; Letters from New Zealand and Elsewhere*. Auckland, New Zealand: Auckland University Press, 1972.

The Story of the Governesses' Benevolent Institution. Southwick, Sussex, UK: Grange Press, 1962.

Vicinus, Martha. *Independent Women: Work and Community for Single Woman: 1850–1920*. Chicago: University of Chicago Press, 1985.

West, Katharine. *Chapter of Governesses. A Study of the Governess in English Fiction, 1800–1949*. London: Cohen, 1949.

Wollstonecraft, Mary. *Thoughts on the Education of Daughters, with Reflections on Female Conduct in the More Important Duties of Life*. London: J. Johnson, 1787.

4

Madness and Victorian Women: Diagnosis and Treatment

The madwoman is a familiar character in English-language literature of the nineteenth century. From the mad and monstrous
women of Romantic poetry (Wordsworth's "Lucy Grey," Coleridge's Geraldine in "Christabel," Keats's "La Belle Dame Sans
Merci," etc.) to Charlotte Perkins Gilman's *The Yellow Wallpaper*
(1892) and Mary E. Coleridge's heroine in "The Other Side of the
Mirror" at the end of the century, the image of the madwoman
attracted the imaginations of both authors and readers. Feminist
scholars Sandra M. Gilbert and Susan Gubar, in their study of literary depictions of madness in *The Madwoman in the Attic*, provide an explanation for the prevalence of the character of the
madwoman in the nineteenth century, particularly in literature by
women:

> As we explore nineteenth-century literature, we will find that this
> madwoman emerges over and over again from the mirrors women
> writers hold up both to their own natures and to their own visions
> of nature. Even the most apparently conservative and decorous
> women writers obsessively create fiercely independent characters
> who seek to destroy all the patriarchal structures which both their
> authors and their authors' submissive heroines seem to accept as
> inevitable. . . . [B]y projecting their rebellious impulses not into

their heroines but into mad or monstrous women (who are suitably punished in the course of the novel or poem), female authors dramatize their own self-division, their desire both to accept the structures of patriarchal society and to reject them. What this means, however, is that the madwoman in literature by women is not merely, as she might be in male literature, an antagonist or foil to the heroine. Rather, she is usually in some sense the *author's* double, an image of her own anxiety and rage. (77–78)

As a woman writing and publishing in a field dominated by men, the Victorian female author stepped out of the traditional role of the proper nineteenth-century lady. For a woman of genteel education and heritage to do so was to put herself into a position that was often considered madness, since madness was often defined (for a woman) as a determination to be "active," to have a place in the world other than that of mother, wife, and caregiver for others. A woman writer, therefore, by her very act of writing, made herself susceptible to charges of unwomanliness, often itself a precursor to the charge of madness.

Women writers of the nineteenth century often published their works anonymously or under pseudonyms, in part to avoid drawing public attention to their private lives, thus making the connection between themselves and their work less obvious. Jane Austen, for instance, published her novels anonymously. She closely guarded the secret of her authorship, allowing no one outside the immediate family to know of it for several years. She was quite upset when she discovered that her brother had leaked the secret to numerous people throughout London, enabling people as far from her own family circle as the Prince of Wales to know she was the author of *Pride and Prejudice*. The Brontë sisters, Charlotte, Anne, and Emily, published under the pseudonyms of Currer, Acton, and Ellis Bell, keeping their own initials as a kind of public code by which to indicate their authorship without allowing it to be revealed for those not privy to the code. Such secrecy and self-division was, of course, completely unnecessary for male writers of the period. Writing was considered to be an active profession, suitable for a man, but a woman who chose to engage in it was subject to suspicion and, as a result, often hid her identity.

The madwoman is not, however, merely a representation of the *author's* "anxiety and rage." She also represents the anxiety, rage, frustration, and will to an active, though respectable, life that other women also feel. In *Jane Eyre*, Bertha sometimes acts as Jane would act were she not so hemmed in by societal expectations that she believes such actions would be ineffective or immoral. For example, shortly before Mr. Rochester and Jane plan to be married, Jane finds in her room the box that contains an extravagantly beautiful and expensive veil that Mr. Rochester has bought for her, despite her insistence on wearing her own simple clothing until after the wedding (at which point she feels she will have to give in to her husband's desire to dress her according to his station in life, whether she wants to dress that way or not). She tells him how she had thought to "teaze [him] about his aristocratic tastes and [his] efforts to masque [his] plebian bride in the attributes of a peeress" (341). She details how she had intended to

carry down to you the square of unembroidered blonde I had myself prepared as a covering for my low-born head, and ask if that was not good enough for a woman who could bring her husband neither fortune, beauty, nor connections. I saw plainly how you would look; and heard your impetuous republican answers, and your haughty disavowal of any necessity on your part to augment your wealth, or elevate your standing, by marrying either a purse or a coronet. (341)

She talks about her intentions as a "teaze," something she is merely toying with him about, nothing important. Yet, it is important to Jane that she bring herself to her husband without frills, with nothing that she cannot claim to be hers by right. As a good and respectable woman, however, she cannot force the issue; she must agree to let Mr. Rochester have his way, at least about something as insignificant as the veil. But the veil is not, in fact, insignificant. It is the symbol of marriage, of her granting him access to her virginity and power over the rest of her life.

Jane was incapable of refusing Rochester's veil. As a result, Jane's "double," the madwoman who *is* capable of such action, enters Jane's room during the night before the scheduled wedding, puts the veil on her own head as a symbol of her own wedding to Rochester, and then tears it in two, "and flinging both [parts] on the floor, trampled on them" (345). Bertha, as mad as she is, seems to recognize the veil as a symbol of marriage, and of the prison that marriage has been for her. Her destroying of the veil enables Jane to wear "the square of unembroidered blonde" she had prepared as a symbol of giving herself in marriage to Mr. Rochester (341). Bertha, therefore, accomplishes what Jane, as a respectable woman, is incapable of accomplishing for herself.

That madwomen so pervade nineteenth-century literature seems odd until one investigates the ways in which madness and other diseases were diagnosed and treated in the nineteenth century. Illness, in general, was closely associated with women in British society. Illness was, in fact, considered an essential part of being female.

In the nineteenth century, the dominant medical model for the diagnosis and treatment of women was one in which the uterus was considered central. Each woman was considered to have been born with a given amount of energy. That energy was intended to be used in the conception, delivery, and nurturance of children. Since she had only a fixed quantity of energy, however, any expenditure of energy that was not in direct relationship to her preparation for or achievement of her biological purpose in life was considered wasteful. If she insisted on using that energy to accomplish goals unrelated to preparation for and achievement of motherhood, she was behaving in an unwomanly fashion and, therefore, must, by definition, be ill.

This economy of energy in woman was considered essentially unstable. As Mary Poovey writes,

> This instability was considered a function of what medical men denominated female "periodicity," a state inaugurated by puberty, signaled by menstruation, and epitomized in childbearing. Theoretically, this periodicity had no counterpart in the male; in the female it was considered so decisive because it was held to be so pervasive. (36)

This theory about women's basic biological instability led medical professionals to conclude that women were subject to a "doctrine of crisis," a doctrine which had to do with a regular system of recurrence in women of various illnesses, in particular various nervous disorders (Poovey 36). The nervous disorders of women, particularly such illnesses as hysteria, were, therefore, founded upon imbalances created by a woman's natural biological instability and exacerbated by any activities a woman participated in that were not supportive of her natural, biological processes. The seeds of hysteria, thus, were always present in the female human being; women were, by their very nature, always on the verge of mental illness.

The most dramatic result of these theories about women's biological makeup was to define women as weak, yet dangerous. Women needed, it seemed, the protection and guidance of men in order to safeguard their energies so that they could be used for the purpose God intended. Yet many women balked at the kinds and degrees of restrictions to which men subjected them. If a woman balked too overtly, refusing to live life as a civilized respectable woman was supposed to live it, she was diagnosed as ill. If her resistance was particularly strong, she was diagnosed as insane and locked away where she could not endanger others by her actions or her attitudes. In *The Horrors of the Half-Known Life*, G. J. Barker-Benfield quotes Dr. Issac Ray, a nineteenth-century American physician, who presented the prevailing view quite explicitly: "With women, it is but a step from extreme nervous susceptibility to downright hysteria, and from that to overt insanity. In the sexual evolution, in pregnancy, in the parturient period, in lactation, strange thoughts, extraordinary feelings, unseasonable appetites, criminal impulses, may haunt a mind at other times innocent and pure" (83). In other words, insanity for a woman could be defined as the actions of a normal female human body taken to their logical extreme. Madness was, then, according to the medical authorities of the nineteenth century, the very nature of femaleness in the human race.

Nervous disorders and insanity were not diagnoses restricted to women in the nineteenth century; men also became mad. But women were diagnosed with nervous disorders and madness in substantially greater numbers than men were. Women were expected to spend considerable portions of their lives in one form of illness or another, and disorders of the nerves were expected of creatures who were as constitutionally weak as women were considered to be in nineteenth-century England.

The excerpts that follow are from medical treatises of the nineteenth century. Some focus on the form and function of women's biological processes. Others expound on the theories behind and experiences of nervous disorders and insanity as they were understood in the nineteenth century. Although there was certainly not a madwoman in every attic, all families seemed to have to deal with some form of what was defined as nervous disorder at one time or another, and many had the specter of madness hanging over them in the form of a living relative or ancestor.

DR. HENRY MAUDSLEY

Dr. Henry Maudsley (1835–1918) was an eminent English physician and medical philosopher of that late Victorian period. He was the founder of the Maudsley Hospital in England as well as editor, for a time, of the *Journal of Mental Science*, the most prominent journal of its type in late Victorian England. Maudsley focused much of his research and writing on the diagnosis, care, and treatment of mental illness. Like most medical practitioners of his time, he accepted the concept of a woman's physical and mental health being centered in the balance that is maintained within her reproductive system. When that system is out of balance, through organic means or because she is using her energies for other, unwomanly, purposes, the woman will, according to that theory, become ill. That illness will often manifest itself in nervous disorders or outright insanity, the symptoms of which can range from a complete abhorrence of anything related to the creation and care of children to unbridled lust or extremely violent tendencies.

Maudsley does not hypothesize about female madness exclusively. He writes about the factors that cause mental imbalances in men as well as in women. But he, like other medical experts of his time, believed mental disorders to be unusual in men, usually generated by a problem in the bloodline (in other words, passed on to him in his mother's womb) rather than something that is expected. For women, lengthy periods of nervous disorder, at least, were considered to be normal, not unusual.

Maudsley was also very interested in and concerned about the freedom with which those who exhibit signs of hereditary insanity continue to marry and have children. By their actions, he believed, greater numbers of the insane were created, causing more problems for society. Those suffering from mental disease have, he asserted, a responsibility not to breed.

Bertha's madness in *Jane Eyre* seems to have begun with a tendency to behave in ways that Rochester considered disreputable for a woman. She drank alcohol to excess and behaved lasciviously, at least so Rochester tells Jane. Such behavior was unwomanly, according to Maudsley's definitions. Bertha was also the daughter of a woman who was known to be a lush and who ended her own life as a madwoman. According to Victorian ideas, that fact made Bertha much more likely to become mad herself than if her mother had been a respectably sane woman.

FROM HENRY MAUDSLEY, *BODY AND MIND*
(London, 1873)

The monthly activity of the ovaries which marks the advent of puberty in women has a notable effect upon the mind and body: wherefore it may become an important cause of mental and physical derangement. Most women at that time are susceptible, irritable, and capricious, any cause of vexation affecting them more seriously than usual; and some who have the insane neurosis exhibit of disturbance of mind which amounts almost to disease. A sudden suppression of the menses has produced a direct explosion of insanity; or, occurring some time before an outbreak, it may be an important link in its causation. It is a matter also of common experience in asylums, that exacerbations of insanity often take place at the menstrual periods; but whether there is a particular variety of mental derangement connected with disordered menstruation, and, if so, what are its special features, we are not yet in a position to say positively. There is certainly a recurrent mania, which seems sometimes to have, in regard to its origin and time of its attacks, a relation to the menstrual functions, suppression or irregularity of which often accompanies it; and it is an obvious presumption that the mania may be a sympathetic morbid effect of the ovarian and uterine excitement, and may represent an exaggeration of the mental irritability which is natural to women at that period. The patient becomes elated, hilarious, talkative, passing soon from that condition into a state of acute and noisy mania, which may last for two or three weeks or longer, and then sinking into a brief stage of more or less depression or confusion of mind, from which she awakens to calmness and clearness of mind. In vain we flatter ourselves with the hope of a complete recovery; after an interval of perfect lucidity, of varying duration in different cases, the attack recurs, goes through the same stages, and ends in the same way, only to be followed by other attacks, until at last, the mind being permanently weakened, there are no longer intervals of entire lucidity. Could we stop the attacks, the patient might still regain by degrees mental power; but we cannot. All the resources of our art fail to touch them, and I know no other form of insanity which, having so much the air of being curable, thus far defies all efforts to stay its course. (87–89)

• • •

[T]he irritation of ovaries or uterus . . . is sometimes the direct occasion of *nymphomania*—a disease by which the most chaste and modest woman is transformed into a raging fury of lust. Some observers have, without sufficient reason I think, made of *nymphomania* a special variety, grouping under the term cases in which it was a prominent symptom. But it certainly occurs in forms of mania that are quite distinct—in puerperal mania, for example, in epileptic mania, and in the mania sometimes met with in old women; and the cases in which it does occur have not such characteristic features as warrant the formation of a definite group. We have, indeed, to note and bear in mind how often sexual ideas and feelings arise and display themselves in all sorts of insanity; how they connect themselves with ideas which in a moral mental state have no known relation to them; so that it seems as inexplicable that a virtuous person should ever have learnt, as it is distressing that she should manifest, so much obscenity of thought and feeling. (82–83)

• • •

What are the bodily and mental marks of the insane temperament? That there are such is most certain: for although the varieties of this temperament cannot yet be described with any precision, no one who accustoms himself to observe closely will fail to be able to say positively in many instances whether an insane person, and even a sane person in some instances, comes of an insane family or not. An irregular and unsymmetrical conformation of the head, a want of regularity and harmony of the features, and . . . malformations of the external ear, are sometimes observed. Convulsions are apt to occur in early life; and there are tics, grimances, or other spasmodic movements of muscles of face, eyelids, or lips afterwards. Stammering and defects of pronunciation are also sometimes signs of the neurosis. In other cases there are peculiarities of the eyes, which, though they may be full and prominent, have a vacillating movement, and a vacantly-abstracted, or half-fearful, half-suspicious, and distrustful look. There may, indeed, be something in the eye wonderfully suggestive of the look of an animal. The walk and manner are uncertain, and, though not easily described in words, may be distinctly peculiar. With these bodily traits are associated peculiarities of thought, feeling, and conduct. Without being insane, a person who has the insane neurosis strongly marked is thought to be strange, queer, and not like other persons. He is apt to see things under novel aspects, or to think about them under novel relations, which would not have occurred to an ordinary mortal. Punning on words is, I am inclined to think, sometime an indication of the temperament, and so also that higher kind of wit which startles us with the use of an idea in a double sense; of both which aptitudes no better example can be given than that of Charles Lamb. His case, too, may show that the insane temperament is compatible with, and indeed it not seldom co-exists with, considerable genius. Even those who have it in a more marked form often exhibit remarkable special talents and aptitudes, such as an extraordinary talent for music, or for calculation, or a prodigious memory for details, when they may be a little better than imbecile in other things. (62–64)

FROM HENRY MAUDSLEY, *RESPONSIBILITY IN MENTAL DISEASE*
(London, 1874)

It would scarcely be an exaggeration to say that few persons go mad, save from palpable physical causes, who do not show more or less plainly by their gait, manner, gestures, habits of thought, feeling and action, that they have a sort of predestination to madness. The inherited liability may be strong or weak; it may be so weak as hardly to peril sanity amidst the most adverse circumstances of life, or so strong as to issue in an outbreak of madness amidst the most favourable external circumstances. Now it is certain that if we were interested in the breeding of a variety of animals, we should not think of breeding from a stock which was wanting in those qualities that were the highest characteristics of the species: we should not willingly select for breeding purposes a hound that was deficient in scent, or a greyhound that was deficient in speed, nor a racehorse that could neither stay well nor gallop fast. Is it right then to sanction propagation of his kind by an individual who is wanting in that which is the highest attribute of man—a sound and stable mental constitution? I note this as a question to be seriously faced and sincerely answered, although not expecting that mankind, in the present state of their development, will either seriously face it or sincerely answer it.

When one considers the reckless way in which persons, whatever the defects of their mental and bodily constitution, often get married, without sense of responsibility for the miseries which they entail upon those who will be the heirs of their infirmities, without regard, in fact, to anything but their own present gratification, one is driven to think either that man is not the pre-eminently reasoning and moral animal which he claims to be, or that there is in him an instinct which is deeper than knowledge. He has persuaded himself, rightly or wrongly, that in his case there is in the feeling of love between the sexes something of so sacred and mysterious a character as to justify disregard to consequences in marriage. We have only to look at the large part which love fills in novels, poetry and painting, and to consider what a justification of unreason in life it is held to be, to realize what a hold it has on him in his present state of development, and what a repugnance there would be to quench its glow by cold words of reason. At bottom, however, there is nothing particularly holy about it; on the contrary, it is a passion which man shares with other animals; and when its essential nature and function are regarded, we shall nowhere find stronger evidence of a community of nature between man and animals. (276–277)

SIR ALEXANDER MORISON

Sir Alexander Morison was visiting physician to Bethlehem Hospital, one of the most important mental institutions in Victorian England. He also developed a private practice consulting with the mentally ill outside the asylum system. In addition, he contributed to the academic training of doctors by giving annual lectures on the subject of insanity to colleges in London and Edinburgh. In *Outlines of Mental Diseases*, Morison provides a brief synopsis of the varieties of mental disorders that were most prevalent in England and the United States during the nineteenth century. His interest in this particular text is in documenting types and forms of mental illness rather than writing about treatments and cures. Such documentary information was intended to be of use to laypeople as well as doctors in recognizing and diagnosing mental problems.

Interestingly, Morison suggests that one of the characteristics of societies that contributes to the creation of certain types of insanity is an openness to differing ideas and opinions, particularly on political and religious issues. It is mentally healthier, he seems to say, if people are told precisely what to believe and are allowed no opportunity to evaluate their systems of government or religion for themselves. Such advice certainly flew in the face of the republican ideals that were pervasive in both England and the United States in the nineteenth century. If people were more susceptible to madness when they thought for themselves, Jane Eyre herself would have been likely to go mad.

One of the most popular means by which a tendency toward mental disorder and/or criminal tendencies was detected in the nineteenth century was the use of phrenology. According to phrenologists, an individual's physiognomy (the shape and appearance of his or her head and face) provided objective information about the individual's psychological and moral tendencies. In *Jane Eyre*, the description of Bertha's face, head, eyes, and complexion includes references that those nineteenth-century readers who had an understanding of phrenology would recognize as the physical characteristics of a person who is, or who has a strong tendency toward becoming, insane. In his *Outlines*, Morison provides details about some of the characteristics common to the physiognomy of the mentally ill.

FROM ALEXANDER MORISON, *OUTLINES OF MENTAL DISEASES*
(Edinburgh, 1824)

With respect to Age.

Infants are nearly exempted [from mania], although children under ten years of age occasionally exhibit symptoms of general and of partial insanity. It is sometimes coincident with rapid growth—and with the efforts of the constitution in establishing the menstrual discharge.

In old age, the first appearance of insanity (Dementia excepted) is rare, although instances have occasionally occurred in persons whose age has exceeded 80, and even 100. It is, however, most prevalent between the ages of 25 and 40.

Sex.—In some countries, as in Great Britain and France, there are more females insane than males; but this is not the case in all. Females are exposed to exciting causes from which males are exempted, as when there is hereditary disposition; this cause acts more extensively in the higher than in the lower classes.

The critical period of female life also frequently leads to the development of insanity.

In the treatment of mental disease, it has been observed that there is a beneficial influence exerted by one sex over the other.

With regard to the influence of occupation and condition in life, in the production of insanity, it may be observed, that professions requiring great mental exertion, and those which lead to hazardous speculations, are more liable to insanity than others; persons who are most independent, in consequence of their rank and fortune, are comparatively speaking, more subject to it than the middle class. This may be accounted for in part by intermarriages and excesses.

Education conducted with too great severity may lead to insanity; but the opposite extreme is a more common cause of it—an education not conducted on the principle of bringing the inclinations and affections under the control of religious and moral principles, and of repressing ideas of hurtful tendency, but encouraging false and romantic notions, and ideas above the rank in life.

The minds of some have likewise been weakened by terrifying tales in early life.

Excess of ignorance, and excess of study, both tend to weaken the mind, particularly the latter, when directed to a few ideas. The consequences of this excess of study, or of application to business, are—an irritable state of body and of mind—restless nights—febrile symptoms—diminished power of attention—confusion of ideas—and, if persisted in, insanity.

The predominant ideas of the times, whether religious or political, have great influence in producing mental disorder.

With regard to the influence of religion, although excessive devotion, and contrition or remorse of conscience may occasionally lead to insanity, especially in melancholy dispositions, doubt or doctrines previously professed in general precedes madness from religion: the mind, in suspense as to what regards eternal salvation, is easily overset.

Religion has less influence in this respect in the warmer climates, and in the Catholic countries, than in the temperate climates, and in countries where latitude of religious opinion is permitted; free governments, and political commotions, being favourable to the production of insanity, while despotic governments are not.

The emotions of mind produced by ardent and ungratified desires—by domestic troubles—and by the affections and passions—are frequent causes of insanity.

Some of the latter, as terror, anger, and passions produced by reverse of fortune, act immediately; but more commonly the action is gradual and continued, as that of grief, love, jealousy, disappointed pride . . . the struggle between religious and moral principles and passions. (66–71)

• • •

The appearance of the face, it is well-known, is intimately connected with, and dependent upon, the state of the mind. The repetition of the same ideas and emotions, and the consequent repetition of the same movements of the muscles of the eyes, and of the face, give a peculiar expression, which, in the insane state, is a combination of wildness, abstraction, or vacancy, and of those predominating ideas and emotions which characterize, the different species of mental disorder, as pride, anger, suspicion, love, fear, grief, &c.

Besides this moveable physiognomy, as it has been termed, other external signs, by which the different modifications of mental disorder might be ascertained, have been suggested. Some of those who adopt the phrenological ideas of Dr. Gall, conceiving mental disorder to proceed from disease in the departments of the brain exercising the functions disordered, allege that this disorder is marked, in recent cases, by increased heat in particular parts of the head, and in cases of long standing by external enlargement or diminution, and internal diseased structure in those parts.

Masks of the insane [death masks] have likewise been taken, to ascertain whether or not there exists any connexion between what is termed the fixed physiognomy, or form and position of the bones of the face, and the different species of insanity. (131–132)

WILLIAM WILLIS MOSELEY

Like Sir Alexander Morison, William Willis Moseley was interested in classifying mental illnesses by their causes as well as their symptoms in the Victorian era. In *Eleven Chapters on Nervous and Mental Complaints*, Moseley examines nervous disorders and mental illnesses from a slightly different perspective than Morison does. In his analysis of predisposing and exciting causes, he spotlights the inheritance factor underlying mental illness that may create Bertha's predisposition toward madness as well as a variety of exciting causes (the result of passion, which Rochester admits Bertha has exhibited), some of which may well have been factors in Bertha's illness. Jane, while not having predisposing causes of mental disorder in her own background, does indulge her passions on many occasions. Such indulgence could, according to Moseley's theories, lead her into madness as well.

FROM WILLIAM WILLIS MOSELEY, *ELEVEN CHAPTERS ON NERVOUS AND MENTAL COMPLAINTS*
(London, 1838)

There are several agencies, one of which is sufficiently powerful, to cause the brain that is healthy to sink into a morbid state.

These causes are of two kinds—predisposing and exciting.

If there exists in us any physical preponderance in favour of any *inclination, passion*, or *practice*, we are said to be under the influence of a predisposing cause. . . .

1st. Family connections. In all ages, in civilized countries an opinion has prevailed that certain tendencies exist in some families to certain principles, practices, and diseases. This opinion has grown up on the evidence of plain and numerous successive facts. The working of hereditary tendencies is too obvious to be disputed in consumption and scrofula; nor is it less generally admitted in diseases of the mind. Times of great national excitement are very fertile in the production of proof of this kind. . . .

2ndly. Ill-conducted nurseries, hot cradles, cribs, and beds; heated rooms without air, constant indulgence or continual severity, infantine and youthful days passed in constant excitement, cause a large race of both sexes to be constitutionally feeble and tremulously weak. These sink soon into nervousness and timidity, become incompetent to bear the trials of time or discharge its duties, fall beneath the load of life, deprecate their birth, and sigh for the grave.

3rdly. Strong passions are dangerous adjuncts to all, but especially to youth. The violence of passion exhibited under circumstances of great provocation, by a spoiled boy or a petted girl, compared with the self-control displayed by a son or a daughter of a Quaker under similar circumstances, demonstrates the position that children are, in their habits and manners, what their education makes them.

Unable to bear the mortification of being denied at the family dinner-table a single article, the petted son of Mr. J—— rose from his chair, fled for a pistol, rushed to the door and in a minute blew out his brains!

How many volumes would the details of the evils of violent passions fill! And who can tell the melancholy, the weariness of life, the suicides, the murders, the insanity, which violent passions have predisposed multitudes to suffer or to commit.

4thly. The absence of appropriate exercise and occupation is another predisposing cause.

"Every organ of the brain should be employed to secure its improvement, and to prevent mental deterioration and daily wretchedness."

The well-being of man and his happiness depend on his activity; and the brain is constituted in conformity to this great law; and, if not exercised, it becomes relaxed, and sinks into a condition of incompetency.

The physiological explanation of this fact is simple and interesting. Arterial or oxygenated blood is the essential element of nutriment to every organ. It is the means of repairing their lost power, and of stimulating their vital energies. The chief local effect of exercise is, to increase the action of the blood-vessels, and the nerves, &c.: to cause a more rapid and plentiful supply of blood and of nervous energy, and thereby to increase the vigour of every part.

Keeping these principles in view, it will excite no surprise, to find that *non-exercise* of the brain and the nervous system, or inactivity of intellect and feeling, is a very frequent predisposing cause of every form of nervous disease and insanity itself. For demonstrative evidence of this position, we have only to look at the numerous victims to be found among females of the middle and higher ranks who have no strong motives to exertion, or any cause to exert themselves for honour or gain: nor interests that call forth their mental energies, or to prevent, by their employments, these energies sinking into feebleness by disuse.

If we look round us we shall see from this cause innumerable examples of nervous or mental debility. Yes! their minds having become apathetic, and possessing no grounds of sympathy in common with others, they have sunken into extreme sensitiveness; shrink within themselves; live in a circle of their own construction, and try in vain to protect themselves against annoyances by living out of society.

To go into society now requires an effort they can no longer make without painful associations. In this state, home, with its little interests, is the center of attraction; and the mind, which is constituted for a wide range of employment and pleasure, is confined within boundaries too limited for the range of a worm.

Among young ladies, of the most respectable circles, from twenty to thirty years of age, as well as among females of the middle ranks of society, many suffer from these and similar causes. We have such now under our care in town and country.

Young men, whose days are entirely without the occupations of the state, church, army, navy, or business, and who find it difficult to kill their time, are sometimes among the sufferers of this class. Nor are military men, when occupying retired positions, and are obliged for weeks to be much alone, strangers to these feelings; feelings which, without much caution, will terminate in very distressing symptoms. But excess of mental activity must be as much guarded against as the want of exercise.

5thly. The brain requires more blood than any other organ, and it requires that it should be of the best kind. . . . Experiments made by oxygen have demonstrated it. The *languor* and *nervous debility* that attend long continuance in crowded places of worship, or amusement, or of business, as factories, &c., are produced by the *bad* air of these places deteriorating the blood. This vital fluid, under such circumstances, cannot receive a sufficient supply of oxygen to keep it in vigorous health, and deprived of this *quickening power*—this essential ingredient of vigour in all nature—languor, nervous debility, &c., follow as naturally and as certainly, as ice will melt on the disc of the sun.

This theory is established by this fact:—Bring those who suffer in these circumstances from the places deprived of a due proportion of oxygen into the open air, and they will soon recover, without any other aids, their lost energy, &c.

The excesses of the excitements of joy, sorrow, watchfulness, weariness, unexpected losses, the unexpected accession of wealth, the excitements of love, mortified ambition, pride or vanity, sudden and unexpected honour, and every other cause of great excitement or heavy depression, will, by degrees, operate as most powerful predisposing causes, when they do not appear at the time to put forth all their vigorous powers, and produce an immediate effect.

The more acute feelings, the greater sensibilities, the more retired and solitary habits, the absence of the bustling occupations, and of the great absorbing *external* interests of Lloyd's, and of the stock exchange, and of the royal Exchange, &c., is each sufficient to predispose females to nervous diseases; and, in proportion as these several agencies combine their *great non-exercise* influence, and act on the nerves of one of this higher class of created beings, she unhappily becomes a victim to strong predisposing agencies. Oh! that she may never fall a victim to the martyrdom of the disease itself.

To these it is unnecessary I should add, that the ardent application of the mind to any study, classics, mathematics, metaphysics, or even the lower branches of intellectual delights, as the composition of poetry, &c.: indeed, close reading on any subject, and sedentary occupations of every kind, will predispose all of both sexes to nervous sufferings, if long and severely pursued.

Let moderation, therefore, govern thee, O, Reader!

Having hastened through a few observations on the predisposing causes of nervous or mental disease and insanity, I must more hastily run through a few observations on the *exciting* causes of their sad complaints.

1st. That the liquids which have an immediate influence on the organ of the brain, should produce disease in it, can create no surprise. Man is so constituted, that all liquids which contain *alcohol* act immediately on the brain, through nerves which it meets with in the *mouth* and in the *throat*, and in its passage to as well as when it arrives in the stomach.

And this action of *alcohol* is as certain to produce a deteriorating effect on the brain, as the spur which stimulates the horse, inflicts a wound in his flesh, and the cruel goad makes a deeper wound in the sensitive legs of the poor ox. But wounds of this kind will also inflame and suppurate: and so will the wounds of alcohol produce disease in the brain.

The repeated use of liquids containing alcohol cannot, therefore, leave the brain of any undisturbed.

In fact, these liquids are the destructive agents which have caused mutinies in our navy, disobedience to orders in our army, have filled our prisons with all kinds of victims; our hospitals and mad-houses with every description of mental and bodily disease; our domestic circles with strife; our cellars and garrets with want and misery; and our streets with blasphemy and obscenity.

Inebriation is temporary madness. If often repeated it may become permanent madness. But wines, spirits, malt liquors, cider, peery, &c., are not the only liquids which contain alcohol, and are in daily use. No! Eau de Cologne, and other *waters*, scents, &c., are common odoriferous accompaniments of the toilet. These, yes! these have alcohol, and these are no less causes of mental disturbance, and will produce low spirits, nervous debility, *delusion, irresolution, sleepless nights*, wretchedness, &c. They may brighten the eye for the moment, but they will inflict deadly wounds in the head and the heart by and by.

2ndly. Determination of blood to the head is another common exciting cause. It is not my intention to detail the various assigned causes of the determination of blood to the head, or to examine these various assigned causes with a view to ascertain the correctness of any particular theory of such causes.

No; this would carry my reader from the point in view; which is the simple fact, that when this diseased state of the circulation exists, it is an absolutely certain cause of nervous or mental disease, and not unfrequently of insanity itself.

3rdly. Solar heat. Exposure of the head to the heat of the sun can never do good. The harm it does varies in kind, depending on the constitutional tendencies of the patient, and on the intensity of the heat, regulated by the climate, season of the year, time of the day, &c.

Head-ache, fever, sickness, nervous debility, delirium, idiocy, insanity, are some of the various effects produced by this powerfully exciting agent.

4thly. Tumours in the head sometimes (not often) become the exciting causes. It is not correct to suppose that tumours exist, unless the constitution is deteriorated by the scrophulous virus [syphilis]. A gentleman, well read on this disease, can at once from the lips, eye-lids, or complexion, determine if this virus is making its ravages on the health. . . .

5thly. Extreme cold and heat produce nervous diseases, and insanity in some constitutions. The retreat of the French army from Moscow, and the voyages of Captain Parry [*sic*], supply proof of this; and the log-books of many vessels, sailing eastward, as well as the domestic history of the three Asiatic capitals: Calcutta, Madras, and Bombay, supply too many sad details in confirmation of the effects of heat on the nerves.

Many visitors say, "I have been in India, and I trace my nervous sufferings to the influence of the heat of that climate."

6thly. Long-continued watchfulness. This ought to be guarded against, as it often produces nervous disease. Mrs. T——, through watchfulness during [her husband's] illness, became very nervous. Numerous subsequent cases of a similar kind are before us among our correspondents.

7thly. Suppressed discharges. If eruptions, discharges, or evacuations of any kind, whether cutaneous, uterine, or intestinal, are suppressed, the first effect must be the increased fullness of the vessels. As the number of these suppressed discharges increases, and the period of their suppression is extended, the vessels must become gorged.

The vessels of the head suffer in common with the rest.

In some cases the force of suppression will fall on the lungs and produce consumption; but in many it will fall on the brain and produce nervous diseases, perhaps madness. . . .

8thly. Wealth and poverty, affliction, speculations, &c., all create a deep interest in most minds. The acquisition and losses of wealth often rouse strong emotions and excite intense and incessant feelings. These create violent cerebral action, indicated by pain in the head, fever, sleeplessness, diseased elevation, vertigo, fear, aberration, &c. Out of one hundred and sixty-four patients in the private mad-house of Esquirol, fifty were merchants. Two respectable brothers, out of three, were torn away as conscripts for the army, during the French revolution . . . and one being shot by the side of the other, the survivor instantly went mad; and when he was conducted home to the third brother, the excitement occasioned in his brain by this sight, and the tale of the shooting, caused him to go mad also. . . .

9thly. Nymphomania. This is another name for certain strong feelings which keep the brain in a state of feverish excitement; it is sometimes called the cerebellar disease, and at other times amativeness. The cause is, no doubt, the size and peculiar sensitiveness of the nympha. The enlargement of the cerebellum is the consequence or sign of this, and not the cause. This disease is unjustly attributed to a worse nature and a more corrupt heart: to a class of human passions of a demoralizing tendency; to the want of a good education; and to the absence of good moral and religious feelings. But the reverse of all this is true, and has been so fully and frequently demonstrated to us, by the facts in our practice, as to teach us to *pity, sympathise*, and not to *blame*. Yes! it is an *organic disease*, against the tide of which neither the firm resolutions, or good principles, nor *frequent fervent prayers* of Miss A——, more of Miss S——, the daughter of a clergyman, nor of Mrs. ——, a married lady, with children, could make sufficient head to stifle these feelings, or keep their distressed minds in a state of self-approval.

10th. Strong attachments, separation, &c. Strong attachments arise from many causes. Their influence is often increased by the concentration of our best and strongest passions, and all the tender sympathies and kindly feelings of our nature. Tranquility, happiness, peace, and life itself, are felt at the moment to depend on their continuity; and if any cause rend this bond of union asunder, the separation is often attended with great mental disturbance. This evil, so powerful, and so frequent, has obtained an appropriate position in the list of diseases, under the name *Nostalgia*. Many extraordinary instances of its power have been displayed in this country during war, when *press gangs*, as in former years, were allowed to tear husbands from the arms of their wives, and children from the embraces of their parents! The revolution in France supplied numberless strong illustrations of the evils of breaking the bonds of attachment, by producing all kinds of mental disease. Dr. Perfect has given us, in his "annals of Nervous Disease and Insanity," several interesting proofs of lacerated attachments. Among others, he names a lady, aged thirty, who sunk into the depth of despair by the death of a friend. She passed days and nights without uttering a word. Sometimes she shed floods of tears, and, at other times, uttered the most piercing shrieks! Her face became pale and swelled, her spirits melancholy, and her mind deranged! Mrs. T——, of B——, Northamptonshire, became melancholy when separated from her husband. Arrangements were made for Miss —— to go out to her brother, holding a high civil appointment in India; her passage was paid, her dress prepared; all her family, that was in England, were with her, to accompany her to the ship. In a state of the greatest excitement, from reluctance to leave England and be separated from her friends, she fled here. *The scene was painfully interesting!*

Incapable of enduring separation from her mother, another young lady became herself mad, when her mamma was sent to a mad-house, by the advice of the medical man who kept it!

11thly. Domestic disturbances and quarrels have made more husbands, wives, and daughters nervous, than the sword has slain; and ought, on this ground, to be most religiously guarded against.

12thly. Disappointed love has ruined the constitutions, broken down the mental powers, and inflicted more intense misery on a great number of females, than Love ever made happy. The number which become nervous from this cause is greater than from most others.

13thly. Onanism [masturbation and coitis interruptus]. To this baneful practice, the deterioration of early beauty, the loss of brilliancy in the eye, and a smooth surface of the forehead; the appearance of premature age; fidgetiness, eccentricity, *unevenness of temper*, unnatural quickness, or great dullness and stupidity; incompetency, impotency, idiocy, wretchedness, and aberration of mind, are to be frequently ascribed. It is true, that it is not always, but very often, to *this cause*, in both sexes, these symptoms can be traced.

14thly. The excessive desire of children.

15thly. Extreme hunger, continued some days.

16thly. Love of admiration.

17thly. Self-esteem.

18thly. Great fear.

19thly. Mistaken perceptions of real relation and of Christian doctrines, and the grounds of acceptance both of our prayers, duties, and persons with God.

20thly. Hard, intense, and *long-continued studies*.

21stly. Blow on the head.

22ndly. Malformation of the *cranium*.

23rdly. Lightning.

24thly. Gambling.

25thly. Jealousy.

26thly. The sudden death of persons in our presence.

27thly. The horrors of a storm at sea.

28thly. The fearful associations of being awoke from sound sleep while the house is on fire.

29thly. The sight of a public execution.

30thly. Sudden and unexpected changes of fortune.

31stly. And Influenza—are but a few of the exciting causes of nervous disease that have come under our notice. (123–140)

ANDREW WYNTER

In *Jane Eyre*, Mr. Rochester discusses his sense of betrayal by his father, brother, and Mr. Mason over the fact that the mental illness of Bertha's mother was not revealed to him until after he and Bertha were married. As we are well aware today, some forms of mental illness can be inherited. In Victorian times, the fear of such inheritance was excessively strong, especially the fear of such inheritance by a daughter from her mother. In *The Borderlands of Insanity* Andrew Wynter, a Victorian physician specializing in mental illness, presents the Victorian perspective of such hereditary transmission of madness.

FROM ANDREW WYNTER, *THE BORDERLANDS OF INSANITY*
(London, 1875)

It is agreed by all alienist physicians [physicians specializing in insane patients], that girls are far more likely to inherit insanity from their mothers, than from the other parent, and that the same rule obtains as regards the sons. The tendency of the mother to transmit her mental disease, is, however, in all cases stronger than the father's; some physicians have, indeed, insisted that it is twice as strong. In judging of the chances of an individual inheriting mental disease, or, indeed, of the insane temperament, it may not be unadvisable to study the general likeness and character. If the daughter of an insane mother very much resembles her in feature and in temperament, the chances are that she is more likely to inherit the disease than other daughters who are not so like. And the reason is obvious; for if the general physical aspect and the temperament are alike, it points to a similar likeness in the structure of the body and nerve. The mental likeness is, however, the most important of the two, as we often see children partaking of the father's features and of the mother's temperament. In such cases the child would possibly inherit the mother's insane temperament, transmuted into some disorder of the nervous system, such as hysteria, epilepsy, or neuralgia; for nothing is more common than to find mere nervous disorders changed, by transmission from parent to child, into mental disorders, and vice versa. (52–53)

GEORGE MAN BURROWS

George Man Burrows spent twelve years as a general medical practitioner, after which he chose to specialize in mental disorders and opened a private asylum for the care and treatment of the insane. He earned a reputation as one of the most prominent experts on mental illness that early Victorian England had to offer. Like Andrew Wynter, George Man Burrows was particularly interested in the hereditary aspects of mental disorders. He writes of "constitutional predispositions to specific diseases," the concept of individuals having a strong likelihood of contracting certain diseases because of particular qualities they were born with. Nineteenth-century medical science was beginning to examine such predispositions through objective scientific methods. Burrows wanted to make certain that the concept of hereditary insanity was treated with the same seriousness in medical science as other hereditary illnesses. He sees the tendency of the families of the insane to keep the problem hidden, as Rochester did, and to deny that insanity runs in the family, as the Masons did, as a serious medical problem for society as a whole.

FROM GEORGE MAN BURROWS, *COMMENTARIES ON INSANITY*
(London, 1828)

The liability of mania, demency, epilepsy, leprosy, &c., to extend through future generations, is an opinion confirmed by the experience of all ages. Some have imagined that insanity moves *per saltum*, and appears in every other, or every third individual, in lineal descent. . . . This, however, is incorrect. The development of insanity may escape one generation, and appear in another; but no rule in this respect obtains.

It is of little real importance whether it be a predisposition, or a malady itself, which descends and becomes hereditary; but no fact is more incontrovertibly established than that insanity is susceptible of being propagated; or, in other words, that a specific morbid condition sometimes exists in the human constitution which, by intermarriage . . . may be perpetuated *ad infinitum*.

Hereditary predisposition, therefore, is a prominent cause of mental derangement.

Mania and melancholia do not propagate their respective types: a maniac may beget a melancholic, and vice versa.

Sometimes, in a large family, we find all the forms and relations of insanity developed in a remarkable manner. Mania, melancholia, hypochondriasis, apoplexy, paralysis, epilepsy, convulsions, chorea, hysteria, &c., or high nervous irritability, are often found to pervade one or the other of the same families. This I have seen exemplified in a respectable family—one son has transcendent talents, the second is inferior, the third has been for years in a state of fatuity, and the fourth is an idiot. That great wit and madness are nearly allied, is not a poetical fiction; but there is this dissimilarity,—the one is rarely ever, the other is generally an inheritance.

Few, I believe, are more particular than myself in endeavouring to trace every case of insanity to its source. It is a duty which I conceive every physician owes to his patient, as well as to himself, to ascertain whether there be an hereditary predisposition; because the correctness of his prognostic greatly depends on a knowledge of the truth.

Hereditary insanity may be as successfully treated as when it arises from an accidental cause; but when we know that a predisposition exists, we can decide with more accuracy the degree of excitement necessary to produce the effect, and the probability of a recurrence of the attack.

Common sense, if not a regard to the welfare of the patient and happiness of his family, one would think to be sufficient to induce the relations of an insane person to give the physician whom they consult every information required on this point. What can be a motive sufficiently strong in such case not only to conceal, but often to deny, an hereditary predisposition is to me quite incomprehensible; yet nothing is more common. I will quote a strong instance: A young lady, of good family and fortune, was placed under my care, in whom mental derangement had been some time developed, till at length she was too violent to be kept at home. I made the usual inquiry into the probable causes of the malady, and whether hereditary predisposition might be suspected. This was positively denied; but it was suggested, that being very fond of hunting, she had several times experienced severe falls from her horse, and might have injured her head. Upon examining the cranium, I actually found a very singular depression of a part of the skull; but whether it was natural or accidental, no one could inform me. I stated to my patient's friends my suspicion that this depression might operate mechanically as a cause of the insanity: and, with their consent, an eminent surgeon was consulted upon the propriety of applying the trephine, with a view of removing such cause. Before any decision upon this question, I learnt from another quarter that several of this young lady's nearest relations had been insane, and that two had died in that state. The operation was, therefore, declined; and she recovered. I believe few cases can occur where the inducements to a candid avowal of hereditary predisposition to insanity were more powerful, yet they were not of sufficient force to elicit the truth. This perverse concealment has often a very baneful effect.

It is very remarkable, that when the desire of concealing hereditary insanity is so great as to run every hazard rather than confess it, yet no care is taken to correct such predisposition; and although a person knows that it is inherent in himself, he is the least careful in betraying proofs to the world. (100–103)

JAMES COWLES PRICHARD

James Cowles Prichard (1806–1848) was a highly respected English physician and ethnologist of the early Victorian period. In *A Treatise on Insanity*, Prichard discusses a condition he calls "moral insanity." Those whom he diagnosed as morally insane were those who refused to follow the dictates of society. Their intellectual capacities were normal, but they experienced and acted upon emotions considered by others to be abnormal. Such individuals might indulge in multiple sexual affairs without any appearance of remorse. They might indulge in excessive gambling or in eccentric behaviors, such as spending vast amounts of money on "improving" their estate in ways that society considers inappropriate. In other words, the "morally insane" were rarely violent or criminal; instead, they tended to act in ways that were severely frowned upon by members of society.

In *Jane Eyre*, John Reed is a young man who grows up to act in ways that could very well have been characterized as "moral insanity." But because he was the heir of his family's fortune and estate, and because he was the only male in the line of descent, it was very unlikely that he would have been so diagnosed. On the other hand, a woman in the position of Bertha Rochester could easily have been diagnosed as morally insane, even before her behavior degenerated into the animalistic form we see when we finally meet her in her attic room. Women who behaved in ways that society did not sanction—especially regarding sexuality—were very often defined as morally insane, the only other option being to declare them disreputable and degenerate.

FROM JAMES COWLES PRICHARD, *A TREATISE ON INSANITY*
(London, 1833)

Moral insanity.—This form of mental disease has been said above to consist of a morbid perversion of the feelings, affections, habits, without an hallucination or erroneous conviction impressed upon the understanding; it sometimes co-exists with an apparently unimpaired state of the intellectual faculties.

There are many individuals living at large, and not entirely separated from society, who are affected in a certain degree by this modification of insanity. They are reputed persons of singular, wayward, and eccentric character. An attentive observer might often recognize something remarkable in their manner of existence, which leads him to entertain doubts as to their entire sanity, and circumstances are sometimes discovered on inquiry which assist in determining his opinion. In many instances it is found that there is an hereditary tendency to madness in the family, or that several relatives of the person affected have laboured under other diseases of the brain. The individual himself is discovered in a former period of life to have sustained an attack of madness of a decided character. His temper and dispositions are found on inquiry to have undergone a change: to be not what they were previously to a certain time; he has become an altered man, and this difference has perhaps been noted from the period when he sustained some reverse of fortune, which deeply affected him, or since the loss of some beloved relative. In other instances the alteration in his character has ensued immediately on some severe shock which his bodily constitution has undergone. This has been either a disorder affecting the head, a slight attack of paralysis, a fit of epilepsy, or some fever or inflammatory disorder which has produced a perceptible change in the habitual state of the constitution. In some cases the alteration in temper and habits has been gradual and imperceptible, and it seems only to have consisted in an exaltation or increase of peculiarities which were always more or less natural or habitual.

In a state such as that above described many persons have continued for years to be the sources of apprehension and solicitude to their friends and relatives. The latter in many instances cannot bring themselves to admit the real nature of the case. The individual follows the bent of his inclinations; he is continually engaging in new pursuits, and again relinquishing them without any other motive than mere caprice and fickleness. At length the total perversion of his affections, the dislike and even enmity manifested towards his dearest friends excite greater alarm. . . .

Individuals labouring under this disorder are capable of reasoning or supporting an argument on any subject within their sphere of knowledge that may be presented to them, and they often display great ingenuity in giving reasons for their eccentric conduct, and in accounting for and justifying the state of moral feeling under which they appear to exist. In one sense, indeed, their intellectual faculties may be termed unsound, but it is the same sense in which persons under the influence of strong passions may generally be said to have their judgment warped, and the sane or healthy exercise of their understandings impeded. They think and act under the influence of strongly excited feelings, and a person accounted sane is under such circumstances proverbially liable to error in judgment and conduct. (14–18)

ROBERT BRUDENELL CARTER

Robert Brudenell Carter was a general practitioner of note in England who began his medical training as an apprentice to a general doctor and then entered London Hospital for formal medical study. He became a member of the Royal College of Surgeons in 1851, but returned to general practice when he could not come up with the money he needed to complete his training for a fellowship at the College. Nonetheless, he kept himself on the cutting edge of medical research throughout his career as a physician.

Carter also became a prominent writer in the medical field, both in the areas of diseases of the nervous system and in ophthalmology, a field he became interested in during his service as a staff surgeon during the Crimean War. Today he is known among medical historians primarily for his ophthalmological work, but his writings on hysteria are equally important. He was one of the few medical experts, it seems, who understood the connection between the restrictive nature of the life that the Victorian lady was expected to live and the onset of nervous disorders. Jane Eyre, who had a passionate desire to lead a more active life than her society allowed, was precisely the kind of woman that Carter believed could become hysterical (in the sense of mental illness). Such restrictions on the liberty of women were, according to Carter, a substantial cause of mental illness among women in Victorian society.

FROM ROBERT BRUDENELL CARTER, *ON THE PATHOLOGY AND
TREATMENT OF HYSTERIA*
(London, 1853)

[I]t is reasonable to expect that [sexual passion], which is strongly felt by great numbers of people, but whose natural manifestations are constantly repressed in compliance with the usages of society, will be the one whose morbid effects are most frequently witnessed. This anticipation is abundantly borne out by fact; the sexual passion in women being that which most accurately fulfills the prescribed conditions, and whose injurious influence upon the organism is most common and familiar. Next after it in power, may be placed those emotions of a permanent character, which are usually concealed, because disgraceful, unamiable, as hatred or envy; after them others equally permanent, such as grief or care, but which, not being discreditable, are not so liable to be repressed. (21)

· · ·

If the relative power of emotion against the sexes be compared in the present day, even without including the erotic passion, it is seen to be considerably greater in the woman than in the man, partly from that natural conformation which causes the former to feel, under circumstances where the latter thinks; and partly because the woman is more often under the necessity of endeavouring to conceal her feelings. But when sexual desire is taken into the account, it will add immensely to the forces bearing upon the female, who is often much under its dominion; and who, if unmarried and chaste, is compelled to restrain every manifestation of its sway. Man, on the contrary, has such facilities for its gratification, that as a source of disease it is almost inert against him, and when powerfully excited, it is pretty sure to be speedily exhausted through the proper channel. (32–33)

JOHN HASLAM

John Haslam was apothecary and chief medical officer of Bethlehem Hospital in England from 1795 through 1816. He was the
subject of a Parliamentary Board of Inquiry into the treatment of
patients at Bethlehem and lost his job due to what the Board considered cruel treatment of his patients. Despite his dismissal from
the hospital, however, Haslam's view on the management of patients were well received generally. In *Considerations on the Moral Management of Insane Persons*, Haslam wrote, not of the
forms mental illness takes, nor of the causes for it or the ways to
avoid it, but of the most efficient and effective ways of maintaining
patients who are insane. In the passage below, he asserts that many
who are insane but not dangerous should be allowed to live in
liberty, but that those who are not "quiet and harmless" need to
be secluded from the rest of the world. He also recognizes the
danger of procreation for the insane, by which means insanity
would be likely to be transmitted to future generations. He would
have approved of Rochester's sequestering Bertha from the world,
as well as his decision not to have children with her.

FROM JOHN HASLAM, *CONSIDERATIONS ON THE MORAL
MANAGEMENT OF INSANE PERSONS*
(London, 1817)

From long established practice, there has been an usual association between *Being Mad*, and confinement in a *Madhouse*. That insanity is a
disease, which for its cure, and also for the prevention of mischief, or-
dinarily requires seclusion, must be admitted; and in many instances, that
persons so confined, enjoy a larger portion of comfort than they could
attain by being at large is equally certain. Still it is my opinion that confinement is too indiscriminately recommended and persisted in. It may
be expected that some rules should be laid down, or directions given on
this important subject, as a guide to practitioners, but this is nearly impossible.

That many persons of deranged intellect are at liberty, and for some
years have been permitted to be so, who have conducted themselves in
a quiet and harmless manner, is well known. Perhaps when insanity exists

without a desire to harm others or themselves, there can be no necessity or even justification for seclusion. But the difficulty is in predicting what will be the conduct of a person whose intellect is deranged: he may be harmless one month and disposed to violence the next, and such conversion of character oftentimes takes place. I recollect a female lunatic, who for many months was of a remarkably placid and amiable disposition, but who without any evident cause became transformed into a most furious and vindictive patient, and in which state she continued for several years.

In many instances an intercourse with the world has dispelled those hallucinations which a protracted confinement, in all probability, would have added to, and confirmed. In its passive state insanity has been often known, if the expression be allowable, to wear off, by permitting the patient to enjoy his liberty, and return to his usual occupation and industrious habits: indeed it might be naturally expected that bodily labour in the open air, with moderate employment of mind, directed to some useful object, would more contribute to health and rationality than immuring a person, so circumstanced, within the walls of a madhouse, provided his derangement be of a mild and inoffensive character. In this view of the subject a pauper has considerably the advantage of a man of rank and fortune. The former being an incumbrance to the parish during the time he is secluded, the parochial officers are disposed to afford him a trial by way of probation, rather than continue him in confinement at a considerable expense. (13–16)

• • •

Before the pure spirit of benevolence and Christian piety devised the foundation of charitable institutions for lunatics, these miserable objects were allowed to wander, and considered as interdicted persons—when they became troublesome or offensive they were whipped from tything to tything, and stocked, punished and imprisoned. The enlightened commiseration of modern philanthropists has afforded them every protection, as the existing public and private asylums sufficiently evince. In these receptacles numbers are temporarily secluded who apparently recover, and afterwards form matrimonial alliances, or if already married, return to their families. The minute investigation of many hundred cases has fully satisfied my own mind that the offspring of a person who has laboured under insanity, is peculiarly liable to become similarly affected. Probably this occasional confinement and premature liberation, when the disease is only quiescent, but not eradicated, may in some degree explain the manner in which it is frequently transmitted. It is not my intention in this place to enter on a discussion of the subject, but leave the reader to form his own deductions. (22–23)

ROBERT GARDINER HILL

Robert Gardiner Hill ran the Lincoln Asylum for the Insane in Enland during Brontë's lifetime. He detested the use of restraints on the patients, many of whom were physically restrained almost twenty-four hours of every day in some asylums. Many of the asylums in nineteenth-century England were simply warehouses for the storage of people who were not and never could be productive citizens. They rarely provided any intellectual stimulation for their patients (mental stimulation of any kind, most believed, would make the patient worse by straining an already strained mind), and what physical activity was allowed, when it was allowed, was seriously inadequate. The conditions in which Bertha lived at Thornfield were precisely the kind of conditions that Hill recommended against for the mentally ill.

Hill's recommended reforms for the traditional treatment of the insane were considered quite revolutionary by some physicians of the time. His assertion that he was able to run Lincoln Asylum without the use of restraints at all was quite startling to most of his contemporaries. Today, most of his suggestions seem to be quite common-sensical.

FROM ROBERT GARDINER HILL, *TOTAL ABOLITION OF PERSONAL RESTRAINT IN THE TREATMENT OF THE INSANE* (London, 1839)

But, it may be demanded, "What mode of treatment do you adopt, in place of restraint? How do you guard against accidents? How do you provide for the safety of the attendants?" In short, what is the substitute for coercion? The answer may be summed up in a few words, viz.— *classification—watchfulness—vigilant and unceasing attendance by day and by night—kindness, occupation, and attention to health, cleanliness, and comfort, and the total absence of every description of other occupation of the attendants.* This treatment, in a properly constructed and suitable building, with a sufficient number of strong and active attendants always at their post, is best calculated to restore the patient; and all instruments of coercion and torture are rendered absolutely and in every case unnecessary.

In order, however, that this plan may be undeviatingly pursued, several essential requisites must unite:—

1. A suitable building must be provided, in an airy and open situation, with ground sufficient for several court-yards, gardens, and pleasure-grounds, commanding (if possible) a pleasing and extensive prospect.

2. There must be a proper classification of the patients, *more especially by night*.

3. There must be also a sufficient number of strong, tall, and active attendants whose remuneration must be such as to secure persons of good character, and steady principle, to undertake their arduous duties. And

4. The House-Surgeon must exercise an unremitting control and inspection, in order that the plan may never, under any circumstances whatever, be deviated from in the slightest degree. (37–40)

• • •

In the treatment of the insane, medicine is of little avail, except (of course) when they are suffering also from other diseases, to which lunatics as well as sane persons are liable. *Moral treatment with a view to induce habits of self-control, is all and every thing*. I have spoken of classification and watchfulness: but these things are done by their guardians, and have little or no reference to their feelings; for they should if possible be watched without leading them to suppose that they are suspected of any thing improper or injurious. But occupation and kindness have especial reference to the patient; and their object is (as I have stated) to induce habits of self-control and cleanliness, which qualities are both essential to recovery, and yet cannot possibly be attained unto by a patient under restraint. Out-door employments with moderate exercise—cheerful society—the occasional presence of friends and even of visitors—healthy recreations and amusements—the enjoyment of the sweet music of spring, or a calm summer evening—the care of a garden, or a shrubbery, or the cultivation of rare and choice flowers—all unite in producing a healthy tone, and giving nerve and vigour to the shattered mind. No patient should be *compelled* to work in any way; but many of them, both males and females, will voluntarily make themselves useful and be industrious; and in many cases their services are very valuable. Sedentary employments are not good. The offices of religion have a soothing and favourable effect on many:—I have found the use of evening service, and the calm and sober strain of piety which pervades the

Liturgy, to be well adapted to these unfortunate beings. Religious excitement of the feelings is always bad and has brought great number of patients to this, as well as to every other Asylum. A patient should never be terrified. (45–47)

JOHN MILLAR

John Millar was medical superintendent at Bethhall House Asylum for Lunatics in London in the middle of the nineteenth century. In that position he observed many hundreds of patients. In *Hints on Insanity*, he presents conclusions he formed based on those observations. The purpose of the book, as he states in the introduction to it, is to be "useful to those medical men who have had not opportunity during their professional education of becoming practically acquainted with Insanity, and whose time is too much occupied to permit them to make a special study of a disease which they are seldom called upon to treat" (iii). Millar believed that insanity and nervous disorders had the best chance of being treated successfully if they were recognized and the treatment begun early. His remarks are organized primarily by classification of mental illness. He concludes the book, however, with some general comments about insanity and its medical treatment. Those comments provide us with details about the treatment of the insane in institutions as well as the level of understanding of the "experts" in the field of mental health in the nineteenth century. He also addresses the tendency of many (like Mr. Rochester) of "keeping their insane relatives at home, confined in an attic or some out-of-the-way room, without any medical supervision, and placed under the care of a servant unskilled and inexperienced" (63). Such behavior he believes to be extraordinarily detrimental to the life and health of the patient, who, he believes, would be much better off in an appropriate asylum.

FROM JOHN MILLAR, *HINTS ON INSANITY*
(London, 1861)

When called to attend upon an insane person in the early stages of the disorder, the medical practitioner should bear in mind that his success with his patient will very much depend upon the impression first produced by his own conduct and demeanour. He should, therefore, before visiting him, make himself thoroughly acquainted with every particular connected with the patient's condition. And, that he may gain his confidence, he must approach and treat him as much like a sane person as possible. It is well known that the insane are exceedingly suspicious, and quick to detect any deceit practiced upon them. They are also jealous of the intrusion of strangers; and, as they do not, for the most part, admit the necessity for advice, they decline to have anything to say to a medical man in his professional capacity, though, at the same time, they are often willing to converse with him as a friend upon the subject of their aberrations. He should listen attentively to all they have to say, for they regard many inquiries with suspicion; and, if he cannot agree with their observations, he should refrain from direct contradiction. He may ask them for some corroborative evidence as to the correctness of their statement, and whether they have not misinterpreted the facts supported, or otherwise, to which they refer. He should never treat their aberrations, in the first instance, lightly, but should rather with all seriousness sympathize with them in their troubles, and gradually lead them to reason more logically upon the subject. This, however, must be done with care and with truth; for, however unable patients may be to reason correctly themselves, they are quick to detect those who step beyond the bounds of fair reasoning, and never trust nor forgive those who have tried to mislead them. After some general conversation, they may be brought to admit that they do not sleep well, and are otherwise out of sorts, and in this way may be induced to take such remedies as may be necessary for them. During the progress of the case, the aberrations should be referred to as little as possible; and then merely to test their existence and intensity.

In some cases, a question may early arise as to the propriety or possibility of treating the patient at home, or of sending him to an asylum; and, before deciding upon a matter of so much importance, it will be well to consider the advantages or disadvantages of either plan, and the effect each is likely to have upon the patient's position and prospects. In the former, there will be the difficulty of inducing him to submit to any plan for treatment, from the unwillingness to admit that there is anything amiss; nor will it be easy at home to restrain him from a repetition of the excesses or irregularities of which he has been guilty, without exciting strong feelings of resistance. When he finds that he is disobeyed by his servants, unsupported in his orders by his family, and that he is a prisoner instead of a master in his own house, the irritation and annoyance which such a state of things must inevitably set up, will operate powerfully against his acceding to any proper course of domestic treatment. With firmness, discretion, and a competent attendant, however, I believe that this difficulty may be overcome; and the patient, after his recovery, will be much more likely to forgive restraint in his own home, than if he had been sent as a certified lunatic to an asylum.

These observations apply more particularly to professional men, and those who are dependent upon their own exertions, and who may be suffering from an acute or other form of mania, from which they are likely soon to recover. For such is the feeling of distrust and suspicion with which those who have been afflicted with insanity are regarded by the world, that, when once the fact becomes known, it operates as a blight upon their future prospects. This feeling is so general, that it is shared even by the patients themselves, and so heavily does the consciousness of it press upon them, that they often take a dislike to all who were instrumental in affixing the brand upon them; wife, relations, and medical men who signed the certificate, share in the aversion, and in many cases it becomes the source of much domestic misery.

Notwithstanding the many advantages to the patient which are known to result from his removal to an asylum, I am not prepared, for the reasons above stated, to advocate the transference of recent curable cases from private treatment; for, with a correct knowledge of the disease, and by judicious management, the acute symptoms may be as readily overcome as an attack of delirium tremens, when change of scene and temporary removal from accustomed associations will complete the recovery.

In the above remarks, I do not mean to include persons who are afflicted with any of the incurable forms of insanity, or those who may be suffering from attacks which are likely to incapacitate them for further useful employment—such as general paralysis, epilepsy, chronic hereditary mania, imbecility, &c.—for all such persons an asylum is undoubtedly the best place. There every advantage which skill and experience can suggest, is offered to the patient, at little comparative expense, without anxiety to the friends. To avoid the publicity which residence in a private asylum is supposed to entail, relatives excuse themselves from adopting this course, under the popular and fallacious plea that association with other insane persons must be injurious—a plea plausible enough on the face of it, but in itself utterly groundless, and only entertained by those who have no practical knowledge of the subject. With questionable humanity, they prefer keeping their insane relatives at home, confined in an attic or some out-of-the-way room, without any medical supervision, and placed under the care of a servant unskilled and inexperienced. Lest the afflicted patients should be seen and recognized, they are scarcely allowed to pass the door, at least in the daytime, a confinement which in due course tells fatally on their health. They fall into a hopeless state of dementia, and becoming dirty in their habits, are more neglected than ever. At last it is found impossible to keep them in a private dwelling, and they are consigned to an asylum. Here, with proper attention and the treatment derived from the experience of late years, they improve so much as to lead to the well-founded belief that, had they been placed under such care in the first instance, they would have been able, at the least, to enjoy their existence more like one of God's rational creatures than the animal to which they have sunk. Such, indeed, is my own experience with reference to a great number of persons who have been sent to this Asylum after having been so treated for many years, most of them surviving the injudicious friends or relatives to whose pride and prejudice they had been sacrificed. An asylum does in reality offer more privacy than can be secured at home, for domestics amongst immediate friends will gossip about family failings. . . .

As the public generally are quite ignorant of lunacy matters, and they look to their medical attendant for advice and direction, the following observations may not be out of place, premising that they apply solely to the middle classes of society.

Public Hospitals, almost without exception, receive private patients only; that is, persons who are maintained entirely from private means. As they are managed by a committee of gentlemen (and such of them as are situated beyond the metropolitan district are officially visited and inspected quarterly by a committee of justices of the peace annually appointed at quarter session), a degree of publicity is given to all proceedings connected with them, which cannot but be gratifying to the friends of those patients who have any fear of the improper detention of their relatives.

Most of these hospitals devote the profits derived from the rich inmates to the general expenses of the institution, and are thus enabled to assist the less wealthy. They therefore maintain many of the poorer patients at a less sum than their actual cost. As each hospital has its own special arrangements, the rules connected with which can be read upon application, it is unnecessary to allude to them further. There are two, however, in London—Bethlehem and St. Luke's—which offer such advantages to the poor and educated classes, by receiving curable patients, free of all expense, for a period not exceeding twelve months. . . . I cannot do better than copy the special instructions which appear on the face of the forms supplied by them.

BETHLEHEM HOSPITAL

"All poor lunatics, presumed to be curable, are eligible for admission into this hospital, for maintenance and medical treatment, except—

1. Those who have sufficient means for their suitable maintenance in a private asylum,

2. Those who have been insane for more than twelve calendar months,

3. Those who have been discharged uncured from any other hospital for the reception of lunatics,

4. Those who are pregnant,

5. Those who are in a state of idiotcy, or are afflicted with any form of paralysis, or are subject to epileptic or convulsive fits,

6. Those whose condition threatens speedy dissolution of life, or requires the permanent exclusive attendance of a nurse,

7. Those whom disease or physical infirmity renders unfit to associate with other patients.

N.B. A preference will be given to patients of the educated classes; to secure accommodation for whom, no patient will be received who is a proper object for admission into a County Lunatic Asylum."

ST. LUKE'S HOSPITAL

The first five rules above quoted also apply to this hospital. The remaining objections—

"6. Being under the age of 12, or above 70 years.

7. Being brought in a state of infectious disease, or extreme debility, or in a dirty condition, or without a proper supply of clothing.

8. Being in receipt of parochial relief or alms from his or her parish."

There are other rules as to securities for the removal of the patient when called upon, the supply of clothing, &c., which are easily complied with.

County Asylums receive those patients only who are sent to them through a parish, and are consequently pauper asylums; though a few of them admit persons in humble circumstances for a small weekly payment, but without making any other distinction from the other inmates.

Private Asylums differ chiefly in being under the entire direction and control of the proprietor or superintendent, who is not hampered by the formal rules which must exist in all public institutions; and whilst the arrangements are more like those of a private family, they offer a greater degree of privacy to those who do not wish it to be generally known that they have a relative insane. All asylums are subject to strict official inspection, and in this respect are much upon a par. Those situated within the metropolitan district derive much advantage from being specially under the supervision of the Commissioners in Lunacy—a body of gentlemen whose general experience, from careful comparison of the different modes of treatment and arrangement of asylums which are brought before them during their official visits to the various asylums in the kingdom, gives them a qualification to advise and direct which is possessed by no other body of asylum visitors.

Private asylums also offer greater facilities for the visitation of friends, one of the best safeguards against neglect or ill-treatment of patients. On this point I have to remark, that patients who are not dangerous should always be seen alone, that they may have every opportunity afforded them of stating unreservedly any grievance or complaint. If these appear to interfere with the comfort of the patient, the friend ought not to leave the establishment without ascertaining their validity by communicating with those in authority. Patients often make unfounded charges, and exaggerate and distort ordinary or trifling occurrences, for the purpose of acting upon the feelings of the friends, in order to effect their liberation, as indeed I have known them to confess; or the charges may be made to annoy to get rid of an attendant to whom they may have taken a dislike. Yet, if complaints are really founded on fact, the sooner they are known the better. (59–73)

TOPICS FOR ORAL OR WRITTEN EXPLORATION

1. Read the novel *Wide Sargasso Sea* by Jean Rhys, which presents a twentieth-century version of the story of Rochester meeting Bertha, their courtship, and their early marriage. Then discuss whether you believe that the difference in cultures between England and the Caribbean may have played a part in Bertha's madness. Discuss what the difference between cultures may have had to do with the problems that developed between Rochester and Bertha.

2. Write an essay in which you discuss the extent to which the societal role of "lady" in Victorian society did or did not have an impact on the large numbers of Victorian women of the middle and upper classes who were diagnosed with nervous disorders and insanity.

3. Examine the various descriptions of insane behaviors in this chapter. Then determine which behaviors would still be considered "insane" and which are now considered lifestyle decisions instead of mental illness.

4. In *Jane Eyre*, we hear the story of Bertha from Mr. Rochester, filtered through the perspective of Jane. Bertha, therefore, does not have the opportunity to tell her own story, even to Jane. In groups, determine what you think Bertha's version of her story would be. Then write that story.

5. Grace Poole spends twenty-three hours a day, seven days a week, guarding Bertha in her attic room. Imagine what Grace's life is like. Discuss how you believe Grace Poole manages to avoid becoming mad herself. Then write a letter from Grace to a dear friend of hers in which she describes her life as Bertha's attendant.

6. Why do you believe that Rochester keeps Bertha in the attic rather than sending her to an asylum? Discuss the issues involved. Then develop a debate in which one side argues that Bertha would be better off in an asylum while the other argues that she is taken better care of in the attic.

7. Behaviors that led to a diagnosis of insanity were very different for Victorian men than for Victorian women. Do you believe that men and women generally tend to display different behaviors when they are mentally unbalanced? If so, what behaviors and why? If not, why not?

SUGGESTED READINGS

Abercrombie, John. *Culture and Discipline of the Mind*. Edinburgh: William Whyte & Co., 1837.

Acton, William. *The Functions and Disorders of the Reproductive Organs in Youth, in Adult Age, and in Advanced Life: Considered in Their Physiological, Social, and Moral Relations*. London: John Churchill, 1857.

Barker-Benfield, G. J. *The Horrors of the Half-Known Life: Male Attitudes Towards Women and Sexuality in Nineteenth-Century America*. New York: Harper and Row, 1976.

———. "The Spermatic Economy: A Nineteenth-Century View of Sexuality." *Feminist Studies* 1 (1972): 45–74.

Bucknill, John Charles. *Unsoundness of the Mind in Relation to Criminal Insanity*. London: Longman, Brown, Green & Longmans, 1854.

Burrows, George Man. *Commentaries on Insanity*. London: Underwood, 1828.

Carter, Robert Brudenell. *The Influence of Education and Training in Preventing Diseases of the Nervous System*. London: John Churchill, 1855.

———. *On the Pathology and Treatment of Hysteria*. London: John Churchill, 1853.

Chesler, Phyllis. *Women and Madness*. Garden City, NY: Doubleday, 1972.

Ehrenreich, Barbara, and Deidre English. *For Her Own Good: 150 Years of the Experts' Advice to Women*. Garden City, NY: Anchor Press/ Doubleday, 1979.

Gilbert, Sandra M., and Susan Gubar. *The Madwoman in the Attic: The Woman Writer and the Nineteenth-Century Literary Imagination*. New Haven, CT: Yale University Press, 1979.

Haslam, John. *Considerations on the Moral Management of Insane Persons*. London: R. Hunter, 1817.

Hill, Robert Gardiner. *Total Abolition of Personal Restraint in the Treatment of the Insane*. London: Simpkin, Marshall & Co., 1839.

Laycock, Thomas. *An Essay on Hysteria: Being an Analysis of Its Irregular and Aggravated Forms; Including Hysterical Hemorrhages, and Hysterical Ischuria*. Philadelphia: Haswel, Barrington, and Haswel, 1840.

———. *A Treatise on the Nervous Diseases of Women: Comprising an Inquiry into the Nature, Causes, and Treatment of Spinal and Hysterical Disorders*. London: Longman, Orme, Brown, Green, and Longmans, 1840.

Maudsley, Henry. *Body and Mind*. London: Macmillan, 1873.

———. *Responsibility in Mental Disease*. London: Henry S. King, 1874.

Millar, John. *Hints on Insanity*. London: Henry Renshaw, 1861.

Morison, Alexander. *Outlines of Mental Diseases*. Edinburgh: MacLachland & Stewart, 1824.

Moseley, William Willis. *Eleven Chapters on Nervous and Mental Complaints*. London: Simpkin, Marshal & Co., 1838.

Packard, Elizabeth P. Ware. *The Liabilities of the Married Woman*. New York: Pelletreau and Raynor, 1873.

———. *Modern Persecution or Insane Asylums Unveiled*. New York: Pelletreau and Raynor, 1873.

Poovey, Mary. *Uneven Developments: The Ideological Work of Gender in Mid-Victorian England*. Chicago: University of Chicago Press, 1988.

Prichard, James Cowles. *A Treatise on Insanity*. London: Marchant, 1833.

Veith, Ilza. *Hysteria: The History of a Disease*. Chicago: University of Chicago Press, 1965.

Wynter, Andrew. *The Borderlands of Insanity*. London: Robert Hardwicke, 1875.

5

Inheritance and Marriage Law and Custom

The laws controlling property and inheritance were very strict in Victorian England. Who owned what, who was entitled to inherit what, and what an owner could do with what he owned were all issues that were determined by an immense and complicated set of laws and customs. At the moment of one's birth, therefore, one's future status and wealth could often be approximated to something very close to the eventual reality.

Among the landed classes, those people whose families had owned property for many generations, the law of primogeniture held the greatest influence over who owned what and who was entitled to inherit it. Primogeniture was essentially the inheritance by the eldest son in a family of all of his father's holdings at the time of his father's death. Primogeniture was a tenet of English common law, which is the foundation of most law even today in both England and the United States. It was not, however, a part of English common law that had great influence in the United States, since most of the early male settlers were either younger sons or men from families without landed estates in England, men who believed they should have a right to do what they wanted with their own property and that their children (at least their male children) generally should be treated equally. But in England, primogeniture was the foundation for transmission of "real" property (real estate) within most families until well into the twentieth century.

In Victorian England, primogeniture was common law, but it could be superseded if the owner of the property chose to do so and left a will that changed the inheritance structure. Only the property of individuals who died intestate (without a will) was subject to the law of primogeniture. Therefore the *custom* of primogeniture was of even greater importance than the law in terms of the *actual* transmission of property. It was generally accepted that all landed estates would, in fact, be left to the eldest son, and wills were written accordingly, leaving little, if any, substantial property to the younger sons—much less daughters—in the family.

Edward Fairfax Rochester was born a younger son. As such, he was not raised to expect to inherit his father's fortune and estates. His elder brother expected to be the sole heir. Younger sons of extremely wealthy families were sometimes given minor estates belonging to the family; Ferndean could, therefore, have been given to Edward to provide him with a home and income. Younger sons of less wealthy families were often expected to enter into professions through which they could provide for their futures. Such professions included the military, the law, and the church. Younger sons were also frequently encouraged to marry into money and property. Such was the fate of Edward Rochester. Bertha Antoinette Mason was the daughter of a successful planter in the Caribbean Islands. He wanted his daughter to be taken care of by a traditional Englishman and was willing to provide her with a substantial dowry in order to win her a husband. Edward Rochester's father wanted his son to be provided for in a style that would honor the family's social position, but he did not want to reduce the value of the estate he would leave his eldest son in order to provide for his younger son. Therefore, Mr. Mason's offer of his daughter as wife for Edward was extremely desirable to Edward's father and brother. Through various subterfuges perpetrated by his father and Mr. Mason, Edward, who might not have appreciated the idea of his marriage being entirely a financial affair, was enticed into going to the Caribbean, meeting Bertha, and marrying her. It was not until after he and Bertha were legally married that he discovered his family's motivation for the match.

Edward Rochester's father was particularly pleased with the

match between Edward and Bertha not only because Bertha had great wealth but because, upon their marriage, her wealth would be transferred to his son, becoming his completely and totally. Under common law, a woman's money and property automatically belonged to her husband once they were married because of the rule of law called "feme covert." Under the principle of "feme covert," a woman, upon her marriage, became one with her husband in the eyes of the law. Her identity, therefore, was "covered" by the identity of her husband. She becomes a covered (or hidden) woman, thus the French term "feme covert."

Arrangements of various kinds could be made by the family of an heiress to protect her financial interests, such as establishing trustees who would control her property on her behalf, but Mr. Mason made no such arrangements for Bertha. Instead, her property belonged to her husband the moment the marriage was legally concluded. Such an arrangement was exceptionally pleasing to Edward's father and brother, both of whom felt they had provided well for the younger son without having to reduce the size or value of the family estate, which would be transferred intact to the elder son. Whether Bertha was a woman of strong moral fiber with a character that would be compatible with Edward's was of no concern to them. Being "well married" in nineteenth-century England had everything to do with money and property, nothing to do with personality and compatibility. What neither Edward's father nor his brother could have predicted was that the former would die soon after Edward's marriage to Bertha, and that the latter would follow him to the grave shortly thereafter, leaving Edward the heir of all the Rochester property, just as if he had himself been the eldest son. Therefore, his marriage to Bertha was not useful to him, even on financial terms, for very long. And the basic incompatibility between them, the result, from Edward's perspective, of her drinking and lascivious desires, which eventually degenerated into outright lunacy, became significantly more pronounced in his eyes as her financial value to him diminished.

Legally, Bertha was Mrs. Rochester. Divorce was not an option. In the first place, divorces were extraordinarily difficult to obtain in Victorian England. In Brontë's time, only an Act of Parliament could dissolve a marriage. Such an Act was quite expensive. It also made the divorce a very public experience, more public than a private man like Edward Rochester was willing to be. But even if he had decided that a divorce was worth the public exposure, Edward's hands were tied. Since Bertha had entered into the marriage with him willingly, and since she was presumed to be sane at the time of her marriage, Edward could not legally divorce her now that she was insane. If it could be proven that she had been insane at the time of the marriage, the marriage could be declared void, but such proof was non-existent. Edward Rochester was, therefore, legally tied to Bertha until death broke the marital bond. The only kind of marriage he could even consider until that time would be a bigamous marriage of the sort he almost engaged in with Jane Eyre.

GEORGE C. BRODRICK

George C. Brodrick published *English Land and English Land-lords* in 1881. This treatise is a lengthy examination of England's property laws throughout the Victorian period, including the history of that property law system's development over several centuries, as well as a discussion of the advantages and disadvantages of such a system. Brodrick was a proponent of land law reform at the end of the Victorian period, a time in which a serious movement for land law reform was under way.

The following is taken from Brodrick's explanation of primogeniture as it had been practiced in England for many generations. As is clear from *English Land and English Landlords*, Brodrick believed that the law and custom of primogeniture was not a productive way of operating in late Victorian England and that primogeniture was, in fact, the first part of English land law and custom that should be reformed.

FROM GEORGE C. BRODRICK, *ENGLISH LAND AND ENGLISH LANDLORDS: AN ENQUIRY INTO THE ORIGINS AND CHARACTER OF THE ENGLISH LAND SYSTEM, WITH PROPOSALS FOR ITS REFORM*
(London, 1881)

The Law of Primogeniture, in its strictest form, has now determined the descent of land on intestacy [dying without a will to determine the transmission of one's property] in this country for more than six centuries. It has been shown that not long after the Norman Conquest the right of an eldest son to inherit his father's estate, if held by knight service, was fully recognized. . . . It has also been shown how this right has survived all recent attempts to abolish it, so that, while all personalty [personal property] is divided on the death of his widow and children, all realty [landed property] still devolves, by common law, on the eldest male descendant of the eldest line. The Custom of Primogeniture, under which landed property is usually settled by deed or will upon the eldest male descendant of the eldest line, is of less ancient origin . . . but has prevailed with little variation for the last two centuries. . . . (89–91)

By the great majority of [the landed aristocracy and those wanting to enter its ranks], embracing the whole nobility, the squires of England, the lairds of Scotland, and the Irish gentry of every degree, Primogeniture is accepted almost as a fundamental law of nature, to which the practice of entails [legal settlements of the estate on the eldest sons through future generations] only gives a convenient and effectual expression. Adam Smith [renowned eighteenth-century economist and philosopher] remarks that "in Scotland more than one-fifth, perhaps more than one-third, part of the whole lands of the country are at present supposed to be under strict entail." . . . Mr. McCulloch, writing in 1847, calculated that at least half Scotland was then entailed. . . . In England, where so much land is in the hands of corporations or trustees for public objects, and where almost all deeds relating to land are in private custody, we cannot venture to speak with so much confidence on this point. Considering, however, that in most counties large estates predominate over small, and that large estates, by the general testimony of the legal profession, are almost always entailed either by will or settlement, while small estates, if hereditary, are very often entailed, there is no rashness in concluding . . . that a much larger area is under [entailed] settlement than at the free disposal of individual landlords.

It is well known that in families which maintain the practice of entailing, the disparity of fortune between the eldest son and younger children is almost invariably prodigious. The charge of the portions [inheritances] of the younger children, when created by a marriage settlement, is created at a time when it is quite uncertain how many such children there will be. It is rarely double of the annual rental, and often does not exceed the annual rental; indeed, in the case of very large estates, it may fall very far short of it. In other words, supposing there to be six children, the income of each younger brother or sister from a family property of £5,000 a year will consist of the interest on a sum of £1,000, or, at the utmost, of £2,000; and, even if there were but one such younger child, his income from the property would probably not be more than one-twentieth or one-thirtieth of his elder brother's rental. Nor does this represent the whole difference between their respective shares of the family endowment; for the eldest son, who pays no probate duty, finds a residence and garden at his disposal, which he may either occupy rent-free or let for his own private advantage. Of course, where a father possesses a large amount of personalty, he may partially redress the balance; and there are exceptionally conscientious landowners who feel it a duty to save out of their own life incomes for younger children. But it is to be feared that [such savings] are too often employed, not exclusively nor mainly to increase the pittances allotted for portions, but on the principle of "To him that hath shall be given," to relieve the eldest son in conforming to a conventional standard of dignity.

It is, indeed, wholly delusive to contrast the Law with the Custom of Primogeniture, as if the harsh operation of the former were habitually mitigated by the latter. The contrary tendency is assuredly far more prevalent in the higher ranks of the landed aristocracy; and the younger members of families in this class would generally have reason to congratulate themselves if the law alone were allowed free scope, instead of being aggravated by the effects of the custom. For instance, in the case last supposed, if a family estate of £5,000 a year were charged with no portions for younger children, but left to descend under the law of intestate succession, each of five younger children would lose £1,000, or, at the utmost £2,000. But then, if the last owner were possessed of £90,000 in personalty, and this also were left to be divided among the children under the Statute of Distributions, each child would receive a share of £15,000. Suppose, however,—and it is no improbable supposition—that portions have been charged for younger children, but that one-third of the personalty, or £30,000, is bequeathed to the head of the family to keep up the place, the fortune of each younger child will be reduced to £12,000, so that he would lose £3,000, and would gain no more than £1,000 or £2,000. But it is not very often that a landowner with a rental of £5,000 a year has £90,000 to leave among his children. The same imaginary obligation to preserve that degree of state and luxury which is expected of country gentlemen with a certain status and acreage offers an obstacle to saving which the majority find insuperable. Besides, nine out of ten men who inherit their estates burdened with charges for their father's widow and younger children would think it Quixotic to lay by out of their available income, as men of business would do, for the benefit of their own children. Hence the proverbial slenderness of a younger son's fortune in families which have a "place," and especially in those which have a title, to be kept up. (99–102)

• • •

It is too often forgotten that Primogeniture, as secured by modern settlements, compels many a territorial family to support, not one "drone" only, but two, with separate establishments yielding no agricultural return. The head of the family, however, is usually a man of mature age, and, feeling the weight of actual responsibility, may well be impelled by the salutary influence of public opinion, as well as by the dictates of his own good conscience, to set a good example. But can this be said with equal truth of the eldest son, upon whom no such responsibility is cast, whose right to succeed is indefeasible, for whom a present income has been reserved out of the rental upon resettlement, and whose power of raising money upon his expectations is unlimited? It is contended, indeed, that an heir born to a great position, and trained from his earliest years to make himself worthy of it, will acquire habits and will be fortified by motives which are powerful securities for his future virtue and capacity. No doubt it may be so, and it would be easy to cite instances of landowners, especially in the higher ranks of the nobility, who devoted themselves in youth to laborious preparation for territorial duties, as others do to a lucrative profession. These instances must be duly taken into account, nor must it be lightly assumed that the choicest results of English Primogeniture could be produced under an opposite system. But are these instances common enough to be treated as typical? Would it be difficult to cite a larger number of instances where the heirs of ancestral estates have been spoiled and demoralized by their great expectations, even if they are afterwards reformed by the effect of realizing these expectations? Would not the senseless frivolities and reckless extravagance of the London season, the scandals of turf speculation, the restless passion for amusement, and the ignoble race of social competition, be sensibly checked by the withdrawal of this *jeunesse doreé* from English society, and especially from those circles in which match-making is the supreme end of human ambition? . . . Would the wisdom of Parliament be diminished if the number of young country members were lessened by the subtraction of those who owe their seats to mere acreage and family names? These are questions which cannot be answered by reference to statistics, but on which a knowledge of the world may throw some light, and which must be faced by those who imagine that Primogeniture is maintained at the cost of younger sons alone, and not also at the cost of the country. It may be too much to assert that family settlements induce unprincipled or careless landowners to neglect the education of their eldest sons, knowing that, however worthless or dissipated they may prove, neither the estate nor the social estimation of the family can be diminished. . . . But they assuredly guarantee wealth and power to men who may be utterly unworthy of either, yet whose conduct and manners are too apt to become a standard for imitation in their own class, and even in the classes below them. If the general effect of such a provision be indeed as beneficial as it is represented to be, we must support the ordinary laws of human nature to be reversed for the purpose of justifying the English Law and Custom of Primogeniture. (114–116)

SIR WILLIAM BLACKSTONE

Sir William Blackstone was one of the most famous and prominent legal experts in English history. He was born early in the eighteenth century, in 1723, the son of Charles Blackstone, a silk merchant, and Mary Bigg Blackstone, daughter of a member of the landed aristocracy. Blackstone was raised and educated in London by his uncle, Dr. Thomas Bigg, a successful surgeon. Bigg provided Blackstone with an extensive liberal education, after which Blackstone entered Oxford University at the age of fifteen.

In 1753, Blackstone became the first professor of English law at Oxford. In the 1760s Blackstone began writing his *Commentaries* on English law. These four volumes have served as some of the most important documents for interpreting British law (and all systems of law based upon it, including U.S. law) ever since.

Blackstone's *Commentaries* define and interpret English law, particularly English common law, in language that is accessible to lay readers as well as legal experts. They provide some of the clearest statements about English law as it was practiced and understood in the eighteenth and nineteenth centuries. Although the *Commentaries* were written approximately eighty years before Charlotte Brontë wrote *Jane Eyre*, their definitions and interpretations of British law were as valid then as they were in the years in which they were written. The legal predicament that prompted Rochester's marriage to Bertha, his financial situation, and his attempted bigamous marriage to Jane would all have been dealt with according to the laws defined in Blackstone's *Commentaries*.

FROM SIR WILLIAM BLACKSTONE, *COMMENTARIES ON THE LAWS OF ENGLAND*
(London, 1765)

[THE COMMON LAW]

The municipal law of England, or the rule of civil conduct prescribed to the inhabitants of this kingdom, may with sufficient propriety be divided into two kinds: the *lex non scripta*, the unwritten, or common law; and the *lex scripta*, the written, or statute law.

The *lex non scripta*, or unwritten law, includes not only *general customs*, or the common law properly so called; but also the *particular customs* of certain parts of the kingdom. . . .

When I call these parts of our law *leges non scripta*, I would not be understood as if all those laws were at present merely *oral*, or communicated from the former ages to the present solely by word of mouth. It is true indeed that, in the profound ignorance of letters which formerly overspread the whole western world, all laws were entirely traditional, for this plain reason, because the nations among which they prevailed had but little idea of writing. . . . But, with us at present, the monuments and evidences of our legal customs are contained in the records of the several courts of justice in books of reports and judicial decisions, and in the treatises of learned sages of the profession, preserved and handed down to us from the times of highest antiquity. However, I therefore style these parts of our law *leges non scripta*, because their original institution and authority are not set down in writing, as acts of parliament are, but they receive their binding power, and the force of laws, by long and immemorial usage, and by their universal reception throughout the kingdom. . . .

As to general customs, or the common law, properly so called; this is that law, by which proceedings and determinations in the king's ordinary courts of justice are guided and directed. This, for the most part, settles the course in which lands descend by inheritance: the manner and form of acquiring and transferring property: the solemnities and obligations of contracts [including marriage contracts]; the rules of expounding wills, deeds, and acts of parliament; the respective remedies of civil injuries; the several species of temporal offences; with the manner and degree of punishment; and an infinite number of minuter particulars, which diffuse themselves as extensively as the ordinary distribution of common justice requires. (Book 1: 42–45)

[ON MARRIAGE LAW]

The second private relation of persons is that of marriage, which includes the reciprocal rights and duties of husband and wife; or, as most of our elder law books call them, of *baron* and *feme*. In the consideration of which I shall in the first place, inquire, how marriages may be contracted or made; shall next point out the manner in which they may be dissolved; and shall, lastly, take a view of the legal effects and consequence of marriage.

Our law considers marriage in no other light than as a civil contract. The *holiness* of the matrimonial state is left entirely to the ecclesiastical law; the temporal courts not having jurisdiction to consider unlawful marriage as a sin, but merely as a civil inconvenience. The punishment therefore, or annulling, of incestuous or other unscriptural marriages, is the province of the spiritual courts; which act *pro salute anima*. And, taking it in this civil light, the law treats it as it does all other contracts: allowing it to be good and valid in all cases, where the parties at the time of making it were, in the first place, *willing* to contract; secondly *able* to contract; and, lastly, actually *did* contract, in the proper forms and solemnities required by law.

First, they must be *willing* to contract. *"Consenses non concubitus, facit nuptias,"* is the maxim of the civil law in this case: and it is adopted by the common lawyers, who indeed have borrowed, especially in ancient times, almost all their notions of the legitimacy of marriage from the canon and civil laws.

Secondly, they must be *able* to contract. In general, all persons are able to contract themselves in marriage, unless they labour under some particular disabilities and incapacities. What those are, it will be here our business to inquire.

Now these disabilities are of two sorts: first, such as are canonical, and therefore sufficient by the ecclesiastical laws to avoid the marriage in the spiritual court; but these in our law only make the marriage voidable, and not *ipso facto* void, until sentence of nullity be obtained. Of this nature are precontract; consanguinity, or relation by blood; and affinity, or relation by marriage; and some particular corporal infirmities. And these canonical disabilities are either grounded upon the express words of the divine law, or are consequences plainly deducible from thence: it therefore being sinful in the persons who labour under them, to attempt to contract matrimony together, they are properly the object of the ecclesiastical magistrate's coercion; in order to separate the offenders, and inflict penance for the offence, *pro salute animarum*. But such marriages not being void *ab initio*, but voidable only by sentence of separation, they are esteemed valid to all civil purposes, unless such separation is actually made during the life of the parties. For, after the death of either of them, the courts of common law will not suffer the spiritual courts to declare such marriages to have been void; because such declaration cannot now tend to the reformation of the parties. And therefore when a man had married his first wife's sister, and after her death the bishop's court was proceeding to annul the marriage and bastardize the issue, the court of king's bench granted a prohibition *quoad hoc*; but permitted them to proceed to punish the husband for incest. These canonical disabilities being entirely the province of the ecclesiastical courts, our books are perfectly silent concerning them. But there are a few statutes, which serve as directories to those courts, of which it will be proper to take notice. . . . [I]t is declared, that all persons may lawfully marry, but such as are prohibited by God's law; and that all marriages contracted by lawful persons in the face of the church, and consummated with bodily knowledge, and fruit of children, shall be indissoluble. And, because in the times of popery, a great variety of degrees of kindred were made impediments to marriage, which impediments might however be bought off for money, it is declared, by the same statute, that nothing, God's law except, shall impeach any marriage, but within the Levitical degrees; the farthest of which is that between uncle and niece. By the same statute all impediments arising from precontracts to other persons were abolished and declared of none effect, unless they had been consummated with bodily knowledge: in which case the canon law holds such contract to be a marriage *de facto*. But this branch of the statute was repealed by statute. . . .

The other sort of disabilities are those which are created, or at least enforced, by the municipal laws. And, though some of them may be grounded on natural law, yet they are regarded by the laws of the land, not so much in the light of any moral offence, as on account of the civil inconveniences they drew after them. These civil disabilities make the contract void *ab initio*, and not merely voidable; not that they dissolve a contract already formed, but they render the parties incapable of forming any contract at all: they do not put asunder those who are joined together, but they previously hinder the junction. And, if any persons under these legal incapacities come together, it is a meretricious and not a matrimonial, union.

The first of these legal disabilities is a prior marriage, or having another husband or wife living; in which case, besides the penalties consequent upon it as a felony, the second marriage is to all intents and purposes void: polygamy being condemned both by the law of the New Testament, and the policy of all prudent states, especially in these northern climates. . . .

The next legal disability is want of age. This is sufficient to avoid all other contracts, on account of the imbecility in judgment in the parties contracting: *a fortiori* therefore it ought to avoid this, the most important contract of any. Therefore if a boy under fourteen, or a girl under twelve years of age, marries, this marriage is only inchoate and imperfect; and, when either of them comes to the age of consent aforesaid, they may disagree and declare the marriage void, without any divorce or sentence in the spiritual court. This is founded on the civil law. But the canon law pays a greater regard to the constitution than the age, of the parties; for if they are *habiles ad matrimonium*, it is a good marriage, whatever their age may be. And in our law it is so far a marriage, that, if at the age of consent they agree to continue together, they need not be married again. If the husband be of years of discretion, and the wife under twelve, when she comes to years of discretion he may disagree as well as she may: for in contracts the obligation must be mutual; both must be bound, or neither: and so it is, *vice versa*, when the wife is years of discretion, and the husband under.

Another incapacity rises from want of consent of parents or guardians. By the common law, if the parties themselves were of the age of consent, there wanted no other concurrence to make the marriage valid: and this was agreeable to the canon law. But, by several statutes, penalties of 100*l.* are laid on every clergyman who marries a couple either without publication of banns, which may give notice to parents or guardians, or without a licence, to obtain which the consent of parents or guardians must be sworn to. And . . . whosoever marries any woman child under the age of sixteen years, without consent of parents or guardians, shall be subject to fine, or five years' imprisonment: and her estate during the husband's life shall go to and be enjoyed by the next heir. The civil law indeed required the consent of the parent or tutor at all ages, unless children were emancipated, or out of the parents' power: and if such consent from the father was wanting, the marriage was null, and the children illegitimate; but the consent of the mother or guardians, if unreasonably withheld, might be redressed and supplied by the judge, or the president of the province: and if the father was *non compos*, a similar remedy was given. These provisions are adopted and imitated by the French and Hollanders, with this difference: that in France, the sons cannot marry without consent of parents till thirty years of age, nor the daughters till twenty-five; and in Holland, the sons are at their own disposal at twenty-five, and the daughters at twenty. Thus hath stood, and thus at present stands, the law in other neighbouring countries. And it has lately been thought proper to introduce somewhat of the same policy into our laws, by statute . . . whereby it is enacted, that all marriages celebrated by license (for banns suppose notice) where either of the parties is under twenty-one, (not being a widow or widower, who are supposed emancipated,) without the consent of the father, or, if he be not living, of the mother or guardians, shall be absolutely void. A like provision is made as in the civil law, where the mother or guardian is *non compos*, beyond sea, or unreasonably forward, to dispense with such consent at the discretion of the lord chancellor: but no provision is made, in case the father should labour under any mental or other incapacity. Much may be, and much had been, said both for and against this innovation upon our ancient laws and constitution. On the one hand, it prevents the clandestine marriages of minors, which are often a terrible inconvenience to those private families wherein they happen. On the other hand, restraints upon marriages, especially among the lower class, are evidently detrimental to the public, by hindering the increase of the people; and to religion and morality, by encouraging licentiousness and debauchery among the single of both sexes; and thereby destroying one end of society and government, which is *concubitu prohibibere vago*. And of this last inconvenience the Roman Laws were so sensible, that at the same time that they forbad marriage without the consent of parents or guardians, they were less rigorous upon that very account with regard to other restraints: for, if a parent did not provide a husband for his daughter, by the time she arrived at the age of twenty-five, and she afterwards made a slip in her conduct, he was not allowed to disinherit her upon that account. . . .

A fourth incapacity is want of reason; without a competent share of which, as no other, so neither can the matrimonial contract, be valid. It was formerly adjudged, that the issue of an idiot was legitimate, and consequently that his marriage was valid. A strange determination! since consent is absolutely requisite to matrimony, and neither idiots nor lunatics are capable of consenting to any thing. And therefore the civil law judged much more sensibly when it made such deprivations of reason a previous impediment; though not a cause of divorce, if they happened after marriage. . . .

Lastly, the parties must not only be willing and able to contract, but actually must contract themselves in due form of law, to make it a good civil marriage. Any contract made, *per verba de presenti*, or in words of the present tense, and in case of cohabitation *per verba de futuro* also, between persons able to contract, was before the late act deemed a valid marriage to many purposes; and the parties might be compelled in the spiritual courts to celebrate it *in facie ecclesia*. But these verbal contracts are now of no force, to compel a future marriage. Neither is any marriage at present valid, that is not celebrated in some parish church or public chapel, unless by dispensation from the Archbishop of Canterbury. It must also be preceded by publication of banns, or by licence from the spiritual judge. Many other formalities are likewise prescribed by the act; the neglect of which, though penal, does not invalidate the marriage. . . .

I am next to consider the manner in which marriages may be dissolved; and this is either by death, or divorce. There are two kinds of divorce, the one total, the other partial; the one *a vinculo matrimonii*, the other merely *a mensa et thoro*. The total divorce, *a vinculo matrimonii*, must be for some of the canonical causes of impediment before mentioned, and those, existing *before* the marriage, as is always the case in consanguinity; not supervenient, or arising *afterwards*, as may be the case in affinity or corporal imbecility. For in cases of total divorce, the marriage is declared null, as having been absolutely unlawful *ab initio*: and the parties are therefore separated *pro salute animarum*: for which reason, as was before observed, no divorce can be obtained, but during the life of the parties. The issue of such marriage as is thus entirely dissolved, are bastards.

Divorce *a mensa et thoro* is when the marriage is just and lawful *ab initio*, and therefore the law is tender of dissolving it; but, for some supervenient cause, it becomes improper or impossible for the parties to live together: as in the case of intolerable ill temper, or adultery, in either of the parties. For the canon law, which the common law follows in this case, deems so highly and with such mysterious reverence of the nuptial tie, that it will not allow it to be unloosed for any cause whatsoever, that arises after the union is made. And this is said to be built on the divine revealed law; though that expressly assigns incontinence as a cause, and indeed the only cause, why a man may put away his wife and marry another. The [Roman] civil law, which is partly of pagan original, allows many causes of absolute divorce; and some of them pretty severe ones: as, if a wife goes to the theatre or the public games, without the knowledge and consent of her husband; but among them adultery is the principal, and with reason named the first. But with us in England adultery is only a cause of separation from bed and board: for which the best reason that can be given, is, that if divorces were allowed to depend upon a matter within the power of either of the parties, they would probably be extremely frequent; as was the case when divorces were allowed for canonical disabilities, on the mere confession of the parties, which is not prohibited by the canons. However, divorces *a vinculo matrimonii*, for adultery, have of late years been frequently granted by act of parliament.

In case of divorce *a mensa et thoro*, the law allows alimony to the wife which is that allowance which is made to a woman for her support out of the husband's estate: being settled at the discretion of the ecclesiastical judge, on consideration of all the circumstances of the case. . . . It is generally proportioned to the rank and quality of the parties. But in case of elopement, and living with an adulterer, the law allows her no alimony.

Having thus shewn how marriages may be made, or dissolved, I come now, lastly, to speak of the legal consequences of such making, or dissolution.

By marriage, the husband and wife are one person in law, that is, the very being or legal existence of the woman is suspended during the marriage, or at least is incorporated and consolidated into that of the husband; under whose wing, protection, and *cover*, she performs every thing; and is therefore called in our law-french a *feme-covert, foemina vire co-operta*; is said to be *covert-baron*, or under the protection and influence of her husband, her *baron*, or lord; and her condition during her marriage is called her *coverture*. Upon this principle, of an union of person in husband and wife, depend almost all the legal rights, duties, and disabilities, that either of them acquire by the marriage. I speak not at present of the rights of property, but of such as are merely *personal*. For this reason, a man cannot grant any thing to his wife, or enter into covenant with her: for the grant would be to suppose her separate existence; and to covenant with her, would be only to covenant with himself: and therefore it is also generally true, that all compacts made between husband and wife, when single, are voided by the intermarriage. . . . The husband is bound to provide his wife with necessaries by law, as much as himself; and if she contracts debts for them, he is obliged to pay them; but for any thing besides necessaries he is not chargeable. Also if a wife elopes, and lives with another man, the husband is not chargeable even for necessaries; at least if the person who furnishes them is sufficiently apprized of her elopement. If the wife be indebted before marriage, the husband is bound afterwards to pay the debt; for he has adopted her and her circumstances together. If the wife be injured in her person or her property, she can bring no action for redress without her husband's concurrence, and in his name, as well as her own: neither can she be sued without making the husband a defendant. There is indeed one case where the wife shall sue and be sued as a feme sole, viz. where the husband has abjured the realm, or is banished, for then he is dead in law; and, the husband being thus disabled to sue for or defend the wife, it would be most unreasonable if she had no remedy, or could make no defense at all. (Book 1: 345–360)

WILLIAM ALEXANDER

In 1779, William Alexander published *The History of Women from the Earliest Antiquity, to the Present Time*. In it he details many of the laws that have affected women throughout English history. Some, he admits, are restrictive, especially for married women; but most, he believes are ultimately beneficial to women as well as to the society of his time. Alexander, unlike Brodrick, supports British law as it stands. He is not in favor of significant reform.

By twenty-first–century standards, of course, the restrictions women have faced throughout Western history are difficult for most to justify. Women in the time that Alexander was writing gave up almost all rights upon marriage to their husbands. They rarely inherited property in the first place, and had to turn over what property they might own to their husbands upon marriage. They had no rights over their own children, nor were they permitted to determine where they wanted to live. Only the husband could legally make that decision. It was generally agreed that husbands had the right to "discipline" their wives as though they were children, even including the right to inflict corporal punishment on them. If Jane Eyre had not complained of the restrictions on her life as a single woman with barely the means to support herself, it would be difficult to understand why she would agree to give up the relative liberty of singleness for the legal restrictions of married life. Understanding the restrictions placed upon married women in English society makes Bertha's position easier to understand as well. As a half-Creole single woman in the West Indies, she would have had much greater freedom than as an English Victorian wife. Being forced to submit to her husband's legal rights to her body and her property might well have caused, or at least exacerbated her mental problems.

FROM WILLIAM ALEXANDER, *THE HISTORY OF WOMEN FROM THE EARLIEST ANTIQUITY, TO THE PRESENT TIME*
(London, 1779)

By the laws of this country, the moment a woman enters into the state of matrimony, her political existence is annihilated, or incorporated into that of her husband; but by this little mortification she is no loser, and her apparent loss of consequence is abundantly compensated by a long list of extensive privileges and immunities, which, for the encouragement of matrimony, were, perhaps, contrived to give married women the advantage over those that are single. Of all the privileges which nature has conferred upon us, none are so precious and inestimable as personal liberty. Men of all ranks and conditions, and women who are unmarried, or widows, may be deprived of this for debts contracted for themselves, or by others for whom they have given security; but wives cannot be imprisoned for debt, nor deprived of their personal liberty for any things but crimes; and even such of these as subject the offender only to a pecuniary punishment must be expiated by the husband. No married woman is liable to pay any debt, even though contracted without the knowledge, or against the consent of her husband; and what is still more extraordinary, whatever debts she may have contracted while single, devolve, the moment of her marriage, upon the husband, who, like the scape-goat, is loaded by the priest who performs the ceremony with all the sins and extravagances of his wife. . . .

So long as a wife cohabits with her husband, he is, by the laws of his country, obliged to provide her with food, drink, clothing, and all other necessaries suitable to her rank and his circumstances, even although he received no fortune with her. If he leaves her, or forces her to leave him by ill usage, he is also liable to maintain her in that same manner; but if she runs away from him, and he is willing that she should abide in his house, he is not liable to give her any separate maintenance, nor to pay any of her debts, unless he take her again; in which case he must pay whatever she contracts, whether she behave herself ill or well. . . .

Every married woman is considered as a minor, and cannot do any deed which affects her real or personal property without the consent of her husband, and if she does any such deed, it is not valid, and the husband may claim the property of what she disposed of, as if no such disposal had been made. As married woman cannot dispose of her property while living, so neither does the law give her that power at her death. In the statute of wills, she is expressly prohibited from devising land, and even from bequeathing goods and chattels without the leave of her husband; because all such goods and chattels are, without any limitation, his sole and absolute property; whether they were such as the wife brought along with her at the marriage, or such as she acquired even by her labour and industry afterward.

The laws of this country not only deny to a married woman the power of making a will, but also dissolve and render of no effect upon her marriage all and every will she may have while single; and even when a single woman who has made her will, marries, and her husband dies, the will which she had made, being invalidated by her marriage, does not recover its validity by the husband's death. (323–324)

• • •

When a husband and wife agree to live separate, and the husband covenants to give her so much a year, if at any time he offers to be reconciled and to take her home, upon her refusal, he shall not any longer be obliged to pay her a separate maintenance. If a legacy be paid to a married woman who lives separate from her husband, the husband may file a bill in chancery to oblige the person who paid it to his wife to pay it again to him with interest. If a wife proves insane, the husband, as her proper guardian, has a right to confine her in his own house, or in a private mad-house; but should the husband not be inclined to release her when her senses return, a court of equity [if someone brings the problem to its attention on her behalf] will give her that relief which the husband denies. The power which a husband has over the person of his wife does not seem perfectly settled by the laws of this country; it is nevertheless certain, that she is not to go abroad, nor to leave his house and family, without his approbation; but what coercive methods he may make use of to restrain her from so doing, or whether he may proceed any farther than to admonition and denying her money, seems a point not altogether agreed upon. (339–340)

SIR FREDERICK POLLOCK AND
FREDERIC WILLIAM MAITLAND

In 1898, Sir Frederick Pollock and Frederic William Maitland published *The History of English Law Before the Time of Edward I*. In it, Pollock and Maitland, like Brodrick, examine English law over time and trace the history of its changes. Like Brodrick, Pollock and Maitland were part of the land law reform movement of the late Victorian period and their discussion of the history of the English law reflects that perspective. Among the many legal concepts discussed in their *History* is the concept of coverture. Their interpretation of the development of the "courteous" rule of coverture provides insight into the seemingly contradictory concepts of marriage and property rights more clearly than any other text I have found. Since the "courteous" rule of coverture is central to the marriage of Rochester and Bertha (metaphorically, as well as legally, since she is literally the "hidden" woman, the *feme covert*), an understanding of its development can shed some light on the reasons that it was allowed to exist as fully as it did in England while other European countries were much less restrictive to women.

FROM SIR FREDERICK POLLOCK AND FREDERIC WILLIAM
MAITLAND, *THE HISTORY OF ENGLISH LAW BEFORE THE TIME
OF EDWARD I*
(London, 1898)

Our law institutes no community even of movables between husband and wife. Whatever movables the wife has at the date of the marriage, become the husband's, and the husband is entitled to take possession of and thereby to make his own whatever movables she becomes entitled to during the marriage, and without her concurrence he can sue for all debts that are due to her. On his death, however, she becomes entitled to all movables and debts that are outstanding. . . . What the husband gets possession of is simply his; he can freely dispose of it. . . . If she dies in his lifetime, she can have no other intestate successor. Without his consent she can make no will, and any consent he may have given is revocable at any time before the will is proved. . . .

During the marriage the husband is in effect liable to the whole extent of his property for debts incurred or wrongs committed by his wife before the marriage, also for wrongs committed during the marriage. The action is against him and her as co-defendants. If the marriage is dissolved by his death, she is liable, his estate is not. If the marriage is dissolved by her death, he is liable as her administrator, but only to the extent of the property he takes in that character.

During the marriage the wife can not contract on her own behalf. She can contract as her husband's agent, and has a certain power of pledging his credit in the purchase of necessaries. . . . The tendency . . . has been to allow her no power that can not be thus explained, except in the exceptional case of desertion. (404–405)

• • •

[W]e may now turn back to the twelfth and thirteenth centuries. If we look for any one thought which governs the whole of this province of law, we shall hardly find it. In particular we must be on our guard against the common belief that the ruling principle is that which sees an "unity of person" between husband and wife. This is a principle which suggests itself from time to time; it has the warrant of holy writ; it will serve to round a paragraph, and may now and again lead us out of or into a difficulty; but a consistently operative principle it can not be. We do not treat the wife as a thing or as somewhat that is neither thing nor person; we treat her as a person. Thus Bracton tells us that if either the husband without the wife, or the wife without the husband, brings an action for the wife's land, the defendant can take exception to this "for they are *quasi* one person, for they are one flesh and one blood." But this impracticable proposition is followed by a real working principle:—"for the thing is the wife's own and the husband is guardian as being the head of the wife." The husband is the wife's guardian:—that we believe to be the fundamental principle: and it explains a great deal, when we remember that guardianship is a profitable right. . . . [T]he husband's right in the wife's lands can be regarded as an exaggerated guardianship. The wife's subjection to her husband is often insisted on; she is "wholly within his power," she is bound to obey him in all that is not contrary to the law of God; she and all her property ought to be at his disposal; she is "under the rod." (405–406)

• • •

We are not contending that the law of England ever definitely recognized a community of goods between husband and wife. We have, however, seen many rules as to what takes place on the dissolution of the marriage which might easily have been explained as the outcome of such

a community, had our temporal lawyers been free to consider and ad-
minister them. Unfortunately about the year 1200 they suffered the ecclesiastical courts to drive a wedge into the law of husband and wife
which split it in twain. The lay lawyer had thenceforth no immediate
concern with what would happen on the dissolution of the marriage
[since the ecclesiastical courts made complete dissolution of marriage
during the lifetime of the marital partners impossible]. He had merely to
look at the state of things that existed during the marriage. Looking at
this, he saw only the husband's absolute power to deal with the chattels
inter vivos. Had he been compelled to meditate upon the fate which
would befall this mass of goods so soon as one of the spouses died, he
might have come to a conclusion which his foreign brethren accepted,
namely, that the existence of a community is by no means disproved by
the absolute power of the husband, who is so long as the marriage endures "the head of the community." As it was, he saw only the present,
not the future, the present unity of the mass, not its future division into
shares. And so he said boldly that the whole mass belonged to the husband. "It is adjudged that the wife has nothing of her own while her
husband lives, and can make no purchase with money of her own." "She
had and could have no chattel of her own while her husband lived."
"Whatsoever is the wife's is the husband's, and the converse is not true."
"The wife has no property in chattels during the life of her husband."
"This demand supposes that the property in a chattel may be in the wife
during the life of her husband, which the law does not allow."

Once more we see the lawyers of the thirteenth century making a short
cut. A short cut it is, as all will allow who have glanced at the many
difficulties which the idea of a "community" has to meet. When they gave
to the husband the ownership of the wife's chattels, they took an important step. Having taken it, they naturally set themselves against the wife's
testamentary power [her power to make a will] (for how can Jane have
a right to bequeath things that belong to John?) and they set themselves
against every restraint of the husband's testamentary power (for why
should not a man bequeath things that belong to him?), they secured for
the widow nothing but the clothes upon her back. (432–433)

• • •

[T]he right given to the husband by English law is a large, a liberal
right. It comprehends the wife's lands by whatever title she may have
acquired them, whether by way of inheritance or by way of marriage
portion, or by any other way; it endures though there is no longer any
issue [child] of the marriage in existence; it endures though the husband
has married another wife; it is given to a second husband, who can
thereby keep out a son of the first marriage from his inheritance. About

these points there has been controversy, but at every point the husband has been victorious. . . .

If we compare our law with its nearest of kin, we see a peculiar favour shown to the husband. Norman law deprives him of his right when he marries again; at any rate he must then give up two-thirds of the land. Scottish law gives him his "curtesy" only in lands which his wife has inherited, not in lands which have been given to her. The English lawyers know that their law is peculiar, believe that it has its origin in some "specialty." This being so, it is by no means unnatural that they should call it "courteous," or as we might say "liberal" law. They look at the matter from the husband's point of view; this is the popular point of view. (416–417)

TOPICS FOR WRITTEN OR ORAL EXPLORATION

1. Write a paper or make a class presentation in which you explain the details of the inheritance structure that allowed Edward Fairfax Rochester to inherit Thornfield and Ferndean.

2. Write a paper or make a class presentation in which you explain the legalities involved in Rochester controlling Bertha's inheritance after their marriage.

3. Divide the class into two teams. Then prepare and initiate a debate, one side arguing for the positive effects of the law and custom of primogeniture on nineteenth-century English society, the other arguing for the negative effects of the law and custom on that society.

4. Write an essay about your own family structure and how you would fare personally if the law and practice of primogeniture applied in the United States at the present time. Would the application of primogeniture change your life? The lives of your siblings? The lives of your parents? How would these lives be changed?

5. When women married in England in Charlotte Brontë's time, any property they owned became the property of their husbands. Any property they were given or earned also became his property. How do you think this transfer of property affected relationships between husbands and wives? What would be the advantages of such a system? What would be the disadvantages?

6. Research the marriage laws regarding property in your state. Then write an essay explaining how fair or unfair those property laws are. Be sure to argue your position based on specific evidence.

7. At the end of *Jane Eyre*, Jane inherits money from her uncle. She then decides that she can freely marry Mr. Rochester because she brings an inheritance into the relationship. Legally, that inheritance will become his as soon as they marry. Why do you think she felt it so necessary to have property of her own before their marriage since it will no longer be hers once the marriage takes place?

8. When Edward Rochester married Bertha Mason, he had no fortune of his own. Once they were married, he had complete control of her relatively large fortune. Write a journal entry in the voice of Bertha explaining how you believe she would have felt after her marriage to Rochester about his now being in control of her fortune.

9. The laws in Brontë's time that regulated the relationship between husband and wife treated the wife as though she were the minor child of the husband, allowing her no freedom to make any decisions of which he did not approve. If you were an early nineteenth-century

woman, do you think you would be willing to marry under these circumstances? If so, why? If not, what would you do instead?

10. Mr. Rochester has every right under English law to keep Bertha locked in the attic, since she is his wife and has exhibited insane behavior. Do you believe that a man should have the right to lock his mate away, making certain that she has a caretaker, without having medical authorities first declare her to be insane? Should he be allowed to lock her away in his own home even if she is declared insane by medical authorities? Discuss the moral and practical ramifications of his having or not having that right.

SUGGESTED READINGS

Alexander, William. *The History of Women from the Earliest Antiquity, to the Present Time.* 2 vols. London: W. Strahan and T. Cadell, 1779.

Blackstone, Sir William. *Commentaries on the Laws of England: In Four Books.* Philadelphia: J. B. Lippincott, 1910.

Bonfield, Lloyd. *Marriage Settlements, 1601–1740: The Adoption of the Strict Settlement.* Cambridge: Cambridge University Press, 1983.

———. "Strict Settlement and the Family: A Differing View." *Economic History Review*, 2nd ser., 41 (1988): 461–466.

Brodrick, George C. *English Land and English Landlords: An Enquiry into the Origin and Character of the English Land System, with Proposals for Its Reform.* London: Petter, Galpin, and Co., 1881.

Clark, J. C. D. *English Society 1688–1832: Ideology, Social Structure and Political Practice during the Ancien Regime.* Cambridge: Cambridge University Press, 1985.

Clay, Christopher. "Marriage, Inheritance, and the Rise of Large Estates in England, 1660–1815." *Economic History Review*, 2nd ser., 21 (1968): 503–518.

Cooper, J. P. "Patterns of Inheritance and Settlement by Great Landowners from the Fifteenth to the Eighteenth Centuries." *Family and Inheritance: Rural Society in Western Europe, 1200–1800.* Ed. Jack Goody, Joan Thirsk, and E. P. Thompson. Cambridge: Cambridge University Press, 1976: 192–312.

Davidoff, Leonore, and Catherine Hall. *Family Fortunes: Men and Women of the English Middle Class, 1780–1850.* Chicago: University of Chicago Press, 1987.

English, Barbara, and John Saville. *Strict Settlement: A Guide for Historians.* Hull, England: University of Hull Press, 1983.

Erickson, Amy Louise. "Common Law Versus Common Practice: The Use of Marriage Settlements in Early Modern England." *Economic History Review*, 2nd ser., 43 (1990): 21–39.

Goody, Jack. "Inheritance, Property and Women: Some Comparative Considerations." *Family and Inheritance: Rural Society in Western Europe, 1200–1800*. Ed. Jack Goody, Joan Thirsk, and E. P. Thompson. Cambridge: Cambridge University Press, 1976: 10–36.

———. "Strategies of Heirship." *Comparative Studies in Society and History* 15 (1973): 3–20.

Harding, Alan. *A Social History of English Law*. Harmondsworth: Penguin, 1966.

Kenny, C. S. *The History of the Law of England as to the Effects of Marriage on Property and on the Wife's Legal Capacity*. London: Reeves and Turner, 1879.

Lawrence, Basil Edwin. *The History of the Laws Affecting the Property of Married Women in England*. London: Reeves and Turner, 1884.

The Laws Respecting Women, as They Regard Their Natural Rights, or Their Connections and Conduct. 4 vols. London: J. Johnson, 1777.

Milsom, S. F. C. *Historical Foundations of the Common Law*. London: Butterworths, 1969.

Mingay, G. E. *English Landed Society in the Eighteenth Century*. London: Routledge and Kegan Paul, 1963.

———. *The Gentry: The Rise and Fall of a Ruling Class*. London: Longman, 1976.

Perkin, Harold. *Origins of Modern English Society, 1780–1880*. London: Routledge and Kegan Paul, 1969.

Pollock, Sir Frederick. *The Land Laws*. 2nd ed. London: Macmillan, 1887.

Pollock, Sir Frederick, and Frederic William Maitland. *The History of English Law Before the Time of Edward I*. 2nd ed. London, 1898.

Simpson, A. W. B. *A History of the Land Law*. 2nd ed. Oxford: Clarendon, 1986.

Spring, David. *The English Landed Estate in the Nineteenth Century: Its Administration*. Baltimore: Johns Hopkins University Press, 1963.

Spring, Eileen. *Law, Land, and Family: Aristocratic Inheritance in England, 1300–1800*. Chapel Hill: University of North Carolina Press, 1993.

Staves, Susan. *Married Women's Separate Property in England, 1660–1883*. Cambridge, MA: Harvard University Press, 1990.

Stone, Lawrence. *The Family, Sex, and Marriage in England, 1500–1800*. New York: Harper and Row, 1977.

Stone, Lawrence, and Jeanne C. Fawtier Stone. *An Open Elite? England, 1540–1880*. Oxford: Clarendon, 1984.

Thirsk, Joan. "Younger Sons in the Seventeenth Century." *History*, ns 54 (1966): 358–377.

Thompson, F. M. L. *English Landed Society in the Nineteenth Century*. London: Routledge and Kegan Paul, 1963.

Trumbach, Randolph. *The Rise of the Egalitarian Family: Aristocratic Kinship and Domestic Relations in Eighteenth-Century England*. New York: Academic, 1978.

6

Jane Eyre: Issues in the Twenty-first Century

Jane Eyre was published in 1847, over a century and a half ago. It became popular immediately and has continued to find appreciative audiences throughout every decade since its initial release.

Many of the social issues *Jane Eyre* deals with continue to be of concern today. The subject of male/female relationships fills countless pages of books and hours of radio and television talk shows. The sizable gap between the rich and the poor continues to create social problems and misunderstandings between individuals and groups of people. Therapists' offices are filled with clients who are working through problems they developed growing up in "dysfunctional" families. How to best educate girls in our society—what to emphasize in their educational content and what methods work best with them—has been the subject of numerous studies over the past several decades. A divorce rate of 50 percent in the United States is generally accepted now as normal, though almost everyone agrees that such a high rate of divorce is problematic for the society; yet the thought of a society in which divorce is not an option, like that in which Charlotte Brontë lived, seems much too restrictive to most twenty-first–century Americans. How to most successfully treat and care for those who suffer from mental illnesses also continues to be a strongly debated issue in many venues.

Each of the topics above is worthy of more exploration and development than is possible within the confines of a single chapter. I encourage students to pursue individual topics in greater detail.

POPULAR MEDIA AND *JANE EYRE*

The popularity of books in the twentieth century is often determined not only by sales of the books themselves, but also by the creation and popularity of other art forms and merchandising based on those books. Motion picture and theatrical adaptations are often the best gauge of how important a novel from a previous century has become to the popular sensibility of our times. *Jane Eyre* is an example of a novel that has been sufficiently a part of the popular consciousness to be part of movie history almost from the very beginnings of the popular movie industry in the United States. Since the initial movie production of *Jane Eyre* in 1914, no decade has been without at least one new feature movie or television version of *Jane Eyre*.

In 1914, a silent production of *Jane Eyre*, starring Lisbeth Blackstone, appeared on movie screens throughout the United States. It was followed by another black and white silent version in 1921 directed by Hugo Ballin. This version starred Norman Trevor as Mr. Rochester and Mabel Ballin as Jane Eyre. The year 1934 saw the release of the first adaptation of the novel with sound, directed by Christy Cabanne. Like the earlier versions, this one was in black and white. It starred Virginia Bruce as Jane Eyre and Colin Clive as Mr. Rochester. In 1944, the film adaptation of the novel that often appears on late-night television and the classic movie channels was produced. It was directed by Robert Stevenson, had a script adapted from the novel by John Houseman, and starred Orson Welles as Mr. Rochester and Joan Fontaine as Jane Eyre. Other cast members contemporary readers may recognize include Margaret O'Brien as Adele Varens and Agnes Moorehead as Mrs. Reed. It was also the first full-length film version of the story and tends to be the version best remembered by most film viewers prior to the 1990s.

In 1956, *Jane Eyre* was first produced for television, followed by two television versions in the 1960s, two in the 1970s, and one in the 1980s. The 1970 version with George C. Scott as Edward Rochester and Susannah York as Jane Eyre is generally considered to be the most faithful to the novel of the various television adaptations. In 1983, a BBC production of *Jane Eyre*, which aired in both Britain and the United States, starred Timothy Dalton as Edward Rochester and Zelah Clarke as Jane Eyre. This adaptation seems to be the favorite of most contributors to online discussion groups for *Jane Eyre*, who often express their preferences with tremendous passion.

The last decade of the twentieth century saw considerable activity in productions of *Jane Eyre* as well. Franco Zeffirelli directed the feature film with William Hurt as Mr. Rochester, Charlotte Gainsbourg as the adult Jane Eyre, and Anna Paquin as the younger Jane. This feature's release in 1996 precipitated much conversation on the Internet comparing these performances and the movie as a whole with previous filmed versions, particularly the 1944 Orson Welles/Joan Fontaine version and the 1980s version with Timothy Dalton and Zelah Clarke. In 1997, one year later, yet another television version of the story was produced in England, this one starring Samantha Morton as Jane Eyre and Ciara Hinds as Mr. Rochester.

But film adaptations are not the only tributes to *Jane Eyre* available to viewers who are moving into the twenty-first century. In a one-woman production of *Jane Eyre*, Lisa Hayes portrays each member of the 25-person cast in her stage adaptation of the novel. Hayes has presented her production at such events as the Edinburgh Fringe Festival, the Columbia Festival of the Arts in Maryland, and at New York's Womenkind Festival, as well as performing at a variety of National Trust castles and stately homes throughout England and at the King's Head Theatre in London.

The newest addition to the history of stage productions of *Jane Eyre* is a musical version of the novel, directed by John Caird with music and lyrics by Paul Gordon. It was originally produced in December 1995 at the Wichita Center for the Performing Arts in Kansas. In spring 2000, it opened in a revised version at the La Jolla Playhouse in southern California which moved to Broadway in November 2000.

Each film and stage version of *Jane Eyre* has won a substantial audience in its time. And many of the film versions produced in earlier decades continue to reach millions who have access to cable and satellite television as well as videotapes of many of the adaptations.

The World Wide Web is a source of considerable information and a place for companionship for those who love *Jane Eyre*, in particular, and the works of the Brontë sisters in general. There are ongoing mailing lists and listservs dedicated to discussion of *Jane Eyre* as well as the other Brontë novels. Internet discussions of Brontë's work occur at the scholarly level as well as at the more general level. There are Web sites dedicated to historical information about the Brontës, about Victorian life and times, and about reactions to *Jane Eyre* as novel, as film adaptation, and as stage adaptation. Web sites dedicated to the study of Victorian history and literature, such as Victoriana.com (www.Victoriana.com) and The Victorian Web (http://landow.stg.brown.edu/victorian/victov.html), often have specific subdivisions for information about the Brontës and their writings. Several sites even have the e-text of *Jane Eyre*, along with e-texts of other novels written by the Brontë sisters. The fact that *Jane Eyre* is so popular on the Web as well as on film and in bookstores is a tribute to the appeal of the novel and its issues across time.

MARRIAGE LAW IN TWENTY-FIRST–CENTURY ENGLAND AND THE UNITED STATES

In the early Victorian period, laws relating to the relationships between men and women were predominantly those that determined who could marry whom and what rights a man had to the property his wife brought to the marriage. Divorce was not an option according to British statutory law; in order for a couple to become truly divorced and free to remarry, an Act of Parliament had to be passed, a process which was extremely public, very costly, and usually quite time-consuming. So most couples, even if they found themselves to be totally incompatible, remained married.

At the beginning of the twenty-first century, the legalities surrounding relationships between men and women are much different in England and the United States. The requirements that must be met in order to get married are similar: legal consent of both parties, both parties being of age, both parties being of sound mind, fulfillment of the legal requirements of a marriage license, and a ceremony to solemnize the contract. But marriage is no longer considered by law necessarily to be a lifelong commitment in these countries. Divorce is now common place, with approximately 50 percent of marriages in the United States ending in divorce rather than death. Stepfamilies are rarely created now through the remarriage of widowed individuals, whereas in the nineteenth century, combinations of step-, half-, and full-blooded siblings were almost always the result of the marriage of widows and widowers. At the beginning of the twenty-first century, women and men are generally considered (legally, at least) to be equal partners in a marriage. The money and property belong to both, to be divided fairly (as judged by a court of law) if they divorce. Debts are also (at least in community property states in the United States) considered to be shared equally between the marital partners. In custody arrangements, both fathers and mothers have rights, and the ruling is supposed to reflect the best interests of the child, whereas, in early Victorian England, the child was simply considered the property of the father. In the nineteenth century, British law regarding marriage and children was based exclusively on property law and operated according to the concepts of British property law. In the twenty-first century, any intimation that a human being is a piece of property is considered to be grossly inappropriate in English and U.S. courts.

The results of the changes in marriage and family law from a system of law based on property to one based on individual human rights are many. Divorce has become frequent, and in most states in the United States, does not even require provable "grounds." The fact that one or both members of the marital union wants out of that union is now reason enough for most courts to grant a divorce. Issues of legal fairness arise in the distribution of property and in custody arrangements, but those arrangements, again, are based on the needs and rights of all parties, not on a strictly interpreted set of property laws.

The definition of marriage itself is being challenged in the United States in the twenty-first century. Since marriage law no longer has its foundation on the legal transmission of property through procreation, but instead on the desires and beliefs of individual human beings, the requirement that marriage be a covenant between individuals of opposite sexes for the purpose of creating and caring for another generation is no longer considered legitimate by many people. As a result, people who have chosen to live together in "domestic partnerships" often want the rights and entitlements of those who are married. Some domestic partners can choose to marry, but among some populations, most notably the homosexual and lesbian populations, legal marriage has not been an option. If, however, marriage is no longer a legal arrangement the sole purpose of which is to legitimize biological heirs to property (which was the basis of marriage in the past), but is now becoming a public and legal recognition of a commitment between two consenting adults to live their lives together as domestic partners, then the *legal* concept of marriage (separate from religious definitions) may provide no logical basis for disallowing same-sex marriage.

Marriage and family law have changed remarkably in England and the United States over the century and a half since *Jane Eyre* was published. But remnants of attitudes toward marriage, toward the proper roles of the husband and of the wife, toward the idea of one's family as "belonging to" the husband, and so forth, all reflect back to a time when the husband had complete rights over his wife, her property, and their children—all of which, under the law, was defined as *his* property. Laws and customs regarding marital relationships have changed dramatically, but attitudes, in some cases, lag far behind.

WOMEN AND PROFESSIONAL LIFE IN TWENTY-FIRST–CENTURY ENGLAND AND THE UNITED STATES

In early Victorian England, the only truly respectable paid occupation for a woman of the genteel classes was as a teacher, working either in a school or in a private home as the governess for a family. Many occupations were available to women of the lower classes, including sewing, nursing, midwifery, running an inn or a pub, doing laundry, and working as a cook or other domestic servant. For individuals of Jane Eyre's class and above, however, only teaching was truly viable. A few respectable women managed to earn livings by writing, though they often wrote under pseudonyms to keep their identities secret. And some hired themselves out as ladies' companions to ladies of wealth who, usually, were not easy to live with, since those who were easygoing usually had members of their own families who stayed with them. But teaching was the occupation that provided the bread and butter for most of England's impoverished gentlewomen. Women who desired to earn their livings in other professions were considered to be un-womanly, as only men were accepted in other, potentially lucra-tive, fields.

In twenty-first–century England and the United States, women are allowed to enter almost any profession (the Roman Catholic priesthood being one of a very few exceptions) and, theoretically, a woman is able to rise as far and as fast as any man in that pro-fession, provided she has the ability and the drive to do so. In fact, however, few women do rise to the top levels of business and industry, in part because of attitudes that continue to reflect some of the ideals of Victorian culture. For example, women are still considered to be the primary caretakers of children. Women who choose to occupy both a professional position and the position of mother often experience a level of guilt over leaving their children in the care of others that fathers rarely experience, having been expected for centuries to be the primary breadwinners for their families, thus fulfilling their family care responsibilities in their pur-suit of financial and professional success. Women of Victorian En-gland's genteel classes received minimal fortunes compared with their brothers. As a result, they rarely brought more money into a marriage than their husbands, and they virtually never earned their own money. Their dependence on their husbands for financial support was therefore total, especially since, once they were mar-ried, he was legally in control of any money his wife brought into the marriage. After generations of being taught that respect-able women should take care of the home and family while being supported financially by their husbands, learning to succeed at business and finance, especially at levels that supersede their hus-bands' successes, has been difficult for women to attempt, let alone to cope with when they succeed.

The fact that women have had to break into business in a world in which professional ties between men began to be forged in all-male institutions such as college fraternities, and even elementary and secondary prep schools, has also created difficulties for women who want to succeed financially. Such all-male institutions, and the loyalties they have created, were developed primarily dur-ing the Victorian period, when feminine intrusion into the world of business was not considered possible. The resulting networks of businessmen have made the struggle for women's entry into the top levels of management and ownership in traditional businesses more difficult than they might otherwise have been.

The "glass ceiling" is a metaphor used to describe the situation in which women tend to be able to rise to a certain level within an organization with relative ease, but beyond that level, they face much greater difficulties than men and often find it impossible to rise any further. But it does not merely describe the situation; it also claims that "the obstacles women face to promotion relative to men systematically increase as they move up the hierarchy" (Baxter and Wright). The numbers of women in the upper levels of the hierarchies of businesses, industries, educational institutions, and the like, therefore, remain excessively small compared to the percentages of women in the organization as a whole because of that systematic increase in obstacles.

Women are succeeding in positions of high management more than ever before, but their numbers remain excessively small compared to the numbers of women in the workplace. In 1993, a study of social work organizations (organizations that tend to employ vastly greater numbers of women than men) found that male social workers hold a disproportionately high number of managerial positions, that they rise to those positions significantly earlier in their careers, and that they generally have greater salaries than female social workers (Gibelman and Schervish). In 1992, an internal committee of the United Nations reported that, despite its charter, which dictates equal participation of men and women within the organization, the hiring and promotion of women into top positions is woefully low (Kirshenbaum). A report from the International Labour Office (ILO) in 1998 finds that "[w]omen are better educated and hold more jobs worldwide than ever before. Yet most women continue to suffer from occupational segregation in the workplace and rarely break through the so-called 'glass ceiling' separating them from top-level management and professional positions" ("Information of Interest"). According to this report, "[w]omen represent more than 40 percent of the world's labor force. Yet their share of management positions remains unacceptably low, with just a tiny proportion succeeding in breaking through the glass ceiling to obtain top jobs" ("Information of Interest").

Although in relatively small numbers, women are moving into

the top ranks of business, industry, the military, and almost all professions, even those most closely associated with men. Women can now choose careers based on their true interests and desires rather than having to enter one of only a couple of occupations that could provide them with subsistence wages. And women's own attitudes are changing. Half a century ago, few women believed that they should work outside the home if their husbands could adequately support the family, and few women sought out professional careers in addition to caring for a husband and children or believed that their value in the marketplace was and should be equivalent to that of men. But today many women choose to pursue careers as well as families; many women want, prepare for, and attain professional careers; and it is the rare woman who believes that her work is not worth equal wages and benefits to a man's for equivalent work. Even governesses (or the closest twenty-first–century equivalent—the nanny) now often make far more than a subsistence wage. Recent reports from the San Francisco area cite advertisements for qualified nannies offering between $40,000 and $60,000 a year, with benefits, private quarters in the home, access to a car, regular hours, and paid vacations. Jane Eyre and her sister governesses would no longer recognize their profession.

EDUCATION FOR GIRLS IN TWENTY-FIRST–CENTURY ENGLAND AND THE UNITED STATES

Just as professional opportunities for woman have changed dramatically in the past century and a half, so have educational opportunities. In the early Victorian period, women of the genteel classes were trained to be "accomplished" rather than "educated." Their education generally consisted of a minimum of reading, writing, and arithmetic (very basic arithmetic), along with training in music, drawing, painting, dancing, speaking and reading French, needlework (the higher the social status of the student, the less practical the kinds of needlework taught), and, in a very few of the more responsible schools, some basic household management, all in a single-sex environment. Too much intellectual training, it was thought, would make a woman unfit to fill a woman's proper role. It would distract her attention from the important things in life: finding a husband, having children, managing a household. It would also, so the medical experts of the day believed, deplete her physical life energy, of which each woman was assumed to have a finite amount, after the depletion of which she would not be able to conceive, bear, or nurture children. Depleting that energy would also make a woman less "womanly," causing her to act more masculine than feminine—so most Victorians believed.

In the twenty-first century, girls are rarely educated differently from boys. In fact, most formal education in the United States at the present time is in mixed-gender settings. Boys and girls are generally believed to need to learn the same basic information from elementary through high school, and are expected to have the same educational opportunities in college and other postsecondary educational environments. There has been a lot of concern in educational circles over the past several decades about the fact that a much smaller percentage of girls chooses to take more than the minimum coursework in areas such as math and science, thereby limiting the professions for which they can be easily and suitably trained. Programs such as GIRLS (Gifted, Intelligent, Real-Life Scientists) are formed to assist girls in determining whether they truly have interests and potential in the sciences, or whether their tendency to avoid science courses and activities is based on an unconscious acceptance of gender stereotyping (Zanelli).

The concern about girls not pursuing math and science is based on the economic fact that individuals who avoid those fields of study essentially lock themselves out of many of the most lucrative careers available in our society—careers in computers, scientific research and development, engineering, and high finance. Boys, who generally avoid taking more than the required courses in the arts and humanities, also shortchange themselves. But in a culture that defines success primarily in terms of financial worth, and which financially values the fields of math and science over those of the arts and humanities, the undertrained in math and science are considered to be at a greater disadvantage than those undertrained in the arts and humanities.

One potential solution to the problem of disparate test scores and course enrollments in certain subject areas based on gender is that of single-sex classrooms. In the March 2000 issue of *The Science Teacher*, one article is dedicated to an examination of the effects of creating single-sex computer classes for women (Crombie). Without the traditionally more competitive and generally more mechanically and technologically minded males in the classroom, the theory suggests, women are likely to learn more, better, and more easily. Such theories are based primarily on the assumption that girls and boys tend to have differing learning styles and might, therefore, be better served by separate methods of training (Alexander).

Some educators are proposing even greater changes. Although the sex-single classroom in an essentially mixed-gender environment might benefit some students, many of the problems that educators believe to be inherent in mixed-gender schools remain. Some of those educators tend to see contemporary public schools as predominantly social institutions in which, on occasion, students choose to spend little of their time and energy learning. According to this view, if girls and boys tend to have differing learning styles and personality types in general, and if the mix of girls and boys together in a school tends to replicate the social world in which adolescents' primary concerns center around relationships and appearances, then the solution is to make school a place where such issues are practically irrelevant. The single-sex school is the solution suggested by those educators. Evidence that girls do not shy away from science classes and activities as much in all-girls' schools as in mixed-gender schools can be found at Hathaway Brown School, an all-girls' school in Shaker Heights, Ohio. According to an article in the May/June 2000 issue of *Ad Astra*, the girls at Hathaway Brown are contributing to space exploration by designing an experiment that will be part of the Small Self-Contained Payload Program of the United States' space program.

The case for single-sex, girls' schools is being made throughout the United States. In 1997, *Technology and Learning* magazine published a report about a private girls' middle school emphasizing math, science, and technology that was opening in California's Silicon Valley. It also reported that the state of California was, simultaneously, introducing a pilot program for taking a single-sex approach to secondary education, providing districts with the means of offering single-sex public schools to both boys and girls as an educational option (Salpeter). The book *For Girls Only: Making a Case for Single-Sex Schooling*, by Janice L. Streitmatter, was published in 1999. In it, Streitmatter examines the positives and negatives of both mixed-gender and single-sex education and

comes down strongly on the side of single-sex schooling. The issue
is important in England as well. In February 2000, a London *Times
Educational Supplement* headline read, "Girls Feel Valued in
Single-sex Schools." The article focused on a study of women who
had attended all-girls' schools in the United States. The study concluded that those women were, overall, much better prepared for
college and careers than women who had been trained in mixed-
gender settings. The women in the study also significantly outper-
formed both men and women taught in mixed-gender settings on
standardized tests (Marcus).

It is clear that, as we enter the twenty-first century, the education
of girls in the United States and England has changed dramatically
in terms of content from the education of girls in early Victorian
England. Schools today need to prepare girls as well as boys for
careers and lives as active and responsible citizens in their com-
munities and countries. But the methods by which that education
is presented are being seriously questioned, and the single-sex
school, *de rigueur* in Victorian times, may well be making a comeback a century and a half later.

The other primary method of educating the Victorian girl was
by teaching her what she needed to know at home, either by
means of a governess or by relying on her mother to supervise her
education. This method is also making a comeback at the beginning of the twenty-first century. More and more families are opting
to home-school their children. The reasons for choosing home
schooling differ from family to family and from student to student.
Sometimes home schooling is necessary because of health problems or other physical difficulties. But more often parents are
choosing to home-school their children because of their dissatisfaction with the public school system available to their children.
Some parents believe that their children do not learn enough in
school; others disapprove of the lack of religious and/or moral
values taught in their public school system. Others fear violence,
peer pressure, bad teaching, and discipline problems that can prevent children from receiving the quality of education their parents
intend for them.

The reasoning behind single-sex schools and home schooling for
girls is very different in the twenty-first century than it was in Victorian England, but the fact is that single-sex schooling and home
schooling are both being considered as means of improving edu-

cation for both girls and boys as we enter a new century. Some of
the old methods may be worth salvaging after all.

TREATMENT OF MENTAL ILLNESS IN THE
TWENTY-FIRST CENTURY

The advancements in understanding mental illness that have
been made since the time in which Charlotte Brontë lived are tremendous. At the time in which Bertha Mason Rochester would
have been diagnosed as insane, the very word *psychology* had not
yet been coined; Freud and Jung's theories were not even ideas
floating in the air, let alone organized and disseminated; and treatment of the mentally ill was extremely harsh, when not purely
neglectful. The predecessors of psychologists were of two sorts:
(1) phrenologists (individuals who read the shapes and sizes of
heads as well as the shapes and measurements of facial features in
order to determine who was constitutionally predisposed toward
insanity and/or criminality in the population) and (2) doctors specializing in the treatment of the mentally ill with methods that
tended to use physical restraints and/or regimens that were intended either to shock the patient back into "reality" or to provide
the patient with so much rest that any imbalance of improper discharges of energy would be made up for by the additional rest.
Locking patients like Bertha away—often for life, with only general
maintenance care—was more the norm than not among all social
classes in Victorian England.

As we enter the twenty-first century, diagnosis and treatment of
mental illness have dramatically improved. With our greater contemporary understanding of neurology, scientists and doctors have
joined together to diagnose organic mental disease more accurately and to produce treatments that can minimize, reverse, and
sometimes even cure diseases of the mind that once were incurable and resulted in permanently debilitating insanity. The development of psychoactive pharmaceuticals has been a tremendous
boon to treating people with mental illness.

Talk therapy, formalized into psychoanalysis by Sigmund Freud,
the recognized "father" of psychology, has enabled multitudes of
people who have serious mental difficulties to avoid succumbing
to extreme mental illness, or to talk their way back from extreme
mental distress. Psychoanalysis is a very formalized, drawn-out

process of talk therapy that can be of great benefit to many people. But talk therapy has also developed along other lines, ones that focus more on specific problems and solutions, thus making the process shorter, less expensive, and more immediately productive.

Other developments in psychological treatment have included behavior modification therapy, hypnotherapy, group dynamics therapy, rapid eye movement therapy, and the like. Each of these treatment modalities assists some who suffer from mental illness of one kind or another.

In the Victorian period, most individuals suffering from severe mental problems were locked away, either under supervision within their own homes or in an asylum dedicated to the care and maintenance of the insane. Generally, only the poorest of the poor who suffered from severe mental illness roamed the countryside freely. By contrast, as we enter the twenty-first century, the vast majority of mentally ill individuals in the United States are *not* institutionalized or constantly supervised in their homes. Only the most seriously ill, who have injured themselves or others so severely as to be considered a risk to society, tend to be institutionalized for more than a few days or weeks at a time. Mental illness is generally considered to be an outpatient illness at this time in history. Counseling sessions, individually or in groups, are often prescribed, along with medications, if deemed appropriate, as treatment for those experiencing mental or emotional difficulties. But beyond the counseling sessions and the medication, most of the mentally ill are expected to cope with their day-to-day lives in society.

The treatment of the mentally ill who have funds and insurance to pay for the necessary medications and counseling sessions is much better than that of the mentally ill of the Victorian period. But one group of the mentally ill who may not be any better off are those who are severely ill but do not have family that can or will take care of them. Many in this category spent long portions of their younger years in government-funded institutions. Cuts in funding for most of these institutions in the 1960s and 1970s left these individuals with nowhere to go except the streets. For many of these people, the streets, where they receive no care or medication and are completely unsupervised, have been home for decades. The treatment of the homeless mentally ill in today's society is as bad, if not worse, than that provided for the mentally ill in

Victorian England. There, each parish had responsibility for those who were destitute within it, and generally they sent such individuals to a charity asylum for the mentally ill. Those asylums were not always better and safer than the streets, but most of the time patients could at least receive decent food and could be kept safe from those who would take advantage of them on the streets. Such is not the case in the twenty-first century.

Our ability to treat mental illness, like our ability to treat physical illnesses, has improved dramatically over the past century and a half, but public access to that treatment is a different story. Most Americans are provided with access to medical care for physical illnesses through some form of private or government insurance program. While those insurance programs may limit certain kinds of care and may require substantial co-payments for others, the programs do, generally, allow people to receive adequate care of physical ailments. Access to mental health care is more costly. Some insurance programs refuse to cover mental health at all unless the problem is found to be organic, for which a surgical or pharmaceutical treatment is prescribed. Most insurance programs offer extremely minimal coverage for any mental health treatment, and those programs also often tend to decline referrals of a mental health nature more frequently than other kinds of referrals. As a result, most Americans tend to pay almost all the costs of mental health care out of pocket. A recent article in the journal *Health Services Research* reported that "individuals with worse mental health consistently report a deterioration of access to care compared to individuals with better health," but although "[s]ubstantial activity has taken place in state and federal legislation to increase the mental benefits offered by health insurance" the mentally ill "continue to fare significantly worse than the general population" (Sturm and Wells). Therefore, access to mental health care lags far behind access to physical health care for most Americans.

The diagnosis, treatment, and maintenance of the mentally ill is dramatically better at the beginning of the twenty-first century than it was in the Victorian period. The stigma attached to the idea of mental illness, however, still prevents society from dealing with it as seriously and as openly as physical illness. Many people still believe that most individuals with mental disorders need to just "buck up," that mental illness is merely a form of moral weakness that can be overcome by a strong enough will. Others believe that mental illness is a sign of moral guilt, or that it is a punishment from God for one's own sins or the sins of one's parents. These are ideas entrenched in Western society's consciousness for centuries. As a result, even though the diagnosis, treatment, and maintenance of the mentally ill is vastly improved when compared to that in Victorian times, mental illness is not yet treated as seriously as it deserves to be because large numbers of people continue to hold prejudicial attitudes against the mentally ill.

TOPICS FOR WRITTEN OR ORAL EXPLORATION

1. View one or more of the film or television adaptations of *Jane Eyre*. Discuss how the adaptations portrayed Brontë's story. Was it faithful to the events of the book? Was it faithful to the spirit of the book? Where and how did it differ from the book? How was the experience of seeing the story on screen different from the experience of reading it? After class discussion, write an essay in which you explain which version you prefer and why.

2. *Jane Eyre* has been in print continuously since its publication. Plays adapted from it began to be performed within a few years of its publication and continue to be created and performed today. Film and television versions have been produced each decade since the silent movie era. Consider the story of *Jane Eyre* and determine what qualities make it such a universal tale that it has achieved continuous popularity since its initial publication.

3. As a group project, choose a segment of *Jane Eyre* and rewrite it in dramatic form. Then produce your drama, either as a staged production with actions and costumes, or as a readers' theater production.

4. Find ten sites dedicated to Charlotte Brontë and/or *Jane Eyre* on the World Wide Web. Create an annotated bibliography of those sites in which you discuss the contents and quality of the material at each site in your annotation. Be sure to format the bibliography according to the standard format your teacher gives you (probably MLA or APA style).

5. After looking at the British marriage law of Brontë's time (Chapter 5) and contemporary American and/or English marriage law, discuss the advantages and disadvantages of both. Then develop a document detailing the marriage laws that you believe would best serve the needs of society as well as the individuals in that society.

6. Examine the current requirements for an individual to get married in your state. Do you think all the requirements are reasonable? Do you think there should be additional requirements? Create a document in which you detail what you believe would be the best set of requirements for marriage. Be prepared to discuss the reasons for your choices.

7. Do you believe that men and women have equal access to equal careers in our culture? Write an essay in which you develop your thesis on this point.

8. Discuss the advantages and disadvantages of single-sex schools versus mixed-gender schools. Which do you think would be more effective

in teaching the accepted state curriculum? Why? Which would you prefer to attend? Why? Be prepared to present your answers and your reasoning orally to the class.

9. What do you believe should be the content of the curriculum students should have to learn today? Why? Do you believe that male and female students should have the same curriculum? Why or why not? Write an essay that answers these questions.

10. Research the provisions for the mentally ill in your community. Then, as a class, discuss whether those provisions are adequate and why or why not. If they are not adequate, create a plan to fix the inadequacies.

11. View one or more films that depict the experiences of the mentally ill in institutions since 1950 (e.g., *One Flew over the Cuckoo's Nest; David and Lisa; I Never Promised You a Rose Garden; Girl, Interrupted*). Then write an essay in which you compare the attitudes toward and the treatment of the mentally ill in those films with the attitudes toward and treatment of the mentally ill in Victorian times.

SUGGESTED READINGS AND MEDIA

POPULAR MEDIA AND JANE EYRE

Film, Television, and Stage Productions

Jane Eyre. Perf. Lisbeth Blackstone, John Charles, Irving Cummings, Ethel Grandin, Alan Hale, Harrish Ingraham, and Dallas Tyler. Feature film. 1914.

Jane Eyre. Dir. Hugo Ballin. Perf. Norman Trevor and Mabel Ballin. B&W. Silent. 1921.

Jane Eyre. Dir. Christy Cabanne. Perf. Virginia Bruce and Colin Clive. B&W. 1934.

Jane Eyre. Dir. Robert Stevenson. Perf. Orson Welles, Joan Fontaine, Margaret O'Brien, and Agnes Moorehead. 1944.

Jane Eyre. Dir. Marc Daniels. Perf. Sally Ann Howes and Fritz Weaver. Television production. 1961.

Jane Eyre. Dir. Delbert Mann. Perf. George C. Scott and Susannah York. Television production. 1970.

Jane Eyre. Perf. Sorcha Cusack and Michael Jayston. Television production. 1973.

Jane Eyre. Perf. Timothy Dalton and Zelah Clarke. Television production. 1983.

Jane Eyre. Adapted and performed by Lisa Hayes. Stage production. First production 1995.

Jane Eyre. Dir. Franco Zeffirelli. Perf. Charlotte Gainsbourg, William Hurt, Joan Plowright, Anna Paquin. Geraldine Chapman, and Elle Macpherson. Miramax, 1995.

Jane Eyre. Music and lyrics by Paul Gordon. Book and additional lyrics by John Caird. Stage production. First production 1995.

Jane Eyre. Dir. Robert Young III. Perf. Samantha Morton, Ciaran Hind, and Gemma Jones. Television production. 1997.

Internet Sites

Jane Eyre, by Charlotte Bronte—Victoria Turvey's Page. Includes discussion list and board. http://www.vturvey.freeserve.co.uk/JaneEyre.htm

Jane Eyre Mailing List. http://www.angelfire.com/wi/crivello/listinfo.html

Jane Eyre Web Ring. http://members.tripod.com/AthenaIris/ring.html

Mr. Cranky Rates Jane Eyre. Movie review site. http://www.mrcranky.com/movies/janeeyre.html

Online Literature Library—Charlotte Brontë—Jane Eyre. E-text. http://www.literature.org/authors/bronte-charlotte/jane-eyre/

MARRIAGE LAW IN TWENTY-FIRST–CENTURY ENGLAND AND THE UNITED STATES

Crouch, Richard E. *Family Law Checklists.* Deerfield, IL: Clark Boardman Callagher, 1995.

Divorce Online Web Site. http://www.divorceonline.com 9 July 2000.

DivorceMagazine.com: The Ultimate Online Resource on Divorce. Segue Esprit, Inc. copyright 1996–2000. http://www.divorcemagazine.com, 9 July 2000.

Marriage Law Project http://www.eppc.org/programs.marrlaw.html, 9 July 2000.

Perga, Mary Ann. "Marriage Is Not a Private Affair." *U.S. Catholic* (August 1996): 18+.

WOMEN AND PROFESSIONAL LIFE IN TWENTY-FIRST–CENTURY ENGLAND AND THE UNITED STATES

Amonette, Ruth Leach. *Among Equals: A Memoir: The Rise of IBM's First Woman Corporate Vice President.* Missoula, MT: Creative Arts, 2000.

Amott, Teresa L., Julie Matthaei, and Julia A. Mattaei. *Race, Gender, and Work: A Multicultural Economic History of Women in the United States.* Cambridge, MA: South End Press, 1996.

Austin, Linda S. *What's Holding You Back?: Eight Critical Choices for Women's Success*. Boulder, CO: Basic Books, 2000.

Baxter, Janeen, and Erik Olin Wright. "The Glass Ceiling Hypothesis: A Comparative Study of the United States, Sweden, and Australia." *Gender and Society* 14.2 (2000): 275–294. Online. Proquest. 7/31/00.

Carr-Ruffino, Norma. *The Promotable Woman: Ten Essential Skills for the New Millennium*. Franklin Lakes, NJ: Career Press, 1997.

Clegg, Sue. "Negotiating the Glass Ceiling—Careers of Senior Women in the Academic World." *Gender and Education* 10.4 (1998): 464–465.

Driscoll, Dawn-Marie, and Carol R. Goldberg. *Members of the Club: The Coming of Age of Executive Women*. New York: Macmillan, 1993.

Evans, Gail. *Play Like a Man, Win Like a Woman: What Men Know About Success That Women Need to Learn*. New York: Broadway Books, 2000.

Ferguson, Trudi, and Joan S. Dunphy. *Answers to the Mommy Track: How Wives and Mothers in Business Reach the Top and Balance Their Lives*. Far Hills, NJ: New Horizon Press, 1992.

Foegen-Karsten, Margaret. *Management and Gender: Issues and Attitudes*. Westport, CT: Greenwood Publishing Group,1994.

Gearing, Sylvia, and Nancy Brinker. *Female Executive Stress Syndrome*. Arlington, TX: Summit Publishing Group, 1994.

Gibelman, Margaret, and Philip H. Schervish. "The Glass Ceiling in Social Work: Is It Shatterproof?" *Affilia* 8.4 (1993): 442+. Online. Proquest. 7/31/00.

"Information of Interest: International." *WIN News* 24.4 (1998): 78–83. Online. Proquest. 7/31/00.

Kelly, Rita Mae. *Gendered Economy: Work, Careers and Success*. Thousand Oaks, CA: Sage Publications, 1991.

Kirshenbaum, Gayle. "U.N. Exposé: Inside the World's Largest Men's Club." *MS* 3.2 (1992): 16+. Online. Proquest. 7/31/00.

Matteo, Sherri. *American Women in the Nineties: Today's Critical Issues*. Chicago: Northwestern University Press, 1993.

Mendell, Adrienne. *How Men Think: The Seven Essential Rules for Making It in a Man's World*. New York: Fawcett Books, 1996.

Mindell, Phyllis. *A Woman's Guide to the Language of Success: Communicating with Confidence and Power*. Upper Saddle River, NJ: Prentice Hall, 1995.

Morrison, Ann M. *Breaking the Glass Ceiling: Can Women Reach the Top of America's Largest Corporations?* Reading, MA: Addison Wesley Longman, 1994.

Power, Gary N. *Women and Men in Management*. Thousand Oaks, CA: Sage Publications, 1993.

Weiss, Ann E. *The Glass Ceiling: A Look at Women in the Workforce*. New York: Twenty-first Century Books, 1999.

White, Jane. *A Few Good Women: Breaking the Barriers to Top Management*. Upper Saddle River, NJ: Prentice Hall, 1992.

White, Kate. *Why Good Girls Don't Get Ahead . . . But Gutsy Girls Do: Nine Secrets Every Working Woman Must Know*. New York: Warner Books, 1996.

Zobel, Jan. *Minding Her Own Business*. Holbrook, MA: Adams Media Corp, 2000.

EDUCATION FOR GIRLS IN TWENTY-FIRST–CENTURY ENGLAND AND THE UNITED STATES

Alexander, Susanne M. "The Next Generation of Space Scientists (Revised)." *Ad Astra* 12.3 (2000): 36–37.

Antler, Joyce, and Sari Knopp Biklen, eds. *Changing Education: Women as Radicals and Conservators*. New York: State University of New York Press, 1990.

Bailey, Susan McGee. "Shortchanging Girls and Boys." *Educational Leadership* 53.8 (1996): 75+.

Belenky, Mary F., et al. *Women's Ways of Knowing: The Development of Self, Voice, and Mind*. New York: Basic Books, 1986.

Bishop, Jeanne E. "Girls Can Succeed in Science! Antidotes for Science Phobia in Boys and Girls." *The Science Teacher* 67.4 (2000): 77–78.

"Case for an All-Girls Public School." *America* 177.5 (1997): 3–4.

Cohen, Mark Francis. "People's Prep." *The New Republic* 218.24 (1998): 13–16.

Crombie, Gail, Tracy Abarbanel, and Colin Anderson. "All-Female Computer Science." *The Science Teacher* 67.3 (2000): 40–43.

Giele, Janet Zollinger. "Coeducation or Women's Education: A Comparison of Findings from Two Colleges." In *Coeducation: Past, Present, and Future*. Ed. C. Lasser. Urbana: University of Illinois Press, 1987: 91–109.

Hall, Roberta M., and Bernice Sandler. "The Classroom Climate: A Chilly One for Women?" Washington, DC: Project on the Status and Education of Women, 1982.

Marcus, Jon. "Girls Feel Valued in Single-Sex Schools." *The Times Educational Supplement*, London (4 Feburary 2000) 16.

Martin, Jane Roland. "Redefining the Educated Person: Rethinking the Significance of Gender." *Educational Researcher* 15 (1986): 6–10.

Niemi, Rhonda. "The Scientific Education of Girls: Education Beyond Re-
proach?" *The Mathematics Teacher* 90.6 (1997): 500+.

Oates, Mary J., and Susan Williamson. "Women's Colleges and Women
Achievers." *Signs* 3 (1978): 795–806.

Salomone, Rosemary C. "Sometimes 'Equal' Means 'Different.' " *Education Week* 17.6 (8 October 1997): 32+

Salpeter, Judy. "High-tech Schools for Girls." *Technology and Learning*
18.3 (1997): 61+.

Sheffer, Susannah. *A Sense of Self: Listening to Homeschooled Adolescent
Girls*. Portsmouth, NH: Heinemann, 1995.

Streitmatter, Janice L. *For Girls Only: Making a Case for Single-Sex
Schooling*. Albany: State University of New York Press, 1999.

Woyshner, Christine A. "A Sense of Self: Listening to Homeschooled Adolescent Girls." *Harvard Educational Review* 66.3 (Fall 1996):
693+.

Zanelli, Kimberly. "GIRLS: Gifted, Intelligent, Real-Life Scientists." *The Science Teacher* 67.5 (2000): 46–47.

TREATMENT OF MENTAL ILLNESS IN THE TWENTY-FIRST
CENTURY

Chadda, Dolly. "Discrimination 'Rife' against Mental Health Patients."
British Medical Journal 320.7243 (2000): 1163.

Horn, Miriam. "A Bedlam in Ruins." *U.S. News & World Report* (26 May
1997): 58.

Isaac, Rael Jean, and D. J. Jaffe. "Toward Rational Commitment Laws:
Committed to Help." *National Review* (29 January 1996): 34+.

McLean, Candis. "Return of the Mental Asylum." *Alberta Report* 26.33
(1999): 32+.

Morse, Jennifer Roback. "Mind Games." *Forbes* (29 May 2000): 126.

Sturm, Roland, and Kenneth Wells. "Health Insurance May Be Improving—But Not for Individuals with Mental Illness." *Health Services
Research* 35.1 (2000): 253+ Infotrac. 5 July 2000.

Index

About the Author

DEBRA TEACHMAN teaches English literature and composition at New Mexico State University, Alamogordo. She is the author of *Student Companion to Jane Austen* (Greenwood, 2000) and *Understanding* Pride and Prejudice: *A Student Casebook to Issues, Sources, and Historical Documents* (Greenwood, 1997).